Communicating the Past in the Digital Age

Proceedings of the International Conference on Digital Methods in Teaching and Learning in Archaeology (12–13 October 2018)

Sebastian Hageneuer

]u[

ubiquity press
London

Published by
Ubiquity Press Ltd.
Unit 322–323
Whitechapel Technology Centre
75 Whitechapel Road
London E1 1DU
www.ubiquitypress.com

Text © the authors 2020

First published 2020

Cover design by Amber MacKay
Cover images by Sebastian Hageneuer
Original cover concept by Sandra Grabowski

Print and digital versions typeset by Siliconchips Services Ltd.

ISBN (Hardback): 978-1-911529-84-2
ISBN (PDF): 978-1-911529-85-9
ISBN (EPUB): 978-1-911529-86-6
ISBN (Mobi): 978-1-911529-87-3

DOI: https://doi.org/10.5334/bch

The full text of this book has been peer-reviewed to ensure high academic standards. For full review policies, see http://www.ubiquitypress.com/

Suggested citation:
Hageneuer, S. (ed.) 2020. *Communicating the Past in the Digital Age: Proceedings of the International Conference on Digital Methods in Teaching and Learning in Archaeology (12–13 October 2018)*. London: Ubiquity Press. DOI: https://doi.org/10.5334/bch. License: CC-BY 4.0

To read the free, open access version of this book online, visit https://doi.org/10.5334/bch or scan this QR code with your mobile device:

Contents

Acknowledgements

This publication would not have been possible if I had not been awarded with a Fellowship for Innovation in Digital Academic Teaching in 2017, which enabled me not only to buy equipment for our (then) brand-new master's programme in archaeoinformatics at the University of Cologne but also to host a two-day international symposium, of which this volume represents the results. I am therefore very grateful to the insightful funding of teaching projects by the Ministry of Culture and Science of the German state of North Rhine Westphalia. To the Stifterverband, which administered the funding, I am thankful for the counsel I received during my fellowship time.

I am also very grateful for the friendly environment in which I was able to conduct my fellowship and my work as a research associate at the Archaeological Institute of the University of Cologne, namely to the head of my department, Professor Eleftheria Paliou, who supported me in my endeavours, and my colleague Sophie Schmidt, who assisted me whenever I needed her to. I also want to thank Christine Avenarius and Laurenz Hillman, who helped as student assistants throughout the symposium and made our guests feel very welcome. Thanks also go out to Visa Immonen, Andrew Reinhard and on other anonymous peer reviewer, whose insightful comments on the draft helped to improve the publication. Finally, I want to thank all the participants of the symposium, whose acquaintances I enjoyed making and whom I hope to meet again in the near future.

Contributors

Ariese, Csilla E.
University of Amsterdam and VALUE Foundation
Dr Csilla E. Ariese is a museologist and post-doctoral researcher at the University of Amsterdam, the Netherlands. Within the Horizon 2020 ECHOES Project, she studies how the Amsterdam Museum is (dis)engaging with the complex colonial pasts of the museum and the city. She is also a co-founder of the VALUE Foundation, which playfully engages with gaming and academia, among others resulting in the edited book *The Interactive Past* (Sidestone, 2017). Csilla is a storyteller at heart, who is passionate about shipwrecks, ruins, the underwater world, games and museums. In 2018, she completed her PhD, *The Social Museum in the Caribbean*, as part of the ERC-Synergy project NEXUS1492 at Leiden University. The same year, she was the curator for the exhibition Culture Arcade at the Prince Claus Fund Gallery in Amsterdam. Besides her PhD, she holds an MSc in international museum (2012) and a BA in maritime archaeology (2010), both from Gothenburg University.
ORCID: https://orcid.org/0000-0002-6555-6814

Boom, Krijn H.J.
Leiden University and VALUE Foundation
Dr Krijn Boom is a post-doctoral researcher and heritage manager with the Economies of Destruction (VICI)-project at the Faculty of Archaeology of

Leiden University, the Netherlands. In this combined function, he studies the social and economic impact of Bronze Age depositions in north-west Europe and manages public outreach and knowledge utilisation. Krijn also has a position as Project Manager Blended Learning at the University of Amsterdam, Faculty of Science, combining his love for media and science in order to innovate teaching and provide students with a meaningful, yet fun way of learning. Krijn is co-founder of the VALUE project – for research and outreach on the past, heritage and video games, which was later formalised as the VALUE Foundation, opening up to other academic sectors.
ORCID: https://orcid.org/0000-0001-5634-3289

Champion, Erik Malcolm
Curtin University
Professor Erik Champion is UNESCO Chair of Cultural Visualisation and Heritage at Curtin University and theme leader for visualisation at the Curtin Institute of Computation, Australia (http://computation.curtin.edu.au). He researches virtual heritage, game design, interactive media, and architectural computing. Prior to joining Curtin University, he was project leader of DIGHUMLAB Denmark, hosted at Aarhus University. Here he worked with EU research infrastructures and projects, such as http://dariah.eu. His publications include *Organic Design in Twentieth-Century Nordic Architecture* (Routledge, 2019), *Critical Gaming: Interactive History and Virtual Heritage* (Routledge, 2015) and *Playing with the Past* (Springer, 2011). He edited *The Phenomenology of Real and Virtual Places* in 2018, co-edited *Cultural Heritage Infrastructures in Digital Humanities* (Routledge, 2017) with Agiati Benardou, Costis Dallas and Lorna Hughes, and edited *Game Mods: Design, Theory and Criticism* (ETC Press, 2012). He is currently writing a monograph, *Rethinking Virtual Places, for the Spatial Humanities Series* (Indiana University Press).
ORCID: https://orcid.org/0000-0002-5362-6176

Cook, Katherine
University of Montreal
Dr Katherine Cook is an assistant professor in public archaeology at the University of Montreal, Canada. Moving through the histories of Canada, the Caribbean and Western Europe, her work examines the ethics, politics and practice of memory and heritage in colonial narratives and present-day research contexts. In particular, her work critically engages with the application of (digital) technologies and the ways in which they are used to generate, preserve, negotiate, modify or even destroy the past, the ways in which we imagine it, and who has access. As an instructor, she also works on pedagogical questions relating to experiential or applied learning, the decolonisation of education (and archaeological training), and transforming closed classrooms into incubators for public archaeology projects.
ORCID: https://orcid.org/0000-0003-2414-751X

Hageneuer, Sebastian
University of Cologne
Sebastian Hageneuer is a Near Eastern archaeologist and currently a research associate in archaeoinformatics (computational archaeology) at the University of Cologne, Germany. In 2008, he co-founded ARTEFACTS, a company for the visualisation of archaeological results that specialised in the virtual reconstruction of ancient architecture (artefacts-berlin.de). Since 2013, he has been part of a research group of the Excellence Cluster TOPOI at the Free University of Berlin, which focuses on the significance of size in the architecture of the ancient Near East. He specialises in the scientific reconstruction of ancient architecture and in 3D methods for archaeology. In 2017, he received a fellowship for innovations in teaching with digital methods by the Ministry of Science and Culture of North Rhine Westphalia. His currently ongoing PhD focuses on the development and reception of reconstruction drawings of the 19th and 20th century in Near Eastern archaeology.
ORCID: https://orcid.org/0000-0001-8973-1544

Hiriart, Juan
University of Salford
Juan Hiriart is a PhD candidate at the School of Arts and Media in the University of Salford, in Greater Manchester, UK, where he teaches games design and production. His research focuses on exploring the suitability of digital games for the representation of historical knowledge, and the ways in which these technologies can be used in formal and informal learning environments. Before starting his doctoral studies, he worked for a range of creative industries, acquiring experience in illustration, animation and interactive design. He also worked for several years in the games industry, developing casual, mobile and serious games. You can read his more recent academic outputs at https://usir.salford.ac.uk/view/authors/58074.html.

Hölscher, David Frederik
Kiel University
David F. Hölscher studied prehistorical and historical archaeology, medieval archaeology, archaeology of the Roman provinces and history between 2009 and 2016 at the Universities of Freiburg i. Br. (Germany), Gothenburg (Sweden) and Kiel (Germany). After working in the field of communication design, he became a member of the scientific staff and a doctoral candidate at KiSOC (Kiel Science Outreach Campus), a joint project of the Leibniz Institute for Science and Mathematics Education (IPN) and Kiel University, in January 2018. His research interests cover (among others) science communication, human–landscape interactions, popularisation and popular perceptions of history and archaeology, experimental archaeology, and the Early Middle Ages in middle and northern Europe. David was an associate member of the graduate school 'Human Development in Landscapes' at Kiel University (end of funding 2018).

Holter, Erika
Humboldt-Universität zu Berlin
Erika Holter is a PhD candidate in classical archaeology at Humboldt-Universität zu Berlin, Germany, writing her dissertation on mosaic floor ensembles in Roman houses. She has experience working on several projects in the area of digital archaeology. The project *digitales forum romanum* uses digital 3D reconstructions of the architecture of the Forum in order to foster and further research into this ancient space. A further project, *Analog Storage Media – Auralizing Ancient Spaces*, applies a wide array of digital tools – acoustic simulations, auralisations, game engines and virtual reality – to reconstructions of ancient spaces, in order to understand what these new tools can offer historical research.

van den Hout, Bram
International Institute of Social History Amsterdam and VALUE Foundation
Bram van den Hout is a junior researcher at the International Institute of Social History (IISH) in Amsterdam, the Netherlands, and a board member of the VALUE Foundation (http://value-foundation.org). In his capacity at the IISH he adapts new technologies and software for use within the institute and has co-written a book and three articles on slavery and the slave trade in the Dutch VOC empire. Together with VALUE, he aims to bring academia and video games together to find (and provide voice to) new research fields and subjects.
ORCID: https://orcid.org/0000-0002-5780-3387

Katifori, Akrivi
Athena Research Center and University of Athens
Dr Akrivi Katifori holds a PhD degree (*An Intelligent System for Managing Historical Archive Documents*), a BSc in informatics and Telecommunications (2000) and an MSc from the Department of Informatics and Telecommunications of the University of Athens, Greece (2003). She has participated in European and national RTD projects, including Papyrus, CHESS, WhoLoDancE and EMOTIVE, and has authored several papers in different research areas of computer science, including information visualisation, virtual museums, digital libraries and digital storytelling.
ORCID: https://orcid.org/0000-0001-6755-2836

Kourtis, Vassilis
Athena Research Center and National and Kapodistrian University of Athens
Vassilis Kourtis is a research associate and software engineer in the Athena Research Center and the National and Kapodistrian University of Athens, Greece. He holds an engineering diploma from the School of Electrical and Computer Engineering of NTUA and he has recently completed his MA in digital communication media and interactive environments from the Department

of Communication and Media Studies of NKUA. His interests include user-centred design and the development of interactive environments for both the digital and the physical space, interactive digital storytelling, gamified experiences and serious games. His work focuses on applications of digital technologies in cultural heritage and education and he is involved in the CHESS (FP7) and EMOTIVE (H2020) European projects. Other works include the creation of cultural heritage experiences for small museums and cultural heritage sites in Greece and abroad, and the development of educational games for high schools in Greece.

ORCID: https://orcid.org/0000-0002-3943-3503

McKinney, Sierra
University of York
Sierra McKinney holds an MSc in Digital Heritage from the University of York, having previously studied Anthropology and Archaeology at the University of Victoria, Canada. She is currently developing digital educational experiences for the EMOTIVE Project, in which she is able to explore her research interests regarding the use of digital technologies to create accessible and emotive heritage.

Martí, Ana
Universitat Politécnica de València
Dr Ana Martí Testón is an associate professor at the Department of Audio-visual Communication, Documentation and Art History in the Universitat Politècnica de València, Spain. Her research profile is specialised in photography, digitalisation of collections, education and cultural management. Over the last five years, she has specialised in the analysis of communication strategies for museum collections through digital media, 4.0 technology, and augmented reality. She also belongs to the Research Institute of Design and Manufacturing, where she has developed several national and international projects related to Europeana, digital heritage and museums.

Mol, Angus A.A.
Leiden University and VALUE Foundation
Dr Angus Mol is an assistant professor at Leiden University's Centre for Digital Humanities, the Netherlands. In his research he combines the study of history using a digital approach with the study of how today's digital cultures are entwined with history. In particular, he looks at how contemporary play functions as a mirror of the past, as well as how games can be used to democratise access to the past. He has authored several papers on the topic and crowdfunded an open-access edited volume with chapters from scholars and professionals from the creative industry. He is one of the founding members of VALUE (http://value-foundation.org). With a PhD in archaeology, Angus also has a keen interest in projects that combine social theory, material culture,

and digital media and tools. For instance, he uses experimental games, network analyses or agent-based models to explore and explain how things and people are entangled over time.
ORCID: https://orcid.org/0000-0001-5448-3712

Muñoz, Adolfo
Universitat Politécnica de València
Dr Adolfo Muñoz García is the professor of the Department of Audiovisual Communication, Documentation and Art History, in the Universitat Politècnica de València (UPV), Spain. He teaches several subjects about digital media and programmation at the Faculty of Fine Arts and the Faculty of Informatics Engineering. He does research in UPV's Institute of Design and Manufacturing (IDF). His research profile specialises in the design of multimedia applications, video games and graphical interfaces, 3D simulations and augmented applications. Currently he directs the AR division of the IDF, where different projects are being developed using the HoloLens augmented reality glasses for productive and cultural industries.

Perry, Sara
University of York
Dr Sara Perry is a senior lecturer in cultural heritage management at the University of York, UK, and a lead on the EU-funded EMOTIVE Project (www.emotiveproject.eu). She has directed heritage interpretation programmes at archaeological sites around the world, including Çatalhöyük in Turkey (www.catalhoyuk.com); Memphis, the capital of ancient Egypt (http://memphisegypt.org); and Pangani in Tanzania (www.conchproject.org).
ORCID: https://orcid.org/0000-0002-9694-000X

Politopoulos, Aris
Leiden University and VALUE Foundation
Aris Politopoulos is a lecturer in the archaeology of the Near East at the Faculty of Archaeology, Leiden University, the Netherlands. He studied archaeology at the National and Kapodistrian University of Athens and did his MA degree at the Faculty of Archaeology at Leiden on the archaeology of the ancient Near East. He is currently finishing his doctorate at Leiden University, researching the creation, construction and function of the capital cities of Assyria. Aris has also been a founding member of the VALUE project, a foundation that works at the crossroads of gaming and academia. Together with VALUE, he hosted the Interactive Pasts Conference, the first conference focusing on the topic of archaeology and video games. He has published several papers on the topic and he is co-editor of the book *The Interactive Past: Archaeology, Heritage, and Video Games* (Sidestone, 2017).
ORCID: https://orcid.org/0000-0002-7613-1264

Quick, Stephan
LVR-Archaeological Park Xanten / LVR-RömerMuseum
Stephan Quick is responsible for education and mediation at the LVR-Archaeological Park Xanten / LVR-RömerMuseum, Germany (LVR-APX). He studied classics and archaeology at the University of Münster and the University of Nottingham. Since his previous work for the LWL-Römermuseum Haltern am See and the *Varusschlacht* im Osnabrücker Land – Museum und Park Kalkriese, he has specialised in the field of museum education. His work at the educational service at LVR-APX focuses on the development of different learning programmes for visitors of all target groups. One of his special interests is finding new and innovative ways to mediate Roman history and archaeology by using digital media tools in the museum.

Remmy, Michael
University of Cologne
Michael Remmy studied classical archaeology, Christian archaeology and ancient history in Bonn and Berlin. After his master of arts with a study on *Greek Sculptures in Roman Contexts*, he went to Cologne to work at the Research Archive for Ancient Sculpture. All his work in different projects connects to the ARACHNE project. This internationally renowned object database opened his eyes to research on the semantic web, ontologies for concepts in cultural heritage documentation and big data. He has worked as a work package leader for the University of Cologne team within the Horizon 2020 project ArchAIDE (Archaeological Automatic IDentification and Classification of cEramics). Michael gathered experience in organising and establishing workflows for this EU project as well as enhancing his knowledge of Roman pottery. Furthermore, his academic research lies in developing concepts to improve teaching archaeology. He teaches classes in classical archaeology and the archaeology of the Roman provinces as well as archaeoinformatics (computational archaeology).
ORCID: https://orcid.org/0000-0003-2121-8327

Riethus, Anna
Neanderthal Museum Foundation
Anna Riethus works as scientific project manager of research project NMsee at the Neanderthal Museum in Mettmann, Germany (a cooperation with BSVN e.V.). Within this project, she researches how app games can help archaeological museums to become more inclusive for people with visual disabilities. Before that, she supported the museum as scientific assistant and marketing officer from 2016. From 2012 to 2016, Anna studied prehistory and historical archaeology in Vienna, as well as archaeology and museum studies in Leiden. Beforehand, she trained as an engineer in garden and landscape design. Anna has joined archaeological excavations in France, Wales, Siberia, Austria and Germany and received training at the NHM Vienna and the Weltmuseum Wien.

Rubio-Campillo, Xavier
University of Edinburgh
Dr Xavier Rubio-Campillo is a lecturer at the University of Edinburgh. His main task at this position is to explore and teach new digital approaches to interpreting and presenting the heritage generated by past human activity. Before joining the school in 2016, he worked as the team leader of the humanities research group at the Barcelona Supercomputing Centre (2009–2016). He participated in several interdisciplinary projects applying computational methods to improve our understanding of the past, such as *SimulPast* and *EpNet*. His research also studies how interactive digital methods can be used to present archaeological findings to a larger audience. From this perspective, he explores how video game design can integrate educational goals within transformational experiences able to promote critical thinking about the human past.
ORCID: https://orcid.org/0000-0003-4428-4335

Schmidt, Sophie C.
University of Cologne
Sophie C. Schmidt is a research associate in archaeoinformatics (computational archaeology) at the University of Cologne, Germany. She studied ancient studies and prehistoric archaeology at the Free University of Berlin and received her MA in prehistoric archaeology there in 2016. Her thesis consisted of a *Geostatistical Analysis of Settlement Patterns from the Neolithic to the Early Iron Age* along a street excavation in Saxony-Anhalt (Middle Germany). In Cologne, she has been teaching quantitative methods for archaeologists, which, advocating for reproducible research, she implements in the programming language R. Recently she taught a class on concepts of the past in computer and video games, for which she received special funding by the University of Cologne. Next to her research interests in quantitative and GIS methods, settlement archaeology and archaeogaming, voluntary work at excavations at Neolithic sites in Turkey, Scotland, Bolivia and Germany reveal her global interest in the Neolithic.
ORCID: https://orcid.org/0000-0003-4696-2101

Schwesinger, Sebastian
Humboldt-Universität zu Berlin
Sebastian Schwesinger studied cultural history and theory, musicology, philosophy and business administration in Berlin, Essen, London and Vlissingen. He works as a research associate at the Institute for Cultural History and Theory at the Humboldt-Universität zu Berlin, Germany. His PhD project focuses on the media history of virtual acoustics. He is coordinator of the project *Analog Storage Media. Auralization of Archaeological Spaces* at the Image Knowledge Gestaltung cluster of excellence at Humboldt-Universität zu

Berlin. His research interests include models of sonic thinking and reasoning, the interplay of sonic materiality and infrastructure design, and cultural economics. Together with Felix Gerloff, he organises the open colloquium and public lecture series KlangDenken (sonic thinking) in Berlin. He is also a member of gamelab.berlin.

Competing Interests

The editor declares that he has no competing interests in publishing this book.

Introduction

Sebastian Hageneuer, Sophie C. Schmidt

University of Cologne

Over recent decades, digital methods have increasingly pervaded every aspect of archaeological knowledge production, from data collection, analysis and interpretation to interaction with the public, as well as exchange between scholars (see e.g. Morgan 2019: 325; Huggett 2019). This development began in the 1960s and has since slowly moved into higher education (Perkins et al. 1992; Schütz-Pitan et al. 2018). University courses on 3D modelling, computer simulation, or serious games – to name just a few – which until a few years ago were considered niche, are gradually included in a growing number of undergraduate and postgraduate archaeology curricula. At the same time, as 3D and interactive technologies are becoming more and more affordable, a proliferation of digital tools, ranging from virtual and augmented reality applications and interactive displays to mobile apps, have been made available for the communication of the past in museums and via the internet. In light of these developments, this volume aims to encourage a productive debate on the potential and challenges of using digital methods for teaching and learning in archaeology.

Unfortunately, academic teaching in general is often thought of as the by-product of the researching scientist. It is not teaching but third party-funded projects that bring academic revenue for the researcher, the institute and the university, whereas good teaching is rarely rewarded (Wosnitza et al. 2014

How to cite this book chapter:
Hageneuer, S. and Schmidt, S. C. 2020. Introduction. In: Hageneuer, S. (ed.) *Communicating the Past in the Digital Age: Proceedings of the International Conference on Digital Methods in Teaching and Learning in Archaeology (12–13 October 2018)*. Pp. 1–10. London: Ubiquity Press. DOI: https://doi.org/10.5334/ bch.a. License: CC-BY 4.0

summarise several studies showing the same attitudes). This leads to an undervaluation of good university-level teaching, which engages students and allows them to develop critical thinking, empathy and integrity. Nevertheless, we firmly believe that teaching is at the very core of universities as well as the archaeological discipline itself and that we need to re-evaluate the way we communicate our knowledge to our students. This holds especially true with the already-mentioned technological developments in the archaeological field. Being an archaeologist today incorporates much more than it did 20 years ago. Today, there is a need for well-educated digital-oriented archaeologists who know and understand the needs of modern-day fieldwork.

Universities and museums are by definition places of teaching and learning (Paletschek 2002; Walz 2016: 9). Outside of these institutions, too, the interest in spreading results was always present. By the 18th and 19th century, researchers such as Johann Joachim Winckelmann and Sir Austen Henry Layard were already not only researching but also disseminating their knowledge to the public in approachable ways (Layard 1851; 1853; Winckelmann 1760). They found a way to relate to the audience. In light of the digital developments outlined above, we therefore want to present methods and tools of today that improve digital teaching and learning in archaeology in- and outside academia.

Since 2016, the Ministry of Culture and Science of the German state of North Rhine Westphalia has been awarding annual fellowships for innovative ways of digital teaching at university level. The aim is to develop and test methods of digital teaching in various fields and in this way transform and strengthen the way we teach at the university. In 2017 the editor of this volume was able to obtain a fellowship which funded not only new technology for the Institute of Archaeology at the University of Cologne but also the organisation of a two-day international symposium on the given topic and its open-access publication, in which you are currently reading these lines.

The symposium was held at the University of Cologne (Germany) from 12 to 13 October 2018, with international scholars from Australia, Canada and Europe, and focused on teaching and learning archaeology with digital methods. In these two days, we had wonderful presentations and discussions of like-minded educators from universities as well as museums that have a shared interest in digital teaching and learning. The symposium was divided into five sessions: archaeogaming, learning in the museum, digital tools in the classroom, digital learning environments, and technical demonstrations. The last session offered participants in the symposium hands-on experience of some of the presented tools. This session did not translate well into a book, but, as the projects are described and published here in detail, we hope readers may get a glimpse into their practical applications. Therefore, the contributions to the volume at hand are divided into the first four sections of the symposium. As is always the case, some of them would have fitted more than one category but were kept in their assigned sessions.

The sessions have been constructed to mirror the variety of applications for the symposium and thus can show only a select view of the possibilities of digital teaching and learning in archaeology. We did not focus on how digitalisation may undermine the old clear-cut division between those who teach and those who are taught (although Remmy or Boom et al. in this volume do) and in this way help to develop a more participatory culture (as put forward by Giaccardi 2012). Citizen science is not just a buzzword but a successful practice (Smith 2014; or see e.g. DigVentures), academic teaching does not need to happen in a classroom and teaching through digital and social media is already part of archaeological education and outreach (MOOCs, Twitter, Skype a Scientist, and much more). Digitalisation and education should also play a role in postcolonial discourses and discourses of decolonisation, as exemplified by Cook's submission to this volume. However, our volume mostly presents techniques and methods of teaching and learning programmes of European, North American or Australian institutions. We express our hope, though, that a successor volume will focus on initiatives that have come to the fore, such as the decolonisation of archives (Cushman 2013) or, more recently, Felwine Sarr and Bénédicte Savoy's report to the French president, in which the sharing of digitised objects of cultural heritage plays a role (Sarr and Savoy 2018: 67). Certainly, the contributions to this volume touch upon topics of decolonialisation and postcolonialism; nevertheless, we do not pretend to cover the theme to its full extent. Digitalisation in archaeology also involves issues of 'democratisation' or at least the hope for that, especially in the realm of knowledge production. We are therefore delighted that a number of speakers focus on free and openly available software solutions (see e.g. Remmy, Rubio-Campillo and Boom et al. in this volume), which undermine established power structures and monetary barriers and thus level the playing field of digital teaching. In this regard, we are also happy to offer this volume as a freely available digital open-access version through the publisher's website.

The first part of this volume consists of chapters related to the relatively new term of archaeogaming (Reinhardt 2018: 2–4), which refers to the archaeology both in and of digital games. In many digital games, reconstructions of the past are created or archaeologists depicted and these representations have largely gone uncommented or are not influenced by historians and archaeologists, who therefore could not impact the kind of knowledge disseminated by these games. The importance of this issue has been recently underlined by Daniel Giere, who developed an empirical study of the influence that digital games have on historical narratives offered by players. He could conclude convincingly that games have an impact on how history is conceived and that game content is being learned and memorised as historical knowledge (Giere 2019). Later contributions in this volume will highlight how players engage with games on an emotional level and how this influences learning behaviour (see Hiriart and McKinney et al. in this volume). The archaeogaming section focuses more on the aspects of how gameplay, game mechanics and representation in different games may further the teaching and learning of archaeology.

Erik Malcolm Champion explains how games can promote learning archaeology. He correctly points to the question of game mechanics and how these are typically used in computer games. He asks us to question what a digital archaeology game should consist of if it is to teach us something, and offers a way to achieve this goal, by proposing a framework within which teachers and students can find, relate, annotate and modify existing 3D models, while exploring the usage of these models with the help of suitable game mechanics.

The joint article by the VALUE Foundation (Boom et al.) shows that video games can be used to teach about the past in a critical, yet fun way, allowing for a deep level of personal and historical learning. Through four case studies, the authors show us how this happens in practice: they used video games to present complicated archaeological topics in the classroom, show us how to use video streaming to not only play but also discuss video games from an archaeological point of view, discuss how the software Twine creates interactive non-linear stories, and finally show us how the popular game Minecraft can help to engage with children and create a first contact with cultural heritage in a fun and creative way.

Xavier Rubio-Campillo gives a real-life example, as he directed the team that created a simulation game with archaeological content. This game allows the player to take the role of the leader of a hunter-gatherer group in different stages of human evolution and try to survive in different eras. He explains how the theme, lore, narrative and game mechanics enabled him to create a challenging and informative game that promotes the understanding of hominid evolution in the Sierra de Atapuerca in Spain.

The second part of this volume examines the topic of learning in the museum. Museums have a long-standing tradition of disseminating knowledge as one of their key functions (Walz 2016: 9). As institutions, they are also changing with the advent of new technologies and interests of the public (Walz 2016: 40–75). Archaeological parks and open-air museums are already an example of this (Walz 2016: 93–103). Nowadays, modern digital tools are being tested and employed to create interactive spaces, engage people of different ages, enhance the experience for impaired visitors and create spaces for polyvocality (Arrigoni & Galani 2019). Engaging with visitors is different from teaching in a classroom and the contributions in this section not only present a whole range of different ways of doing so but also discuss pitfalls and challenges.

Anna Riethus shows us how playing an audio app game during a museum visit can create an inclusive museum experience. Her development of the NMsee app game combines an interactive story with tactile exhibits within the permanent exhibition of the Neanderthal Museum. This innovative approach offers both seeing and visually impaired visitors an audio-tactile way to experience the past that is more immersive than before.

Stephan Quick offers a way to use digital media in an open-air archaeological park and how this aids in experiencing the Roman past. Virtual reconstructions at the exhibition reveal the monumentality of the site as it once was. The response to these elaborate visualisations is positive throughout all target groups.

Adolfo Muñoz and Ana Martí describe a project realised at the La Almoina Museum in Valencia, Spain, where they experimented with a prototype of an application where the visitors could experience the excavated remains of the Roman Republic in Valencia. With the help of the HoloLens, view-through augmented reality glasses, visitors are guided through the museum and can see overlays of reconstructions directly on the actual remains. Additional information is given by a virtual tour guide perceptively superimposed as a video inside the glasses.

Finally, Sebastian Hageneuer discusses how to present archaeological reconstructions to a broader audience and highlights examples of the past and the present. He also risks a look into the future and concludes that the correct communication of archaeological reconstructions is the key, especially in a museum environment. While most displays of virtual reconstructions aim for visually pleasing or impressing effects, the most important aspect of this form of scientific communication, the potential to inform, is often neglected.

Digital tools in the classroom is the third section of this volume and concerns itself with tools that assist us in teaching archaeology to children and adults in schools or universities. Here the volume ties back to the archaeogaming section and links it to gamification. Gamification describes the transfer of playable elements to tasks, which usually are not part of games. This means that rules are created that assign awards or penalties to certain actions; points may be gained, levels reached etc. (Oxford Dictionaries 2019), creating positive feedback for preferred behaviour, which leads to higher motivation. Gamification has been a buzzword for several years, because many studies took the view that gamification has the potential to improve learning, if well designed and used correctly (Dicheva et al. 2015). In this session, Michael Remmy and Juan Hiriart take advantage of these approaches.

The first contribution, though, produces a smooth transition from the last session on museums, as Katherine Cook focuses on higher education courses on public archaeology. She exposes problems involved in teaching archaeology in the global context of postcolonial legacies and neocolonial structures of oppression, challenging the ways in which we learn, teach and do archaeology today. She demands that we find ways to decolonise archaeology and asks what digital technologies can do to help. In two case studies, she explains how bringing together students, instructors, heritage professionals, descendant communities and the public promotes the transformation of the discipline of archaeology itself.

Michael Remmy presents his experience with the application of geocaching software at the university level, where he taught courses in collaboration with the digital humanities (DH). Students of archaeology and DH jointly developed geocaching games that led the user through modern-day Cologne to teach them something about the rich Roman past of that city. The outcome was truly positive, as the students reported a higher motivation and gaining practical experiences.

Juan Hiriart developed a game for primary schools, where one plays the head of an Anglo-Saxon family and learns about cultural meanings and traditions, defining identities, roles and social interactions in post-Roman Britain. By assessing the knowledge of schoolchildren before and after playing the game, Hiriart was able to evaluate that the game was most successful when it was able to engage with the children empathetically. This leads to the conclusion that we need to teach the past in a more thoughtful way, especially in the classroom.

The last section examines digital learning environments and how these affect and help teaching and learning in archaeology. Learning environments may look very different from each other. While in some cases a whole countryside is used as a learning space (see Hölscher in this volume), in other cases purely digital environments (Holter and Schwesinger in this volume) or a mixture of digital and analogue entities (McKinney et al. in this volume) are created. By creating the right learning space, we can engage better with students and the general public. An important aspect here is the experience in itself, which facilitates the learning process.

David Frederik Hölscher showcases ways to base science outreach in archaeology upon educational principles. In his PhD project, visitors in northern Germany are offered GPS-guided cycling tours with ludic elements, inviting them to learn about the local landscape and its cultural history. This connection of outdoor learning, archaeological content and digital media might prove to be a powerful way to facilitate public engagement with heritage sites.

Erika Holter and Sebastian Schwesinger's approach is a completely different learning space, in which they simulate the sound distribution in open spaces in classical Athens. With the help of virtual reality, the user is able to listen to a public speaker in an open space from different points with varying options, like the volume of the surrounding crowd, the position of the speaker or his temper. This way, the user is not only able to see a reconstruction of a certain space but also experience its purpose.

The EMOTIVE Project (McKinney et al.) finally introduces a multi-component digital kit for use in formal and informal learning environments in order to foster prehistorical empathy among young people for cultural heritage. They also emphasise the importance of social interaction and dialogue in learning.

In the last 150 years, archaeology has experienced major transitions and the once-classical archaeology of the elite is now a worldwide profession, with dozens of disciplines and led by a common public interest in our past. The digital turn changes our way of practising archaeology and offers many possibilities to address these issues. Although archaeological projects (gradually) adapt accordingly, with the exception of a few examples, teaching archaeology does this only very slowly and in isolated cases.

Overall, the symposium and the chapters in this volume show a clear trend towards a more playful and empathetic, but also more respectful way of teaching archaeology in the future. Either by play, practical experience or both, the authors of this volume put forward how we should think about knowledge transfer and how we should transform classical forms of teaching in our field.

Through different forms of gaming, the chapters by Champion, Boom et al., Rubio-Campillo, Remmy, Hiriart and Hölscher demonstrate clearly how to engage playfully with students, but also the public. Their results clearly show that learning and interest is raised by playful engagement. The works by Riethus and Cook, especially, focus on the inclusion of marginalised people into the creation of content for museums. This decolonisation of knowledge creation can be much aided by digital media, as has been shown by Arrigoni and Galani (2019). In addition, the division between 'audience' and 'specialist disseminating knowledge' is broken in several contributions by engaging the public and by creating digital spaces, in which the players can create their own content (e.g. Boom et al. or Holter and Schwesinger in this volume).

Several contributions in this publication show how emotional involvement may improve the engagement of pupils, students and the general public with archaeology (e.g. Boom et al., Hiriart, Remmy, McKinney et al. in this volume). It has recently been put forward how entrenched emotions such as excitement and enchantment are in archaeological practice (Perry 2019) and how archaeological narratives reflect personal attitudes as well as the zeitgeist (Hageneuer 2016; Miera 2019; Moser & Gamble 1997). Digital tools offer a multitude of ways to engage users emotionally by creating captivating narratives, interactive spaces and/or lively representations, and games are one of the most proliferative. This does not necessarily mean that we should start playing games with our students or visitors in the museum (although we can!) but it does exemplify that we cannot continue teaching archaeology in the same traditional way, which focuses on frontally disseminating knowledge created by experts, whether this happens in the classroom or the museum.

We therefore need to focus our teaching to a more specialised direction, as it is already partially done in special MA programmes in digital archaeology[1] or archaeoinformatics.[2] These new sub-disciplines train students in the usage of digital technologies designed to help in the field but also to develop methods for the future. Just as well, these methods aid in communicating archaeology

---

[1] For example, at the University of York: [online] Department of Archaeology. Available at: https://www.york.ac.uk/study/postgraduate-taught/courses/msc-digital-Archaeology [Accessed 3 June 2019].

[2] For example, at the University of Cologne: [online] Institute of Archaeology. Available at: http://archaeoinformatik.uni-koeln.de [Accessed 3 July 2019].

to the public in a more relatable way. Comfortable in the digital space, the broader audience understands technologies and visualisations much better than it does scientific publications or traditional museum displays. It responds better to engagement than to passive reception. This volume demonstrates in many ways how we can engage in scientific communication with the public, in contrast to simply telling them what to believe. This holds especially true with a younger audience.

We strongly believe that as archaeologists it is our duty not only to discover the past but also to communicate it to everyone that makes our profession possible and in this way to foster a close relationship to our shared human history. With technologies like virtual or augmented reality, computer games, 3D visualisations or virtual environments, this is easier than ever before, when done responsibly and respectfully.

References

Arrigoni, G. and Galani, A. (2019). Digitally enhanced polyvocality and reflective spaces. Challenges in sustaining dialogue in museums through digital technologies. In: A. Galani, R. Mason and G. Arrigoni, eds, *European Heritage, Dialogue and Digital Practices*, London: Routledge, pp. 37–61. [online] Newcastle University. Available at: https://eprints.ncl.ac.uk/256404 [Accessed 19 August 2019].

Cushman, E. (2013). Wampum, Sequoyan, and story: Decolonizing the digital archive. *College English*, 76: 115–135.

Dicheva, D., Dichev, C., Agre, G. and Angelova, G. (2015). Gamification in education: A systematic mapping study. *Journal of Educational Technology & Society*, [pdf] 18(3): 75–88. Available at: https://www.j-ets.net/ETS/journals/18_3/6.pdf [Accessed 16 August 2019].

DigVentures (2019). *DigVentures Website* [online] Available at: https://digventures.com/ [Accessed 16 August 2019].

Giaccardi, E. (2012). Introduction: Reframing heritage in participatory culture. In: E. Giaccardi, ed., *Heritage and Social Media: Understanding Heritage in a Participatory Culture*, London and New York: Routledge, pp. 1–10.

Giere, D. (2019). *Computerspiele – Medienbildung – historisches Lernen. Zu Repräsentation und Rezeption von Geschichte in digitalen Spielen*. Frankfurt am Main: Wochenschau-Verlag.

Hageneuer, S. (2016). The influence of early architectural reconstruction drawings in Near Eastern archaeology. In: R.A. Stucky, ed., *Proceedings of the 9th International Congress on the Archaeology of the Ancient Near East*, Wiesbaden: Harrassowitz, pp. 359–370.

Huggett, J. (2019). Resilient scholarship in the digital age. *Journal of Computer Applications in Archaeology*, 2(1): 105–119, DOI: https://doi.org/10.5334/jcaa.25.

Layard, A.H. (1851). *A Popular Account of Discoveries at Nineveh*. London: John Murray.

Layard, A.H. (1853). *Discoveries among the Ruins of Nineveh and Babylon; with Travels in Armenia, Kurdistan and the Desert: Being the Result of a Second Expedition Undertaken for the Trustees of the British Museum*. New York: Harper & Brothers, DOI: https://doi.org/10.5962/bhl.title.67558.

Miera, J.J. (2019). *Ursachen, Formen und Konsequenzen des Erzählens in der Prähistorischen Archäologie: eine Synthese der deutschsprachigen Theoriedebatte*, DOI: https://doi.org/10.6105/journal.fka.2019.8.1.

Morgan, C. (2019). Avatars, monsters, and machines: A cyborg archaeology. *European Journal of Archaeology*, 22(3): 324–337, DOI: https://doi.org/10.1017/eaa.2019.22.

Moser, S. and Gamble, C. (1997). Revolutionary images. The iconic vocabulary for representing human antiquity. In: B.L. Molyneaux, ed., *Cultural Life of Images. Visual Representation in Archaeology*, London: Routledge, pp. 184–212.

Oxford Dictionaries (2019). *Gamification*. [online] Available at: https://en.oxforddictionaries.com/definition/gamification [Accessed 15 August 2019].

Paletschek, S. (2002). Die Erfindung der Humboldtschen Universität: Die Konstruktion der deutschen Universitätsidee in der ersten Hälfte des 20. Jahrhunderts. *Historische Anthropologie*, [online] 10(2): 183–205. Available at: https://www.vr-elibrary.de/doi/10.7788/ha.2002.10.2.183 [Accessed 15 August 2019].

Perkins, P., Spaeth, D.A. and Trainor, R.H. (1992). Computers and the teaching of history and Archaeology in higher education. *Computers & Education*, 19(1): 153–162, DOI: https://doi.org/10.1016/0360-1315(92)90021-V [Accessed 15 August 2019].

Perry, S. (2019). The enchantment of the archaeological record. *European Journal of Archaeology*, 22(3): 354–371, DOI: https://doi.org/10.1017/eaa.2019.24 [Accessed 15 August 2019].

Reinhardt, A. (2018). *Archaeogaming. An introduction to Archaeology in and of Video Games*. New York: Berghahn Books.

Sarr, F. and Savoy, B. (2018). *The Restitution of African Cultural Heritage. Toward a New Relational Ethics*, [pdf] Restitution Report. Available at: https://restitutionreport2018.com/sarr_savoy_en.pdf [Accessed 20 August 2019].

Smith, M.L. (2014). Citizen science in archaeology, *American Antiquity*, 79(4): 749–762, DOI: https://doi.org/10.7183/0002-7316.79.4.749 [Accessed 16 August 2019].

Schütz-Pitan, J., Weiß, T. and Hense, J. (2018). Jedes Medium ist anders: Akzeptanz unterschiedlicher digitaler Medien in der Hochschullehre, Die Hochschullehre, 2018(4). [pdf] Hochschullehre. Available at: http://www.hochschullehre.org/wp-content/files/die_hochschullehre_2018_Schutz-Pitan_et_al_jedes_Medium_ist_anders_.pdf [Accessed 15 August 2019].

Walz, M. (2016). *Handbuch Museum: Geschichte, Aufgaben, Perspektiven.* Springer: Stuttgart.

Winckelmann, J.J. (1760). *Description des pierres gravées de feu Baron de Stosch.* André Bonducci: Florenz.

Wosnitza, M., Helker, K. and Lohbeck, L. (2014). Teaching goals of early career university teachers in Germany. *International Journal of Educational Research*, 65: 90–103, DOI: https://doi.org/10.1016/j.ijer.2013.09.009 [Accessed 15 August 2019].

Archaeogaming

Games People Dig: Are They Archaeological Experiences, Systems or Arguments?

Erik Malcolm Champion

Curtin University

Abstract

One of the many but important dilemmas we may encounter in designing or critiquing games for archaeology (Champion 2015) is determining the why: why we should develop, buy, play, and teach specific games for the above disciplines. For archaeology, I propose there is a further important trifurcation: games aiming to convey an experience of archaeology (Hiriart 2018); games aiming to show how systems, methods, findings, and unknowns interact either to produce that experience; or games revealing what is unknown or debated (how knowledge is established or how knowledge is contested).

Keywords

Definitions, Systems, Prototyping, Heritage

How to cite this book chapter:
Champion, E. M. 2020. Games People Dig: Are They Archaeological Experiences, Systems or Arguments? In: Hageneuer, S. (ed.) *Communicating the Past in the Digital Age: Proceedings of the International Conference on Digital Methods in Teaching and Learning in Archaeology (12–13 October 2018).* Pp. 13–25. London: Ubiquity Press. DOI: https://doi.org/10.5334/bch.b. License: CC-BY 4.0

Introduction

Why should we develop, buy, play and teach serious games? If there are insufficient engaging archaeological games, is the problem a lack of photo-realism? Recently, philosophers (Thompson 2016) have accused VR of being parasitic and incapable of simulating the real-world experience but this misses a key value of VR: it can also provide us with explorations of process and predictions. It can act not only as a model of the real world but as an investigation into the processes and interpretations of the real and historic world. For what is visualisation? The London Charter (Denard 2009) defined computer-based visualisation as '[t]he process of representing information visually with the aid of computer technologies'. This implies that visualisation is only visual, that all is required is to represent (in a visual format) content to an end user. It does not explain the cultural significance of the object or process simulated, or reasons for why it should be preserved and communicated. I suggest that cultural learning is a wonderful opportunity for digital archaeology, to explore how different interpretations and world views can be presented and explored.

Digital games, game levels and game mods (modified games) are often easy to change, with simpler development than many CADD systems; it is easy to find students and involve them; and games typically require less maintenance than many expensive VR systems. They have online forums and active modding communities, and inbuilt performance evaluation, and the interaction is typically more intuitive and offers different ways of learning.

Games can help us learn how to:

- manage resources;
- observe and interact with appropriate social behaviour (chat, observation, mimicry);
- visualise or even predict changes in scale, landscape or climate;
- make decisions based on varying levels of uncertainty or probability;
- filter, reconfigure, reconstruct elements of time periods;
- immerse ourselves in the excitement of the times (seen as important to the inhabitants);
- select correct objects or appearance to move about the 'world' or to trade or to advance social role or period of time;
- decipher codes, language, avoid traps;
- follow online or inworld walkthroughs by teachers or inhabitants or students;
- create embedded collaborative storytelling (via film-making or via role-playing, see (Figure 1)).

However, games are based on fast-moving technology. As commercial products they sometimes offer less coding flexibility, they are often looked down upon by academics, they may not offer as much flexibility in transferring content and providing open formats as other software, they have no professional (modding)

Figure 1: Archaeologists roleplay soldiers marching on each other in Dr Stuart Eve's proposed phenomenological *Battle of Waterloo* game, CAA2017, Atlanta, Georgia.

support (as that is not their main market) and they usually favour ludic immersion and artistic creativity over historical accuracy. They can also feature genre baggage, if you mod a game with historical content, players may only play that game in a mind-set calibrated to a specific commercial game genre and under-value or miss the historical content.

And it is still not clear how computer games can communicate cultural significance, overcome changing technologies and platforms, demonstrate archaeological methods, interpretations and principles, convey simulated inhabitants' viewpoints, link large scholarly or intangible heritage data, or help local communities to convey traditions (although *Never Alone* is a worthy exception – see Mol et al. 2017).

Most importantly, games are engaging challenges, a point not always made by game theorists. For example, Salen and Zimmerman (2003) defined a game as '[a] system in which players engage in an artificial conflict, defined by rules, that results in a quantifiable outcome'. Juul (2003) defined a game as '[a] rule-based formal system with a variable and quantifiable outcome, where different outcomes are assigned different values, the player exerts effort in order to influence the outcome, the player feels attached to the outcome, and the consequences of the activity are optional and negotiable'.

With both definitions, where is the engaging challenge? There is an emphasis on conflict (what about Caillois's forms or modalities of mimesis, vertigo, chance?) The definitions discount games that may never have a final outcome (e.g. cricket) and do not emphasise the importance of strategy or the appeal of player agency. Virtual environments have constraints and affordances; games have risks and rewards. What should a digital archaeological game have?

I believe a successful game must have an engaging challenge. I defined a game (Champion 2006) as 'An engaging challenge that offers up the possibility of temporary or permanent tactical resolution without harmful outcomes to the real-world situation of the participant' and I included 'tactical resolution' to emphasise the importance of strategy and options.

This definition arose from my PhD thesis project (2001–2004), which evaluated approximately 80 students in a pilot study of an Internet Explorer browser-based three-dimensional recreation of the Mayan city Palenque in Chiapas, Mexico. The evaluation, in controlled conditions, tested 12 pairs of museum, archaeology and 3D experts, then five pairs of IT experts at the *Lonely Planet* headquarters in Melbourne. There were three different modes of interactivity: exploration and observation; conversation with simple NPCs (non-playing characters); and activity (for example, moving a trapdoor that led down to the sarcophagus of Lord Pakal in the Temple of Inscriptions).

On completion of each archaeological/heritage level, the participants were teleported through a portal to a more imaginative game-like level based on Mayan mythology or Mayan history (like the ball court and the mythical crack in the earth). Xavier Quijas Yxayotl, a musician with Mayan heritage, graciously provided musical tracks he composed and played on traditional instruments inspired by Palenque, and the music was trigged in relation to events and to location (the music also faded when participants moved away from the tasks).

I evaluated task performance, their ranking of the three environments in terms of what I called specific presence questions comparing the three environments in terms of their interest-value, their perceived sense of Mayan-specific inhabitation, environmental recall (if participants noticed certain aspects of the digital environments), and subjective experience of time passed (Table 1).

In my evaluation (Table 1), I had to carefully define 'challenge' to the participants. Challenge means an engaging challenge or something people want to avoid; successful games are always the former. Games have genre baggage as well, many people see a game and assume they know how to play it, but understanding specific cultural situatedness (and ways of doing things) may be obscured by the already-understood conventions of popular game genres. For example, if I said the levels were games, participants knew exactly what to do and where to go, but if I said the levels were archaeological reconstructions, participants were confused but treated the environment with more care and concentration on the content.

My results also indicated that those who were quickest to complete tasks scored the lowest in terms of memory recall or understanding the implications

Table 1: Evaluation questions (Palenque thesis project, 2001–2004).

Evaluation	Content	Objective
Task performance	6 information objects to find per environment	Compare to understanding
Cultural understanding (multiple choice)	6 multiple-choice questions on the Temple of Inscriptions	Compare to preference, task performance and demographics
	6 multiple-choice questions on the Palace	
	6 multiple-choice questions on the Cross Precinct	
Presence survey (rank from 1 to 7)	Which did you find the most challenging to explore, find or change things?	Compare to demographics and task performance. Find personal preference in answers (A to D/E). Rank the 3 archaeological and the 4 imaginative environments from 1 for highest (most, closest), and 7 for least close
	Which was the most interesting to you?	
	Which seemed most interactive to you?	
	Which did you feel most closely represented the way Mayans saw their own world?	
	Which most effectively seemed inhabited by real people?	
	Which felt most like you were in the presence of Mayan culture?	
Environmental Recall: did you notice? (multiple choice)	Shadow?	Compare to demographics, to task performance and to understanding
	Real People?	
	How tall were Mayans compared to modern western people?	

Continued

Evaluation	Content	Objective
	How many real or computer scripted people were in the site?	
	In future, which would you like such environments for?	
Subjective experience of time passing (rate 1–3)	In each environment, did time pass by quickest? (Write in descending order of apparent speed)	Compare to subjective preference and to demographics
	Rank the environments (1 for fastest to 3 for slowest) for how slow they seemed to be for updating the screen	

of Mayan history. Surprisingly, the technical improvements important to me as a designer (such as dynamic lighting) were not noticed by most of the participants.

More important to me than genre and typology is exploring whether the game appeals to a particular type of experience. Roger Caillois's (1961) *Forms of Play* (which I prefer to call modalities of play), goes some way to explaining different types or modes or modalities of playful experience and why they engage players (Table 2). Can game genres or games as interaction modes be compared to what is learned? Can a schematic framework show what can be communicated and why the framework should be undertaken? Plus, can there be criteria revealing when the game is useful while avoiding banal gamification (applying badges and simple reward systems to software and interfaces which are simply routine and boring)?

To break down artificial and conventional categories of game genres, I believe that game modalities of experience and game mechanics are critical: appropriate mechanics help create the feel of the gameplay,

My suggestion is that gameplay related thematically to the goals and setting of the game and game mechanics that are both appropriate and imaginative can help designers avoid the trap of boring games and clumsy gamification. To break down artificial and conventional categories of game genres, I believe that game modalities of experience *and* game mechanics are critical: choosing the appropriate mode of experience for the player, tied to suitable mechanics, help create the immersive and integrated feel of the gameplay; mechanics push the game along via an internal logic to an eventual final game state; they provide the interactional chassis to the experience.

Game mechanics are typically mechanics to progress the player through the game, but they can also be designed to encourage the player to improve and extend their range of skills and judgement), or to progress the player through the game, or bring together one or more apparent story threads in relation

Table 2: Three of Roger Callois's Four Forms or Modalities of Play.

Challenge modes	Engages because you	Archaeology	Pros/Cons
Competition *Agon* (competition/ strategy)	Compete against people, long-term decision-making	*Civilization*-"build an empire" type games	+ Strategic + Engaging – Means to end
Chance *Alea*	Handle unpredictability, humour	Could *Spore* be an archaeology game?	+ Engaging – No causality
Mimicry *Mimesis*	Observation, control and humour and role-playing	Maybe if *Sims 4* were used as anthropological machinima?	+ Builds empathy + Engaging – Difficult for interfaces

to gameplay. They can also help persuade players to develop habits through repeated gameplay, and accustom players to see things in certain ways, or they could shock the player into breaking habits and seeing events, objects or experiences in a new light. We could also imagine insight and reversal mechanics: mechanics that disrupt the in-game or real-world expectations and presumptions of the player acquired previously or during the game in order to reveal to them a viewpoint they may have previously taken for granted or a perspective they never noticed before.

I would agree that games do not normally prioritise interaction to help us understand historical situations. History is usually the backstory; it is not a laboratory to explore. However, it can be a laboratory: my PhD project made use of gamic simulations to retrieve evaluation data about different forms of interaction, but designing games is also a wonderful way of learning about content.

What is the best way of integrating 3D digital models and commercial (and independent) game content into learning for non-archaeology students? The approach I have taken with my students at three different universities has been to design basic game levels and prototypes to explore new ways of interacting with content, but, as I typically taught multimedia students game design, a focus on heritage and history games was not always possible. The students were organised into groups of four; they pitched their game levels, designed prototypes or fully working levels, and evaluated another group's game design. Their evaluation was also part of the final mark. Although I said they were multimedia students, their game levels featured Minoan, Egyptian, Maltese, Mayan, Chinese and Australian archaeological data, and historical content.

We encountered many issues but that was expected, because my goal for them was to explore new ways of interacting with and learning from games,

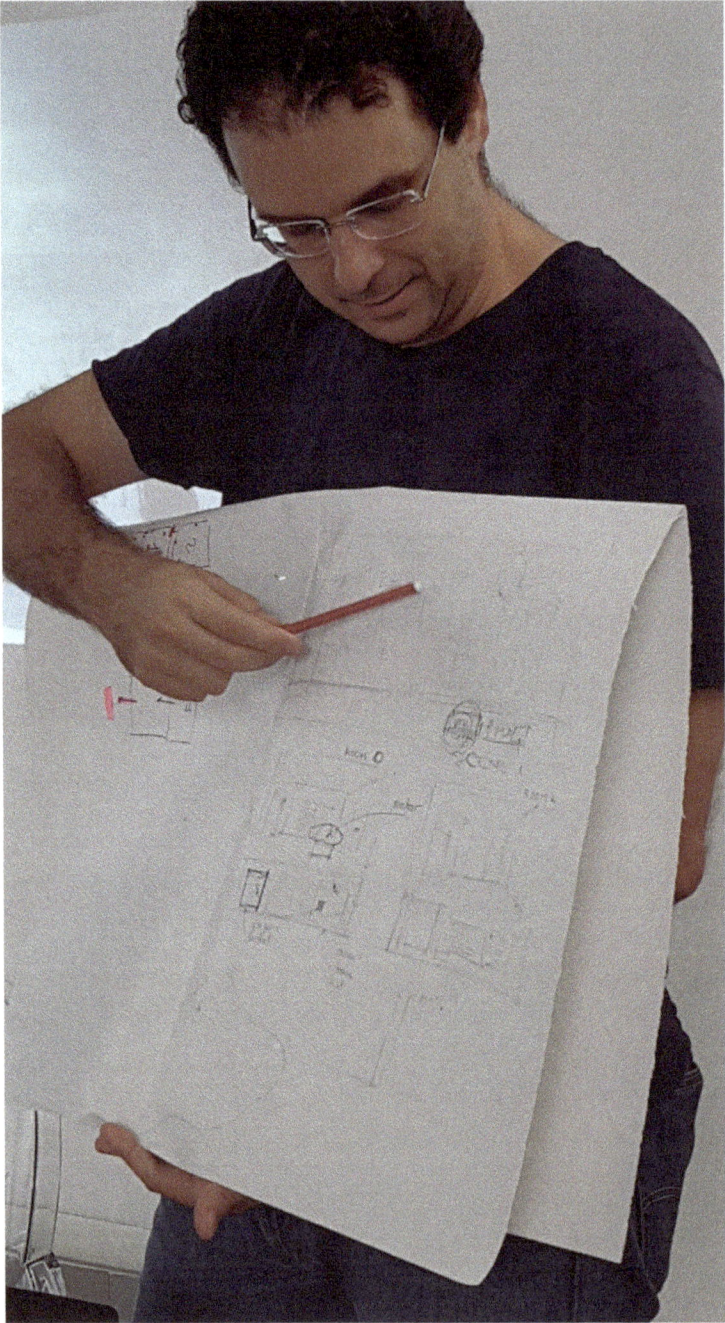

Figure 2: Architect at 2018 Turin Summer School explains a game designed to convey value of artefacts in Brazilian museum fire.

and to learn from design challenges, not to mimic existing game themes or conventional mechanics. One group built their own game engine from code, a few used the *Source* game engine, some used *Unity*, one used *Quest3D*, but most used *Warcraft*, *Neverwinter Nights* or *Unreal Tournament*. A few built their own Flash games, but most were 3D games or game mods (modified game levels).

Typical problems included how to find suitable interaction metaphors that fitted the context, incorporating game balance, resolving copyright issues as mods, unstable versions (especially in the case of *Neverwinter Nights*), how to provide learning content but also to afford agency, and the dilemma of whether the gamer should emphasise priority of learning as the primary aim or design the game to be primarily an enjoyable challenge for its own sake.

For prototyping workshops (and I have run game prototyping panels or workshops to archaeologists, historians, and architects at CAA2016 and Turin 2018 Digital Summer School), the problem is simpler.

- **What** should be experienced and interacted with, as specifically as possible?
- **Why** are we creating a specific experience in a game? (What are our objectives?)
- **Where** will the game be played? (What is the background environment, what is the imaginative setting?)
- **How** do we design prototypes to convey the experience of the site, arte-fact or model? How can the game prototypes be better designed as systems, methods or findings that interact to produce engaging learning experi-ences? Or, can the game prototypes reveal what is unknown or debated (how knowledge is established or contested)? Can games be used as inter-pretative systems or be staged by the player to test or to demonstrate the clash of interpretations or to pose or test a scholarly argument?
- **When** will the player receive suitable feedback?

To design a game prototype for archaeology, history, or heritage (Figure 3), our first steps are:

1. Determine the cultural, historical, or archaeological facts and inter-pretations of the site or model that are significant, hidden or otherwise appropriate, engaging or transformative to explore.
2. We must consider the environment it will be played in. This is not just the type of audience but the environment in which they will play the game: together, alone, on a bus, in a lecture theatre, at a museum?
3. To ensure we are designing a game rather than a virtual environment, we need to find a challenge (it could be based on Caillois's modes of game experience or some other theory), and how the core gameplay affects and is affected by the modality of experience. Steps two and three also give us an idea of a setting and theme.

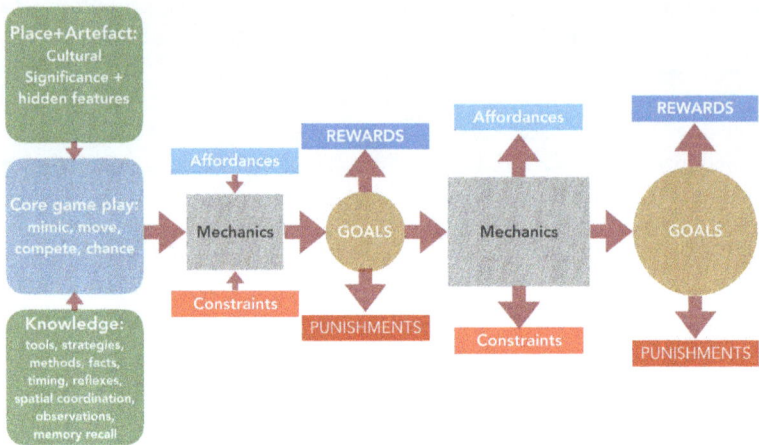

Figure 3: Schematic example of game prototyping components.

4. We need to define the core gameplay. What does the player typically do? Does the game scale, changing in effectiveness and complexity over time? In general, increasing complexity during gameplay keeps players engaged.
5. We also need to develop a reward and punishment system; how do the rewards and punishments interact with the core gameplay and move the game along (i.e. trigger its mechanics)?
6. What is the end state? How will the game mechanics help us get there? Does reaching the end state create an intentional specific reflection, knowledge development, interpretation, experience or other feeling in the player?

Infrastructure

A further issue we have no space for here, but is of critical importance, is how to maintain and preserve the games, and to include our models, paradata and findings in academic literature. Unfortunately, 3D digital recreations, and by extension games, are not typically considered a key scholarly resource (Di Benedetto et al. 2014), nor is there a great deal of available infrastructure to support them. I hope future projects, and publications like this one, challenge that assumption. One solution is to leverage digital real-time reconfiguration to suit the learner, device and task at hand, in other words personalisation; to increase the sense of agency and therefore personal responsibility; to avail one-self of the opportunities for auto tracking and inbuilt valuation in games; and to design a rewards feedback system so that learning is also supported by the game's feedback mechanisms.

I concede that teaching digital heritage and archaeology via existing exemplars is still problematic. Sophisticated but accurate 3D models and related games are hard to find (Tringham & Ashley 2015), to download and to edit. Accessible models are also typically in unwieldy and obsolete formats and standalone meshes. They seldom have comprehensive metadata or information on how data was acquired or how sharable the content is, or the level of accuracy of scanning or modelling, let alone links to paradata. They also typically do not describe the goals of the model (Champion & Rahaman 2019).

Summary

Because of these difficulties I support the development of a scholarly ecosystem: media assets and communities (scholars, shareholders and public) and active participants in game development. I am also heartened by recent development in VR, pushing towards a VR product ecosystem based on consumer level components, phones, head-mounted displays and gaming consoles with additional interface devices.

What is particularly needed, though, is a framework to allow teachers and students to find, relate, annotate and modify existing 3D models and related paradata, and then to comment on them and provide data as to how they could be used for further research and teaching. For example, researchers in Germany have been exploring similar methods to combine metadata, the web and CIDOC CRM to produce Cultural Heritage Markup Language (Hauck & Kuroczyński 2016), but much more integration work and training needs to be done.

I suggest that, rather than just creating 3D models, we should explore how people would and could use them, with suitable archaeological or historical game mechanics. And, if suitable mechanics do not exist, we should create them! This is why I have suggested simple steps both to leverage the engagement potential of game mechanics and to involve as many people as possible in the design of serious games. For designing games and game prototypes is a meaningful, collaborative activity. Even if the conversations and outputs are not easily conveyed in scholarly articles, they are still important.

References

Caillois, R. (1961). *Man, Play, and Games*, Champaign, Illinois: University of Illinois Press.
Champion, E.M. (2006). *Evaluating Cultural Learning in Virtual Environments*. PhD. University of Melbourne, [pdf] Available at: http://nzerik.googlepages.com/PhDBound-Jan2006.pdf [Accessed 6 May 2019].

Champion, E. (2015). Virtual heritage, an introduction. In: G. Robyn and J. Jacobson, eds, *The Egyptian Oracle Project; Ancient Ceremony in Augmented Reality*, London: Bloomsbury.

Champion, E. and Rahaman, H. (2019). 3D digital heritage models as sustainable scholarly resources. *Sustainability*, [online] 11(8): 1–8. Available at: http://www.mdpi.com/2071-1050/11/8/2425 [Accessed 6 May 2019].

Denard, H. (2009). *The London Charter for the Computer-Based Visualisation of Cultural Heritage*. [online] Available at: http://www.londoncharter.org [Accessed 18 July 2016].

Di Benedetto, M., Ponchio, F., Malomo, L., Callieri, M., Dellepiane, M., Cignoni, P. and Scopigno, R. (2014). Web and mobile visualization for cultural heritage. In: M. Ioannides and E. Quak, eds, *3D Research Challenges in Cultural Heritage: A Roadmap in Digital Heritage Preservation*, Berlin and Heidelberg: Springer, pp. 18–35.

Hauck, O. and Kuroczyński, P. 2016. Cultural Heritage Markup Language. In: W. Börner and S. Uhlirz, eds, *Proceedings of the 20th International Conference on Cultural Heritage and New Technologies 2015* (CHNT 20, 2015), 2–4 November 2015, Vienna, Austria. Vienna Austria: Museen der Stadt Wien – Stadtarchäologie, [pdf] Available at: http://www.chnt.at/wp-content/uploads/eBook_CHNT20_Hauck_Kuroczynski_2015.pdf [Accessed 6 September 2019].

Hiriart, J.F.V. (2018). *The Game of Making an Archaeology Game: Proposing a Design Framework for Historical Game Design*. Computer Applications and Quantitative Methods in Archaeology (CAA) International Conference. Tübingen, Germany.

Juul, J. (2003). The game, the player, the world: looking for a heart of gameness. *DIGRA Conference-'Level Up'*, Utrecht, the Netherlands, 4–6 November 2003.

Mol, A.A.A., Ariese-Vandemeulebroucke, C.E., Boom, K.H.J. and Politopoulos, A. (eds) (2017). *The Interactive Past: Archaeology, Heritage, and Video Games*, Leiden: Sidestone Press.

Salen, K. and Zimmerman, E. (2003). *Rules of Play: Game Design Fundamentals*, Cambridge, MA: MIT Press.

Thompson, J. (2016). *Why Virtual Reality Cannot Match the Real Thing*. [online] The Conversation. Available at: https://theconversation.com/why-virtual-reality-cannot-match-the-real-thing-92035 [Accessed 6 May 2019].

Tringham, R. and Ashley, M. (2015). Becoming archaeological. *Journal of Contemporary Archaeology*, 2(1): 29–41.

Ludography

Warcraft (1994–2018). Blizzard Entertainment. [Multiple platforms].
Neverwinter Nights (2002–2003). BioWare. [Multiple platforms].

Unreal Tournament (1999–2020). Epic games. [Multiple platforms].

Civilization series (1991–2016). MicroProse & Firaxis Games. MicroProse, Activision, Infogrames Entertainment & 2K Games. [Multiple platforms].

Never Alone (Kisima Inɲitchuɲa) (2014). Upper One Games. E-Line Media. [Multiple platforms].

Teaching through Play: Using Video Games as a Platform to Teach about the Past

Krijn H.J. Boom[*†§], Csilla E. Ariese[†§],
Bram van den Hout[‡§], Angus A.A. Mol[*§]
and Aris Politopoulos[*§]

*Leiden University
†University of Amsterdam
‡International Institute of Social History Amsterdam
§VALUE Foundation

Abstract

The video game market is a big part of the current popular media landscape and is growing rapidly. Developers of video games are keen to make use of a variety of historical pasts as this provides them with recognisable themes, settings or narrative frameworks. Video games can be seen as the manifestation of experiential learning theory: they provide a unique informal learning

How to cite this book chapter:
Boom, K. H. J., Ariese, C. E., van den Hout, B., Mol, A. A. A. and Politopoulos, A.
2020. Teaching through Play: Using Video Games as a Platform to Teach about the
Past. In: Hageneuer, S. (ed.) *Communicating the Past in the Digital Age: Proceedings
of the International Conference on Digital Methods in Teaching and Learning in
Archaeology (12–13 October 2018)*. Pp. 27–44. London: Ubiquity Press. DOI:
https://doi.org/10.5334/bch.c. License: CC-BY 4.0

environment in which their interactive nature allows for an immersive experience with which a deeper level of personal and historical learning can potentially be reached than in more formal settings. However, pasts incorporated in video games are mostly utilised to provide a fun experience in order to generate revenue. As more and more people depend on video games to teach them about the past, they often take the history presented in them for granted, relying on developers to tell an accurate story. Unmediated, players are prone to miss opportunities for critical engagement with the presented past, and can fall into the trap of presentism.

It is important for those teaching about the past to understand how video games work, and what their potential and impact are. Data-driven approaches allow us to explore what types of games are considered to be 'historical'. Our research shows that 206 million copies of games have been sold through Steam that were tagged as historical, and can be classified as strategy/top-down games, action-adventure narrative-driven games, or first-person action games. These types all have a reliance on some form of violence as central game mechanic, which needs to be taken into account when using video games as an education platform.

Through four case studies, we show that video games can function as a platform to teach about the past in a critical, yet fun way. Firstly, Twine can be used to stimulate critical and multi-linear thinking as it allows the user to create a narrative based on a branching structure instead of a linear one. Secondly, video games can be incorporated into formal classroom settings in order to illustrate certain complex theoretical concepts. Streaming, or creating videos about games that incorporate the past, can be a major avenue for content-focused teaching, as well as a way to reflect on video game pasts – the third case study. Lastly, our RoMeincraft case study shows that participants are not only taught something about Roman heritage but also able to increase their skills in communication and digital media. The goal of this chapter is to provide researchers with practical examples set within a solid theoretical framework of how video games can be implemented as a teaching tool.

Keywords

Experiential Learning Theory, Video Games, Experience, Impact, The Past

Introduction

As the video game market is ever expanding within the contemporary media landscape (ESA 2018a; 2018b; Shieber 2019), big-budget game studios, indie developers, social media influencers and other creatives design their versions of the past, purely or mostly, as entertainment products, where the focus is on making money through designing fun. This is problematic in the sense that such individuals and organisations (1) have not traditionally been and are frequently still not taken seriously in their role of shaping our collective understanding about the past, (2) are not primarily (or at all) concerned with teaching about the past and (3), more and more, the connection many people have with the past is partly or even primarily shaped by video games, including how they learn or teach others about it.[1] Learning about the past through video games can and does take place in the context of formal education or in public heritage institutions (e.g. Koutsabasis 2017; McCall 2016), but the majority of experiences take place through unstructured, informal learning. As video games are still often considered to be 'neglected media', which 'exhibit strong popular appeal and economic relevance, contrasted by a lack of cultural prestige and scientific coverage' (Reichmuth & Werning 2006: 47), not much is known yet about how they shape the ways 'players engage with and think about the past' (Metzger & Paxton 2016: 532). Thus, it is all the more important to research how video games influence people's understanding and experience of the past in order to improve teaching approaches.

The goal of this chapter is to share some practical approaches, based on the experiences of the authors, of how to leverage video games as a platform to teach about the past. While learning theory in the context of video games is discussed to illustrate the necessity of teacher mediation, the focus lies on how teachers can implement video games in their teaching.[2]

We will first discuss some theoretical considerations, as video games are not created in a vacuum and their use for history teaching has many implications, both positive and negative. Secondly, we will consider what kind of pasts people (tend to) play outside of structured heritage or educational experiences. Thirdly, we will discuss four case studies illustrating how the authors of this chapter, who are all part of the VALUE Foundation,[3] have employed video games for teaching purposes in different contexts.

---

[1] The video game market is an ever-expanding giant in the contemporary media landscape. In 2018, video game revenue reached its latest peak of 43.8 billion US dollars, making it one of, if not the, largest grossing entity in the entertainment industry, far surpassing Hollywood figures. More importantly, 64% of US households own a device that they use to play video games and 60% of Americans play video games daily (ESA 2018a; 2018b).

[2] What the impact is on learning, especially as realised upon the different target groups, their individual perceptions and cognitive processes, is a subject that is characterised by a lack of data sets from structured studies. As such, there is a disbalance between teaching experiences and a data-driven understanding of how we learn about the past through games; the authors feel this needs to be a much more pronounced aspect of future research in this field.

[3] The VALUE Foundation 'aims to design, facilitate, and conduct worldwide research, development, and outreach on the crossroads of gaming and academia. Our approach is characterized by playfulness and accessibility.' It consists of six members: Csilla Ariese, Krijn Boom, Angus Mol, Aris Politopoulos, Bram van den Hout and Vincent Vandemeulebroucke. VALUE has three core focus areas: firstly, to organise knowledge activation and dissemination projects (e.g. the RoMeincraft project detailed below); secondly, to bring the gaming industry and knowledge institutions

Experiencing the past

History and archaeology are fascinating subjects for video game developers: many video games revolve around historical settings, characters or ideas
(Chapman 2016; Mol et al. 2017) and developers have many ways to 'deploy'
the past, for instance to guide the game's narrative or to convey a sense of historical representation, but also to send (knowingly or unknowingly) a political
message (e.g. Alexandra 2018) or to glorify a certain historical era (Metzger &
Paxton 2016).

On the one hand, it is a good thing that many video game developers embrace
the past as a way to tell a good story – for example, online discussion forums
for such games are often filled with players taking their game experiences as a
way to discuss actual history and heritage with each other. The unique feature
of video games is that they are interactive: players absorb a particular narrative
while taking part at the same time, enabling players to experience a shift in
their self-perception (Gilbert 2019: 111). In essence, video games are playful
manifestations of experiential learning theory (ELT), which can be defined as
'the process whereby knowledge is created through the transformation of experience' (Kolb 1984: 23). In Gilbert's study, for example, students emphasised
how playing and following stories made them experience the past and feel an
immediate access to history and a sense of human connection to people in
the past – both results contrasting with formal high-school learning (Gilbert
2019). Another core feature of video games is that their narratives can be based
on non-linear storytelling. These branching structures allow players to change
the course of the story, allowing for multiple directions and outcomes (Wolf
2001). While playing *Assassin's Creed* (AC) games, Gilbert's students indeed
perceived these multiple perspectives in history, incorporated into the game
by its developers. Importantly, this narrative structure allowed them to reflect
upon historical events and characters and as such think differently about their
understanding of both history and themselves (Gilbert 2019). The AC franchise
is known for having strong narrative-driven stories, combining linear storytelling with branching structures. The last iterations of the franchise even include
so-called 'Discovery Tours', providing players with a game mode purely focused
on non-combat, educational aspects (Politopoulos et al. 2019). However, the
past as incorporated in the AC games is still rather 'fixed'.[4] Other video games,
such as *Sid Meier's Civilization* (Civ), allow the player much more freedom in
their play with the past. Civ is a strategy game which allows players to 'engage

---

closer together; and, thirdly, to conduct research on gaming and the use of gaming
for research, outreach, and teaching. Most of VALUE's formal learning activities have
focused on tertiary education. For more information: www.value-foundation.org.

[4] On 10 June 2019 a so-called Story Creator Mode was launched, allowing players
to create and share their own stories in the AC-Odyssey universe. See: https://
assassinscreed.ubisoft.com/story-creator-mode/en-us.

with past and present technological advances, social systems, and built heritage in a playful history that is closely analogous to but always slightly different from our own' (Mol, Politopoulos & Ariese-Vandemeulebroucke 2017: 1; more about Civ below). Roberts wrote about the usefulness of this 'counterfactual history' for teaching purposes and concludes that his students, who could experiment with historical cause and effect in Civ, had an increased understanding of and interest in history (Roberts 2011). On the other end of the spectrum are games that allow players to create their own unique version, or representation, of history (see our case studies below for an example of this using *Minecraft*). What these brief examples show is that, in contrast to factual learning, video games allow players to experience the past by interacting with it as they go, deepening their understanding through reflection and experimentation. This is in line with ELT, which presupposes that learners need four different kinds of abilities: concrete experience abilities, reflective observation abilities, abstract conceptualisation abilities, and active experimentation (Kolb 1984). Video games inherently allow players access to all these abilities and act, as it were, as a learning conduit.

Although the above illustrates a quite positive picture of the potential that video games have in teaching about the past, there are certainly also some (known and lesser known) drawbacks. With the ever-growing video game market, students are increasingly positioned to combine their knowledge gained from popular culture media messages with that of formal academic teaching (Metzger & Paxton 2016). In her study, Gilbert also noted that students missed opportunities for critical engagement with the past while playing video games and often took creative design decisions as historical facts, 'fully trusting the designers to present an unbiased view of history' (Gilbert 2019: 127). Furthermore, because of the immersive nature of video games, players are prone to presentism, trusting that their gameplay experience equals people's actual feelings at that time. Also, because video games are perceived as less valuable than more direct academic approaches to teaching about the past (Reichmuth & Werning 2006), players might internalise that message too, giving less critical attention to the pasts they play. Students need guidance in these gameplay experiences. There is an 'absolute necessity for post-game reflective discussions to take place in order to disentangle factual and fictional elements and complement the learning experience' (Lynch, Mallon & Connolly 2015: 35); formal teaching is still required in order for players to be able to critically analyse their more informal experiential learning experiences (Gilbert 2019).

What pasts do people play?

One important step in understanding how to teach about the past using games is to have an overview of the (types of) pasts that people play. There may be one, several or many games that intersect with the region, time period or theme one

seeks to teach and it is good to add (a selection of) these to one's body of popular culture references. Beyond this direct connection, it is perhaps even more
important to have a grasp of what types of narrative, audio-visual, mechanical
and other features are found in games that are, broadly speaking, addressing
the same pasts as we are. Obviously, playing some of these games is the best
way to gain an understanding of the medium, although this is rather time-
consuming. There is now also a growing number of scholarly reviews discussing specific games and their relation to the past (e.g. McCall 2013; 2019; Mol,
Politopoulos & Ariese-Vandemeulebroucke 2017; Politopoulos et al. 2019).
Beyond academic outlets, several blogs and YouTube series focus on the inter-
section of games and the past.[5]

Aside from learning about individual games, data-driven approaches allow
us to explore this corpus on a larger scale. For example, there is SteamSpy, a web
service that collects and allows access to data from Steam, the biggest digital
distribution platform in the game industry. SteamSpy gives, among many other
things, information on games that have been tagged by its users as 'historical',
allowing for insights on playtime and numbers sold of individual games and
the corpus as a whole.[6] With SteamSpy data, it is also possible to explore the
contents of these games, for example through tags, which are one- or two-word
descriptive statements about a game by its players. Figure 1 is a visualisation
that shows how tags in games (that are also tagged as 'historical') are connected
to each other. The figure shows both the great diversity of features in this corpus, but also shows that certain tags are more frequently found together. Based
on these stronger inter-tag relations it is possible to distil three subgroups of
historical games: strategy/top-down games, action-adventure narrative-driven
games, and first-person action games.[7]

---

[5] Such as Shawn Graham's *Electric Archaeology* (https://electricarchaeology.ca),
Andrew Reinhard's *Archaeogaming* (https://archaeogaming.com) – managed by
Kaitlyn Kingsland since mid-2019, Dominik Schott's *ArchaeoGames* (https://
archaeogames.net) and VALUE's *Interactive Pasts* (http://interactivepasts.com).

[6] 'Historical' would be a relatively narrow term or scope in terms of an academic understanding of the past – i.e. taking place in historical times or a subject understood
through the practice of history (Chapman 2016). Yet, the games that are actually
tagged as 'historical' feature pasts that range from 'mythological' (*Age of Mythology*,
Ensemble Studios, 2002) to 'postcolonial' (*Tropico 5*, Haemimont Games, 2014). This
shows that, collectively, Steam users have a loose definition of 'historical', more in line
with a more general conceptualisation of the past.

[7] Using the public SteamSpy API (Galyonkin, 2018), 342 different tags applied to 23,985
games on Steam (at the time of collection on 23 and 24 July 2018) were collected in
a database, including not only if they were applied to a game but also how many
times. This data provides the basis for a two-mode (game-to-tag) network, which can
be transformed to either game-to-game or tag-to-tag similarity networks (Borgatti &
Everett 1997). In this case, the tag-to-tag network has been used to identify groupings
within historical games, using Louvain Modularity network community detection,

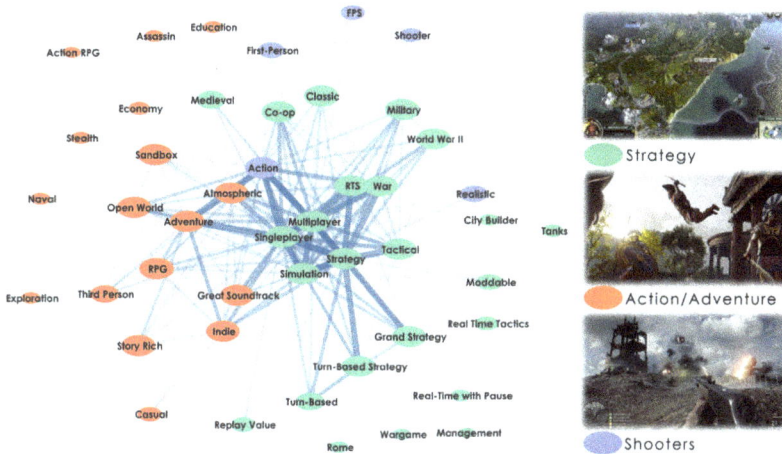

Figure 1: A network of tags applied to games on Steam by its users. These tags describe several aspects of features or themes that can be found in these games. The tags in this network all occur in games that have also been tagged as 'historical'. Width of links in this network indicates how often tags co-occur together (e.g. are found in the same game). The colour of nodes is based on a network community measure (see footnote) and show what family of historical games they belong to: strategy (image from *Sid Meier's Civilization 6*), action-adventure (image from *Assassin's Creed: Odyssey*), and shooters (image from *Battlefield 1*).

It falls outside the scope of this chapter to discuss these individual subgroups in depth, but an element uniting the corpus is the reliance on some form of violence as central play mechanic: from conquering other peoples in *Sid Meier's Civilization* series (Mol, Politopoulos & Ariese-Vandemeulebroucke 2017) to the assassinations and swordplay of *Assassin's Creed* (Politopoulos et al. 2019), and the hyper-realistic gunplay in *Battlefield*. This is, of course, not unique to historical games: violent play has long been a core aspect of video games. Nor is the point here that this is actively harmful – studies on the psychological or social effects of violence in video games are, on the whole, inconclusive (e.g. Anderson, Gentile & Buckley 2007; Przybylski & Weinstein 2019). The point is rather that the vast majority of historical games, while showcasing a large set of features that may be important for players (evidenced by the diversity of tags applied to this corpus), end up with a relatively narrow and shallow experience of the past: only three groups within the corpus, all of them relying on violence

---

which measures the density of links inside network groups to links outside groups (Blondel et al. 2008). The groups that result from this could be conceptually understood as different members within the family of historical games (Mol 2019).

as a mechanic to drive play.[8] The violence of gaming pasts is something that needs to be taken into account when using video games as a teaching platform, and Gilbert's study is a prime example of this (Gilbert 2019). It also provides a challenge to archaeological, heritage and other academic professionals to contribute to or create playful experiences themselves that provide a more nuanced perspective on the past.

Case studies

We have sketched the enormous potential that video games have as learning material, based on their innate interactiveness, but also emphasised that this learning process still needs to be 'mediated' through teaching (Lynch, Mallon & Connolly 2015: 35; Gilbert 2019). As a way to illustrate the teaching potential of video games, in this section we discuss practical examples of how the authors have approached the otherwise often narrow representations of the past in video games. Through four case studies, we showcase practical applications of using video games for teaching purposes in different contexts. They are chosen specifically because they present a wide variety of ways in which video games can be incorporated as (formal and informal) teaching material, as well as each providing an example of different target audiences.

The first case study covers Twine, a tool to create non-linear stories. VALUE organised several workshops on using Twine during our Interactive Past conferences. As such, this case study concerns academic conference delegates as main target audience. Our second case study comes from a formal educational setting: Aris Politopoulos uses game analogies to teach bachelor students about complex archaeological concepts. Thirdly, we discuss how streaming online allows the authors to reach and teach the general public about many historical and archaeological aspects using – and while playing – video games. Lastly, our final case study describes one of VALUE's public outreach activities – RoMeincraft – aimed at the general public but particularly resonating with children aged six to 14.

Learning to tell stories with Twine

Twine, an 'open source tool for telling interactive, non-linear stories,'[9] allows anyone to write and create their own stories and – with some help from online tutorials and a helpful community – create games that range from simple to

---

[8] AC's combat-free Discovery Tour modes form an exception, although it can be argued whether they are still playful and interactive enough to be called games (Politopoulos et al. 2019).

[9] Twine website: https://www.twinery.org.

surprisingly complex designs, with images, audio, branching paths or even advanced gameplay mechanics with Twine macros, HTML, CSS codes and JavaScript. For the fields of archaeology and history (see Copplestone 2016), Twine is particularly interesting as a storytelling device because it works excellently for creating non-linear stories that allow for creative and multi-perspectival engagements with the past.[10] For students or practitioners of the past, it can be a valuable – if conceptually challenging – exercise to design non-linear histories, particularly as most of their previous experience in storytelling will have been linear in the form of essays, papers or monographs.

VALUE has organised two- to five-hour workshop sessions at conferences in which predominantly academic educators and researchers are taught the basic workings of Twine. These short workshops encourage participants to explore the possibilities of Twine and consider whether they can use it for their own research dissemination or educational activities. Some of these participants continued with Twine after the workshop, either to finish their game in progress or to use Twine with their students. Longer workshops were organised as well (such as those during the two-day TIPC@Work in 2017 and the seven-day Game Jam during the Culture Arcade exhibition in 2018; see Figure 2), where more time was available for debate and reflection, as well as for invited game developers to share their expertise.[11] Finally, Twine has also been used in BA-level courses taught by Angus Mol.[12]

Having engaged roughly 140 scholars and students in creating historical stories in Twine, we can make some assessments of the educational value based on our observational evaluations and feedback from participants. Of course, writing your own story in Twine encourages independent and group research into the time period, person(s) or events which are involved in the story; thus, content knowledge is usually gained. Particularly within longer Twine workshops, independent (historical or archaeological) research skills are practised, mainly in the form of literature research, but also research into material culture and (online) museum collections. From a formal education perspective, what is most interesting is the extent to which writing a Twine story forces the writer to think through branching structures (Wolf 2001), alternative storylines and multiple endings, and cause and effect (Roberts 2011). Opposed to traditional

---

[10] There are many great twines available for free or a suggested donation at https://itch.io/games/tag-twine. For a good example of a Twine story that meaningfully incorporates the past, see McCall's *Path of Honors* (2018).

[11] VALUE's Twine workshops were, among others, enriched by the presentations and attendance of game developers and designers Omar Gilani, Mata Haggis-Burridge, Hermen Hulst, Paweł Szyszka, Roy van der Schilden and Guillermo Vizcaíno, as well as archaeologists and Twine-ers Tara Copplestone and Jeremiah McCall.

[12] Examples of Twines made by students include a biography of the early life of philosopher Ludwig Wittgenstein and a detective story based on two 1732 cases from the Old Bailey; see: dahi.lucdh.nl/twines2019.

Figure 2: Two screenshots from the Twine game *Generations: Lucia*, made by Ana
   Barretto, Vera Grosskop and Phillip Morris during the Culture Arcade Game
   Jam, 2018.

linear scholarly writing, Twine can be valuable for interpreting fragments of the
past to recreate or envision diverse possible scenarios.

Game analogies in the classroom

By using game analogies, we can teach difficult and complex terms through a
medium that is popular, visually engaging and interactive, allowing students to
have a hands-on approach – and recognisable examples – for theoretical and,
often, abstract concepts. The examples presented in this chapter have been used
for the purposes of teaching different courses on the archaeology of the ancient
Near East by Aris Politopoulos.[13]

A first example of such an analogy is the historical and archaeological
discussion around cities, city formation, and urban environments (e.g. Marcus &
Sabloff 2008). Discussion around ancient cities can often be too abstract for

---

[13] These courses include 'Archaeology of Empires', 'Early Cities and States of the
   Ancient Near East', and 'Early Complex Societies of the Ancient Near East', and were
   taught at Leiden University, Faculty of Archaeology from 2015/16-2018/19.

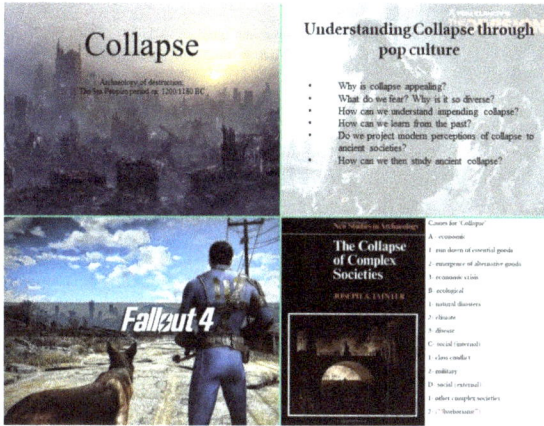

Figure 3: Slides from the course Early Cities and States of the Ancient Near East, discussing the concept of societal collapse as analogy.

students, while comparative examples from our everyday experiences of modern cities can be quite biased towards modern urban spatial conceptions. Games such as *ANNO 1800* or *Ancient Cities* offer diverse and innovative approaches into the urban design of the past. Through these examples, it is possible to visualise, present, discuss and evaluate a number of different models regarding ancient urban design.

In a similar manner, video games can help us present models and conceptions of empire. Critically successful game series such as *Age of Empires* and the *Civilization* series have both shaped and been shaped by popular understanding of empires. They offer a good starting point to familiarise students with terminology, before delving deeper into specifics about the diverse theories of empires and imperialism (e.g. Burbank & Cooper 2010).

Finally, video games offer the opportunity to discuss more contested concepts such as that of societal collapse. The topic of societal collapse has been both popular and controversial in archaeology and other sciences of the past (see most notably Tainter 1988). This has resulted in a convoluted and difficult-to-grasp theoretical framework, which, while fascinating, can be particularly daunting. To solve this, we use examples of video games modelling different cases of collapse such as the *Fallout*[14] series – societal collapse through war and nuclear destruction – or *The Division* series – societal collapse through the spread of disease (Figure 3). This allowed us to deconstruct some of the ideas around the concept of collapse, discuss them from a new perspective, and then

---

[14] For a discussion around collapse and *Fallout 4* see VALUE's stream of the game: https://tinyurl.com/yykf7q39.

proceed to the teaching of past instances of collapse, such as the late Bronze Age collapse.

The use of games as analogies has been very popular among students who participated in these courses. This was reflected in student evaluations, but also in specific comments, such as 'I appreciate the attempt of the lecturer to bring contemporary phenomena into the classroom' (student evaluation form, Early Cities and States course, 2016–2017).

Streaming the past

Video content is another great way to engage with a larger community, in particular with people who already play games. In some cases, YouTube channels like the popular-scientific History Respawned series, have gathered a massive number of followers who are both looking to be entertained and learn. Even if it is extremely difficult – requiring both a lot of hard work and a degree of luck – to reach such a level of popularity, creating video game-based video content is a great way to reach out beyond the classroom or conference rooms. Shawn Graham has, for example, created a quirky but fun YouTube video about video games and agent-based modelling[15] and Andrew Reinhard has directed a small video report about archaeology in the No Man's Sky video game.[16] Sophie Schmidt and Jan Wieners let their students create Let's Play videos, in which students critically comment on video games from an archaeological perspective in a short form video essay, as part of an archaeogaming course at the University of Cologne.[17]

Live streaming offers a different, and arguably even more interactive, way of creating content and engaging an audience than traditional online video formats (Taylor 2018). VALUE has been live streaming via the Twitch platform (https://twitch.tv/valuefnd) since 2016. With our 'Streaming the Past' series, we play and discuss a game together with a live audience. In these roughly two-hour episodes, we discuss specific (archaeological and historical) themes in relation to video games, such as 'Collapse and Fallout 4', 'Historical Agency and Assassin's Creed', and 'Violence in Human Nature and Far Cry: Primal'. Furthermore, all content on Twitch can be live-streamed and recorded at the same time (e.g. with open broadcasting software), which allows for the uploading of recordings of live streams to, for example, YouTube as videos on demand.

There are hurdles to creating live streams and other video content, however. First of all, in the current online video media landscape, discoverability of individual creators is extremely low. Indeed, to gain wider viewership and

---

[15] See: https://youtu.be/eCe5QEnoioI.

[16] See: https://www.youtube.com/watch?v=qORK8SUgM7E.

[17] More information on this course can be found at: http://archaeoinformatics.net/ teaching-concepts-of-pre-history-in-computergames.

popularity, supported by Twitch algorithms, it is necessary to stream regularly, often and extensively: to gain truly large numbers of viewers, daily streams of upwards of four hours are essential. In short, this is not a tool that will magically draw crowds of viewers (our average streaming audience numbers lie between five and 20 individuals), especially if 'production values' – what the videos sound and look like – are low. To create a live stream with solid production values requires the right hardware, software and set-up. Furthermore, there is an art to playing a game while maintaining an active and interesting mono- or dialogue simultaneously. That said, we consider live streams to be a major yet largely unexplored avenue for (video game-based and) content-focused teaching as well as a way to reflect on video game pasts. What happens in our streams is both a deep dive into archaeological and heritage concepts and methods and a communal critical interaction with how games portray the past. In short, this is both a creative, performative and interactive way to play with and teach about the past.

Teaching the past by playing RoMeincraft

The blocky world of *Minecraft* – a game that could be called the digital version of LEGO – offers many opportunities to teach about the past in fun and creative ways.[18] Starting with a pilot event in 2015, the VALUE Foundation has organised various types of events focused on (re)building heritage sites from around the world within *Minecraft*.[19] The largest of these projects was RoMeincraft (Politopoulos et al., forthcoming).[20] The project was designed for the province of South Holland to consist of 10 events, during which visitors and participants would, under our supervision as mediators, reconstruct the Limes (a Roman border in the Netherlands) and some of its heritage sites such as forts, harbours and watch towers. The project was later extended to other provinces and crossed the border into Belgium in 2019. These playful reconstructions were organised, prepared and guided by VALUE but largely executed by the visitors of the events, most of which took place at museums, as part of heritage festivals, or in public places (2017–2019) (see Figure 4). The *Minecraft* world in which these reconstructions took place was based on a digital reconstruction of the provincial landscape from Roman times (CE 200; based on height

---

[18] See projects by Colleen Morgan (https://colleen-morgan.com/2015/06/11/breaking-blocks-and-digging-holes-archaeology-minecraft) and Shawn Graham (https://electricarchaeology.ca/tag/minecraft) as examples.

[19] Similar projects have been organised elsewhere in the world, such as by the Creative Minds team for the DigIt festival in Scotland (McGraw, Reid & Sanders 2017).

[20] RoMeincraft is a wordplay in Dutch, combining the title of the game with the Dutch word for Roman: 'Romein'.

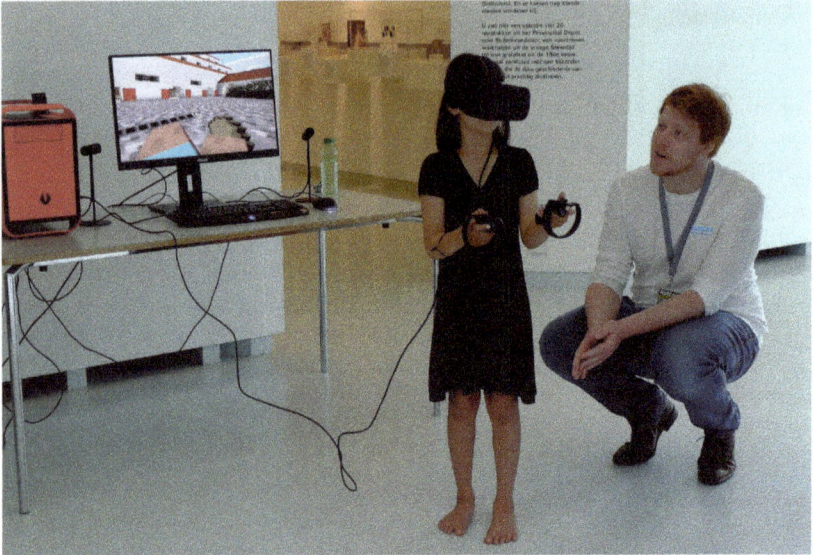

Figure 4: Participant of a RoMeincraft event explores the *Minecraft* reconstruction of Roman Nijmegen in virtual reality, guided by Bram van den Hout, Museum Het Valkhof. © Maud Heldens.

maps); archaeological data in visual form such as site plans and cross-sections of buildings were collected in a booklet for referential purposes.

RoMeincraft events have managed to engage over a thousand participants (players and spectators) with Roman heritage. Generally speaking, players are mostly young children (aged around six to 14), although older children, teens, adults and seniors have also played. At the guidance of VALUE, play was always collaborative – not just with multiple computers connected to the same map but also *in real life* with family members sitting together at one computer – meaning that these events contributed to supporting social skills and interpersonal communication, between family members but also with strangers. It would often happen that children approached each other to ask for help with bigger building projects or they would go back and forth between the computers to consult with each other which material to use or how to design the building, while explaining the purpose of the structure they were working on. Collaboration was key, as players needed to be respectful of what others were building or had built or to engage in large-scale projects simultaneously together.

Mediation by VALUE members and other participants was important here: (grand)parents were often best placed to 'translate' the provided archaeological knowledge; children then interpreted this creatively into their building process. The ongoing, unstructured conversations between participants also often led to exchanges of knowledge about what would have been – or would not have been – accurate for Roman times. We noticed that many visitors – both adults and children – had preconceived notions of what was, or was not, 'Roman'. For instance: yes, the Romans did have heated baths, but, no, they did not have rollercoasters. A core skill in archaeology, namely interpreting fragmentary remains such as foundations into full, detailed 3D structures, was inherently part of the creative RoMeincraft process and experientially learned: spatial skills and a consideration of the materiality of structural elements (i.e. selecting the right type of block) were combined. Finally, RoMeincraft also fostered some digital skills: general computer usage but even some 'coding' through cheats. The majority of our younger visitors were very experienced with *Minecraft*, and some engaged in 'counterplay' rather than contributing to the ongoing building projects. Engaging with Roman heritage in RoMeincraft, whether as a spectator or player, required constant mediation between actual past and digital present and an ongoing conversational knowledge exchange. RoMeincraft follows the principles of ELT, and provided an opportunity for players to learn from experience (Kolb 1984). Yet, while we have indications based on informal conversations and observations, quantitative and qualitative research needs to be undertaken to better understand the educational impact (Metzger & Paxton 2016).

Conclusion

Video games that incorporate the past as part of their narrative, theme or setting provide a great opportunity space for experiential learning. Their inherently interactive character allows for an immersive experience and through this both a deeper and wider understanding of the played past. However, although more and more people are relying on video games to teach them about the past, video games' *raison d'être* is the generation of economic revenue. As such they often provide a relatively narrow and shallow experience of the past, which is framed in a way to make a gripping story or interesting gameplay, or simply to have fun. Oftentimes, these shallow experiences of the past are driven by violence. In order to make more use of video games as an educational platform, both in formal and informal settings, it is important to better understand the educational impact video games have on players, and to find opportunities in which interaction between the players and the past can be discussed or mediated in order for the latter to be more critically assessed. Through the presented case studies we have provided a number of playful opportunities in a wide variety of contexts and for different audiences. We have briefly showcased how pasts could be taught interactively, although research on learning and impact measurements remains necessary. As such, the chapter shows the practical applicability of video games for teaching purposes, illustrating through four selected case studies how a wide variety of audiences can be engaged through different games and particular mediated approaches.

References

Alexandra, H. (2018). *The Division 2 Is Political, Despite What Its Developers Say*. [online] Kotaku. Available at: https://kotaku.com/the-division-2-is-political-despite-what-its-developer-1826776710 [Accessed 3 May 2019].

Anderson, C.A., Gentile, D.A., and Buckley, K.E. (2007). *Violent Video Game Effects on Children and Adolescents: Theory, Research, and Public Policy*, Oxford/New York: Oxford University Press.

Blondel, V.D., Guillaume, J., Lambiotte, R. and Lefebvre, E. (2008). Fast unfolding of communities in large networks. *Journal of Statistical Mechanics: Theory and Experiment*, 2008(10): P10008.

Borgatti, S.P. and Everett, M.G. (1997). Network analysis of 2-mode data. *Social Networks*, 19: 243–269.

Burbank, J. and Cooper, F. (2010). *Empires in World History: Power and the Politics of Difference*, Princeton, NJ: Princeton University Press.

Chapman, A. (2016). *Digital Games as History: How Videogames Represent the Past and Offer Access to Historical Practice*, New York: Routledge.

Copplestone, T. (2016). *Twine for Archaeology Dummies: A Living Book about How to Make Things about and for Archaeology Using the Twine Engine*. [online] GitBook. Available at: https://taracopplestone.gitbooks.io/twine-4-archaeology-dummies/content [Accessed 25 April 2019].

ESA [Entertainment Software Association] (2018a). *2018 Sales, Demographic, and Usage Data: Essential Facts about the Computer and Video Game Industry*. [pdf] Entertainment Software Association. Available at: http://www.theesa.com/wp-content/uploads/2018/05/EF2018_FINAL.pdf [Accessed 19 April 2019].

ESA (2018b). *U.S Video Game Sales Reach Record-Breaking $43.4 Billion in 2018*. [online] Entertainment Software Association. Available at: http://www.theesa.com/article/u-s-video-game-sales-reach-record-breaking-43-4-billion-2018 [Accessed 3 May 2019].

Galyonkin, S. (2018). *Steam Spy API*. [online] SteamSpy. Available at: https://steamspy.com/api.php [Accessed 23 November 2018].

Gilbert, L. (2019). 'Assassin's Creed reminds us that history is human experience': Students' senses of empathy while playing a narrative video game. *Theory & Research in Social Education*, 47: 108–137.

Kolb, D.A. (1984). *Experiential Learning: Experience as the Source of Learning and Development*, Englewood Cliffs, NJ: Prentice Hall.

Koutsabasis, P. (2017). Empirical evaluations of interactive systems in cultural heritage: A review. *International Journal of Computational Methods in Heritage Science*, 1: 100–122.

Lynch, R., Mallon, B. and Connolly, C. (2015). The pedagogical application of alternate reality games: Using game-based learning to revisit history. *International Journal of Game-Based Learning*, 5: 18–38.

McCall, J. (2013). *Playing with the Past: Digital Games and the Simulation of History*, London: Bloomsbury Academic.

McCall, J. (2016). Teaching history with digital historical games: An introduction to the field and best practices. *Simulation & Gaming*, 47: 517–542.

McCall, J. (2018). *Path of Honors: Towards a Model for Interactive History Texts with Twine*, DOI: https://doi.org/10.22215/epoiesen/2017.16.

McCall, J. (2019). Playing with the past: History and video games (and why it might matter). *Journal of Geek Studies*, 6(1): 29–48.

McGraw, J., Reid, S. and Sanders, J. (2017). Crafting the past: Unlocking new audiences. In: A.A.A. Mol, C.E. Ariese-Vandemeulebroucke, K.H.J. Boom and A. Politopoulos, eds, *The Interactive Past: Archaeology, Heritage, and Video Games*, Leiden: Sidestone Press, pp. 167–184.

Marcus, J. and Sabloff, J.A. (2008). *The Ancient City: New Perspectives on Urbanism in the Old and New World*, Santa Fe, NM: School for Advanced Research.

Metzger, S.A. and Paxton, R.J. (2016). Gaming history: A framework for what video games teach about the past. *Theory & Research in Social Education*, 44: 532–564.

Mol, A.A.A. (2019). *Gaming Genres: Using Crowd-Sourced Tags to Explore Family Resemblances in Steam Games*. Digital Humanities Conference 2019.

Mol, A.A.A., Ariese-Vandemeulebroucke, C.E., Boom, K.H.J. and Politopoulos, A. (2017). *The Interactive Past: Archaeology, Heritage, and Video Games*, Leiden: Sidestone Press.

Mol, A.A.A., Politopoulos, A. and Ariese-Vandemeulebroucke, C.E. (2017). From the Stone Age to the Information Age: History and Heritage in Sid Meier's Civilization VI. *Advances in Archaeological Practice*, 5(2): 214–219.

Politopoulos, A., Mol, A.A.A., Boom, K.H.J. and Ariese, C.E. (2019). History is our playground: Action and authenticity in Assassin's Creed: Odyssey, *Advances in Archaeological Practice*, 7(3): 317–323.

Politopoulos, A., Ariese, C.E., Boom, K.H.J. and Mol, A.A.A. (forthcoming). Romans and rollercoasters: Scholarship in the digital playground. *Journal of Computer Applications in Archaeology*.

Przybylski, A.K. and Weinstein, M. (2019). Violent video game engagement is not associated with adolescents' aggressive behaviour: Evidence from a registered report. *Royal Society Open Science*, 6(2): 171474.

Reichmuth, P. and Werning, S. (2006). Pixel pashas, digital djinns. *ISIM Review*, 18: 46–47.

Roberts, S.L. (2011). Using counterfactual history to enhance students' historical understanding. *The Social Studies*, 102: 117–123.

Shieber, J. (2019). *Video Game Revenue Tops $43 Billion in 2018, an 18% Jump from 2017*. [online] Techcrunch. Available at: https://techcrunch.com/2019/01/22/video-game-revenue-tops-43-billion-in-2018-an-18-jump-from-2017 [Accessed 3 May 2019].

Tainter, J.A. (1988). *The Collapse of Complex Societies*, Cambridge: Cambridge University Press.

Taylor, T.L. (2018). *Watch Me Play: Twitch and the Rise of Game Live Streaming*, Princeton, NJ: Princeton University Press.

Wolf, M.J.P. (2001). Narrative in the video game. In: M.J.P. Wolf, ed., *The Medium of the Video Game*, Austin, TX: University of Texas Press, pp. 94–111.

Ludography

Age of Empires series (1997–2018). Ensemble Studios, Relic Entertainment. Microsoft Game Studios. [Multiple platforms].

Age of Mythology (2002). Ensemble Studios. Microsoft. [PC and MAC].

Ancient Cities (In development). Uncasual Games. [PC].

ANNO 1800 (2019). Blue Byte. Ubisoft. [PC].

Assassin's Creed series (2007–2018). Blue Byte, Gameloft, Ubisoft Montréal, Ubisoft Paris, Ubisoft Quebec, Ubisoft Sofia. Ubisoft. [Multiple platforms].

Battlefield series (2002–2018). EA Digital Illusions CE, Visceral Games. Electronic Arts. [Multiple platforms].

Civilization series (1991–2016). MicroProse & Firaxis Games. MicroProse, Activision, Infogrames Entertainment & 2K Games. [Multiple platforms].

Fallout series (1997–2018). Interplay Entertainment, Black Isle Studios & Bethesda Game Studios. Interplay Entertainment & Bethesda Softworks. [Multiple platforms].

Minecraft (2011). Mojang. Mojang & Microsoft. [Multiple platforms].

The Division series (2016–2019). Massive Entertainment. Ubisoft. [Multiple platforms].

Tropico 5 (2014). Haemimont Games. Kalypso Media & Square Enix. [Multiple platforms].

Gameplay as Learning: The Use of Game Design to Explain Human Evolution

Xavier Rubio-Campillo

University of Edinburgh and Murphy's Toast Games

Abstract

Video games are one of the most engaging media at our disposal to communicate knowledge. They offer a unique combination of interaction and storytelling that allows players not only to observe virtual worlds but also to experiment with these imagined universes in ways that cannot simply be matched by any other media.

This potential is explained by the fact that the player needs to take an active role inside the recreated world. The world should always be crafted to strengthen game mechanics and this requirement presents a challenge to anyone that wants to use games for archaeological outreach; the most scientifically accurate version of the past will be meaningless if the story, characters and dynamics of the game cannot capture the interest of the player.

How to cite this book chapter:
Rubio-Campillo, X. 2020. Gameplay as Learning: The Use of Game Design to Explain Human Evolution. In: Hageneuer, S. (ed.) *Communicating the Past in the Digital Age: Proceedings of the International Conference on Digital Methods in Teaching and Learning in Archaeology (12–13 October 2018)*. Pp. 45–58. London: Ubiquity Press. DOI: https://doi.org/10.5334/bch.d. License: CC-BY 4.0

The need for engaging experiences suggests that educational video games should never forget the basic requirement that any game needs to be fun. However, the dialogue between these two parallel goals poses some unique questions: what are the best approaches to combine learning with engagement? How does the goal of scientific dissemination affect gameplay? Can an educational game even compete with high-budget projects while seeking for players' interests?

We explore here how game design provides tools to overcome these challenges exemplified by the case of Ancestors: Stories of Atapuerca. *This project aimed at presenting recent discoveries at the UNESCO World Heritage archaeological site of Atapuerca (Spain). The discussion on the game design principles used for this initiative highlights possible ways to improve the design of video games purposely created for scientific communication on human evolution.*

Keywords

Digital Learning, Video Games, Archaeological Outreach, Game Design, Prehistory

Introduction

Video games have become the most important 21st-century cultural industry in terms of both audience size and economic activity. One of the main reasons for this success is that they are able to open powerful windows to new or past worlds thanks to the combination of embodiment and interactivity they provide (Slater & Wilbur 1997). These two elements generate a strong cognitive link between the player and the experience; games are the only media where character actions are referred in the first person: 'I defeated the enemy', 'I died', 'I am moving to this city'. The strong sense of embodiment does not happen in other media because it requires a high degree of interactivity and immersion that is simply not possible while reading a book or watching a movie.

The way a video game is approached by a player is also unique. In essence, a game is a problem waiting to be solved. The structure of any game is organised as a sequence of increasingly difficult challenges that the player needs to solve using an explicit set of possible actions; this player will engage with a learning process for a simple yet powerful reason: it is the only way to achieve success in the game. Game challenges are based on abstract mechanics that can be enriched through background and narrative, which sometimes can play a major role within the player's experience. Archaeology is a popular source of inspiration for creating these game elements, but the relation between both worlds is still not properly explored. How are archaeologists and their activities presented to the public? Is scientific and historical accuracy relevant for game creators? How is the past experienced and perceived in the worlds they create?

Mainstream games such as *Uncharted* (Naughty Dog, 2007–2016) and *Tomb Raider* (Core Design & Crystal Dynamics, 1996–2016) depict archaeologists in a way that is similar to other popular media and they use Indiana Jones as their main inspiration (Holtorf 2007: 62–63; Meyers Emery & Reinhard 2015; Reinhard 2018: 62–88). The stereotype of the treasure hunter is complemented by mechanics focused on (1) exploration of mysterious ruins, (2) search and looting of mythical artefacts and (3) confrontation with powerful enemies. These products define the relation to archaeology adopted by a majority of games: to recreate the past in a way that reinforces the game mechanics and storytelling irrespective of its accuracy. The perspective is reasonable for a fictional product, but it has limited value as a pedagogical resource; it generates simplistic portrayals incapable of capturing the complexity and richness of past societies (Chapman 2012; Rejack 2007).

On the other hand, games classified as educational are typically focused on transmitting contents over designing a compelling experience. As a consequence, they are not as engaging as other products and are discarded by a majority of players beyond their compulsory use in the classroom (Squire 2008; Klopfer, Osterweil & Salen 2009). The emphasis on heavy educational content combined with basic game mechanics (known as edutainment) is based on the false assumption that learning is boring, so games are used as a device to 'sweeten the pill' (Resnick 2004); by doing so these initiatives do not exploit the essential trait discussed above: beating a game is always a learning process.

Is there any way to blend both goals? A project following this design philosophy is a challenge because it would have to follow two different sets of requirements: (1) to create an engaging playing experience and (2) to transmit specific contents that may be complex to assimilate. These goals are often seen as opposite: either a game is fun or it is educational. We discuss here an alternative approach to achieve both goals: game design should be the main pedagogical tool precisely because any playful experience is a puzzle that requires learning to be solved (Schell 2014). In essence, the process of playing itself is a learning experience that may be used to discover the past in innovative and surprising ways.

This work explores this third approach in the context of archaeological outreach. The next section presents the general setting of *Ancestors: Stories of Atapuerca*. *Ancestors* is a pedagogical project created to promote outreach on human evolution. The third section discusses the relation between the game design of *Ancestors* and learning outcomes related to human evolution; we focus here on four common game design topics often overlooked by educational games: theme, lore, environmental narrative and game mechanics. The chapter concludes with a summary on how this innovative approach to video games as learning devices can improve the impact of scientific outreach activities within our society.

Ancestors: Stories of Atapuerca

The construction of a railway line at the Sierra de Atapuerca in the mid-20th century revealed the existence of abundant archaeological material (Carbonell et al. 2014). The excavations carried out over the last four decades across the area have allowed us to gain a critical understanding of Palaeolithic Europe and human evolution: evidence suggests that at least four different groups of hominins lived in Atapuerca over a timespan of one million years (*Homo antecessor*, *Homo heidelbergensis*, *Homo neanderthalensis* and *Homo sapiens*).

The continued presence of hominin groups around Atapuerca can be explained by its strategic location: the mountain range is located at the crossroads between two rivers (the Duero and Ebro) and at the boundary between different ecosystems. Any group living at the Sierra would be able to access water resources while controlling areas of prairie that would work as perfect hunting grounds. The archaeological complex of Atapuerca is so critical to understand our past that in 2000 it was declared a UNESCO World Heritage Site.

The interest in the landscape of Atapuerca and the long human history that it witnessed made it an ideal setting for a video game on human evolution. The project 'Atapuerca – Evolución. Videojuegos Educativos' was led by the DIDPATRI research group from the University of Barcelona and it aimed at presenting the recent discoveries at this site with video games.

The primary output of this initiative was *Ancestors: Stories of Atapuerca* (Murphy's Toast Games, 2018). Ancestors is a simulation/strategy game where the player takes the role of the leader of a hominin clan living in Atapuerca. The experience is structured as a set of stories told by an elder *Homo sapiens* to her group, as seen in Figure 1. This setting linked all these stories (i.e. game scenarios) depicting different hominin groups through a common starting point. This elder preface to each mission also emphasised the importance that oral tradition had to prehistoric human groups. Each of the four stories released until now tells the legend of an ancestor of the group in a different era, thus exploring the differences on landscape, technology and biology across hominin groups.

The first story is a tutorial designed to allow the player to learn what actions can be used to lead the clan. It can be moved across different camps located at the Sierra de Atapuerca and each of these camps offers different activities, as can be seen in Figure 2. The range of actions include tasks that would be common for Palaeolithic peoples (e.g. hunt animals, gather resources and plants, make tools...). The remaining three stories set out different scenarios where a careful planning of actions, resources and timing will allow the player to achieve a sequential list of goals and advance the story until its ending.

The player needs to achieve these goals by performing required activities while keeping a food reserve. This food reserve works as the health bar of the group: if it ever reaches zero then the clan is forced to migrate and leave Atapuerca for some time. The final score of a story is based on the number of times the player's clan has been forced to migrate.

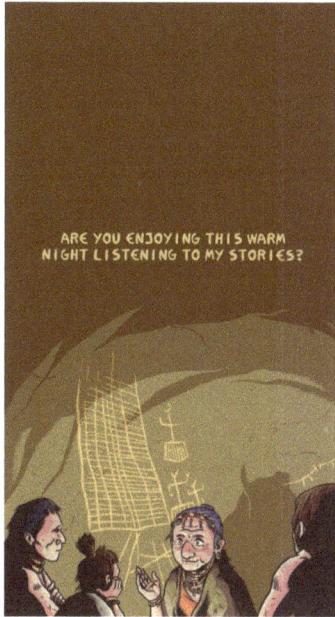

Figure 1: Storytelling structures the different episodes of the game. CC-BY SA 4.0 Murphy's Toast Games.

Figure 2: Each character on the camp defines a different activity that can be performed by the player. CC-BY SA 4.0 Murphy's Toast Games.

Game design as a learning device

Game-based learning is currently recognised as an efficient approach to acquire new skills and knowledge due to its high cognitive gain. While there exist current debates on the difficulties of quantifying this gain, a large corpus of literature suggests that the principles of embodiment, interactivity and problem-solving are key to understanding the effectiveness of games for cognitive learning (see Wilson et al. 2009 for a review).

This learning process can be generally split into three phases (Vogel et al. 2006). Firstly, the learner needs to acquire a specific set of knowledge. Secondly, they need to organise the acquired knowledge by grouping units of information and map these units into mental models. Finally, the learner should be able to devise strategies to apply the organised knowledge to new situations.

The inherent nature of games as virtual worlds explored through problem-solving induces any player to closely follow these three steps if she wants to beat the game. However, this is only true if the learning outcomes for a specific game are integrated within the learning strategies of the game itself (Gee 2005). This is arguably missing in most educational games because they mainly rely on the first step of the process; even large-scale commercial products such as *Assassin's Creed Origins: Discovery Tour* do not follow this approach. In this case, the player can experience Hellenistic Egypt by taking part in a set of virtual guides to a diversity of aspects of daily life and architecture of the period. While this can be fascinating, the tours do not use any of the game mechanics that made the *Assassin's Creed* franchise popular, thus inhibiting any application of the acquired knowledge (i.e. the third step of the learning process).

These three steps can only be fulfilled by using game design principles. Game design can be broadly defined as the process of conceiving and designing the rules and structure of a game (Salen, Tekinbaş & Zimmerman 2004). During the development of *Ancestors* the team identified four main aspects of game design that could be used to integrate educational goals with gameplay: (1) the underlying theme of the game, (2) the lore or background of the game's world, (3) the use of environmental narrative and (4) game mechanics for problem-solving.

Theme

The theme of a game is the unifying concept that permeates all the aspects of the artistic work. It is often an abstract concept (e.g. friendship, treason or hope) that allows game developers to focus the entire creative process of a video game into the most essential traits that should be present in the product. The theme is often not explicitly mentioned, and several players would not even recognise the theme of their preferred games. However, this concept helps to focus the myriad of decisions taken during design because they should always reinforce the theme as a means to provide a cohesive experience.

Creators have absolute freedom on the choice of the theme and for this reason several topics crossing the archaeological discipline could be potentially chosen as the primary theme of a game. These concepts could be rather abstract and accommodate current debates of the discipline (e.g. individuality vs community, social change, agency), but they could also be much more specific, as was the case in *Ancestors*.

The archaeological site of Atapuerca is unique because it has a very long and almost complete sequence of human occupation across hundreds of thousands of years. We wanted to integrate a variety of hominin groups in the game and include at least stories of *Homo antecessor* and *Homo neanderthalensis*. Moreover, all stories would be told from the perspective of a Bronze Age group of *Homo sapiens* so constant human occupation seemed to be a recurrent topic. A theme that could strengthen the temporal dimension was the transcendence of human life: several generations will pass across thousands of centuries, but the essential traits that makes us human are always present, even across groups. The theme would be present in all aspects of the game, as previously discussed, and even the game menus were inspired by this theme, as can be seen in Figure 3.

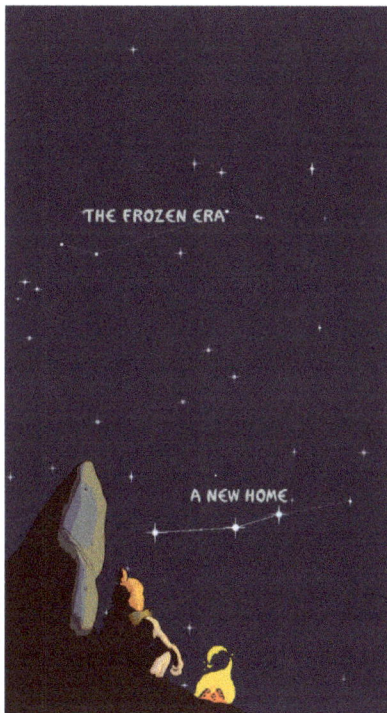

Figure 3: The main menu was uniquely designed to reinforce the theme of transcendence: the human groups that the player leads lived thousands of years apart from each other, but all of them watched the same stars on a clear night sky. CC-BY SA 4.0 Murphy's Toast Games.

Lore and exposition

The lore of an imaginary world is the collection of facts, belief and knowledge crafted to provide context to the narrative. It is transmitted to the audience through the process of exposition, which may take a variety of forms, the most common being dialogue between characters, item descriptions, diary entries and cut scenes.

There is a clear parallel between the lore of a fantasy-themed game and the introduction of knowledge in an educational game. Most educational games use text-based exposition because it is easy to make and it closely resembles classical educational media such as textbooks. While this passive approach to game content may be effective, it often works against the interactive nature of the media.

Ancestors had to provide the lore of a prehistorical period without written records and scarce evidence on the existence of language. This scenario was a double-edged sword; on the one hand, it made knowledge transmission difficult because several aspects of Palaeolithic daily life are speculative; on the other hand, it allowed the team to develop new lore that contributed to an improved gameplay while still based on archaeological evidence.

The oral-based story setting was the main exposition mechanism of the game. The approach allowed us to reinforce the theme of transcendence by integrating the different groups into a common background. This cultural framework was based on myths and legends tailored to the specifics of the archaeological site of Atapuerca. For example, the mountain range itself took an almost mythical status as homeland and sanctuary of the clan that the player would be controlling during the entire game. This approach justified the 'game over' mechanism based on migration; it also strengthened the role that both territory and mobility played for prehistoric peoples.

Environmental narrative

The narrative of a simulation video game is typically secondary compared to other genres because this genre relies on emergent narratives generated by the player's own decisions. However, an engaging story can be used to raise the interest of the experience towards beating the game as a way to know how the story ended and what happened to the characters. In *Ancestors* we decided to use a mixed approach based on four independent stories taking place on different moments of Atapuerca's timeline. Each story is developed as a list of goals or main quests that need to be achieved before moving onwards. The narrative unfolds through the achievement of these goals and for this reason it provides a strong motivation for success: if the player wants to know what happened to the group then she will have to beat the game.

One aspect of video game storytelling that revealed particularly effective for scientific outreach is the use of environmental narrative elements. Environmental narrative uses visual and sound cues to reinforce the main story through a number of small details that provide coherence to the game's universe. This approach allowed us to integrate recent findings on human evolution in the game, including:

• Neanderthal use of tattoos, clothing and body decoration, as seen in Figure 2 (Zilhao et al. 2010).
• Characterisation of plants and animals based on existing evidence.
• Presence of children and elderly people in Palaeolithic groups, which are often invisible in video games.
• No assumptions on sex-based roles as the game alternated males and females for each activity within different groups.
• The cave paintings found in the 'Galería del Sílex' (Bronze Age) were used as the background of the *Homo sapiens* group (Diez et al. 2003).

Environmental narrative proved to be an efficient way of adding content to the game while avoiding the abuse of text-based exposition. The approach may be more indirect as players would never notice some of these subtle details, but it generates a scientifically accurate picture of Palaeolithic life while breaking common stereotypes seen in popular culture.

Mechanics

Game mechanics are the processes available to the player to interact with the game world (Sicart 2008). Any player needs to learn and master these mechanics during gameplay because it is a requirement to solve the problems introduced over the game.

Ancestors's game mechanics were based on activities summarising the essential traits of the hunter-gatherer lifestyle: hunt, make tools, gather resources, move camp etc. All of these activities could be undertaken using a common user interface, as seen in Figure 4, but each of them was unique in terms of options, requirements and outcomes.

Hunting was the task that focused the development team's efforts. Early testing with both high-school students and adults suggested that this activity should be one of the most important game mechanics of the game; feedback suggested that players were expecting hunting to be fun because it is a common mechanic in several commercial video games such as *Red Dead Redemption 2* or the *Monster Hunter* franchises. The team decided to develop a specific mini game for the hunting activity based on a risk vs cost dilemma: should I go for the larger animals or stick to the ones that are easier to catch? Should I organise a large and expensive hunting party or risk it with a smaller group?

A random event system was also implemented to bring life to the world beyond the player's clan. Every time the player moves camp there is a chance than an event will happen; two options are then provided and the player needs

Figure 4: In the hunting activity the player needs to choose the prey and the size of the group (larger groups will require more tools and food). CC-BY SA 4.0 Murphy's Toast Games.

to choose which event will actually happen (see Figure 5). The effect of these events can be quite diverse and the player needs to think which one will provide more benefits (or less damage). Events are text-based and for this reason it was a simple yet effective way to enrich gameplay with other clans, climate change, animal migration or bits of agency.

Concluding remarks

Ancestors: Stories of Atapuerca was freely released during the autumn of 2018 in Google Play and Apple Store. The number of downloads (over 25k in six months) and the high average rating highlight the success of outreach initiatives grounded on video games. This archaeological project joins other experiences in a diversity of fields such as Herald for History (van der Schilden & Heijltjes 2017) or Never Alone for Anthropology (Cook Inlet Tribal Council 2017) to suggest that there is a suitable path to design engaging experiences at the crossroads between pure entertainment and games as pure education. These transformational games (McGonigal 2011; Schell 2014) promote critical thinking and at the same time they are capable of interesting the player beyond

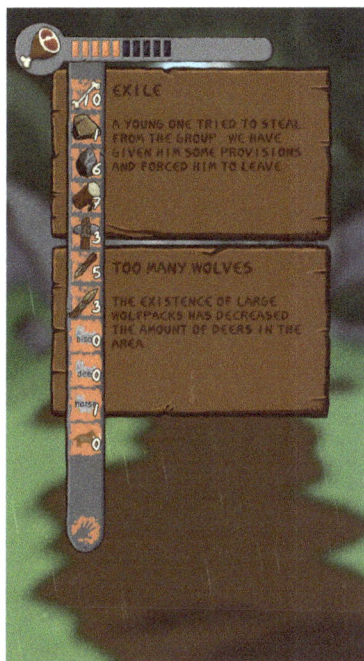

Figure 5: Events can have short- or long-term consequences on the world's state. CC-BY SA 4.0 Murphy's Toast Games.

the educational goals. At their core, transformational games apply common game design elements developed in the industry with a different perspective; they show that it is possible to generate engaging experiences while contributing to a new goal: to enrich the vision of the players about the world that surrounds them and, in the case of *Ancestors*, about the past of our species.

The first steps of video gaming during the 20th century offered a limited diversity of themes and topics to a restricted audience. At present the genre and topics treated by video games are as diverse as the community of gamers in terms of gender, age, interests and preferences. As a consequence, video game design is immersed in a transition phase towards maturity where unique and original language, narrative and mechanics are being introduced by a large number of small-sized projects. At the same time, the explosion of digital platforms such as Steam, the Apple Store and Google Play has simplified the distribution of any video game that can be now played by anyone with internet access (Rubio-Campillo 2013).

This combination of cultural innovation and ease of distribution is a perfect setting to try new ideas on the communication of archaeological knowledge to the main public; it is in our hands to create better cultural products able to promote engaging and critical approaches to our past, present and future.

Acknowledgements

The author wants to thank the ATA-EVE and Murphy's Toast Games teams for their invaluable contribution to this project. ATA-EVE was funded by the BBVA foundation programme on digital humanities. *Ancestors* can be freely downloaded for iOS and Android from Murphy's Toast Games official website at http://www.murphystoastgames.com/sheet.php?p=ancestors.

References

Carbonell, E., Huguet, R., Cáceres, I., Lorenzo, C., Mosquera, M., Ollé, A., Rodríguez, X.P., Saladié, P., Vergès, J.M., García-Medrano, P. and Rosell, J. (2014). Sierra de Atapuerca archaeological sites. Pleistocene and Holocene hunters-gatherers in Iberia and the Gibraltar Strait. In: R.S. Ramos, ed., *Pleistocene and Holocene Hunter-Gatherers in Iberia and the Gibraltar Strait: The Current Archaeological Record*, Burgos: Universidad de Burgos-Fundación Atapuerca, pp. 534–560.

Chapman, A. (2012). Privileging form over content: Analysing historical videogames. *Journal of Digital Humanities*, 1(2): 1–2.

Cook Inlet Tribal Council (2017). Storytelling for the next generation: How a non-profit in Alaska harnessed the power of video games to share and celebrate cultures. In: A. Mol, C. Ariese-Vandemeulebroucke, K. Boom and A. Politopoulos, eds, *The Interactive Past: A Book on Video Games and Archaeology*, Leiden: Sidestone Press, pp. 21–32.

Diez, M.G., i Uixan, J.M., Merino, M.M. and Martínez, A.O. (2003). Dates for rock art at a Bronze Age sanctuary at the Galería del Sílex cave. *Antiquity*, 77(296). [online] Antiquity. Available at: http://www.antiquity.ac.uk/projgall/diez296 [Accessed 6 May 2019].

Gee, J.P. (2005). Learning by design: Good video games as learning machines. *E-learning and Digital Media*, 2(1): 5–16.

Holtorf, C. (2007). *Archaeology Is a Brand!: The Meaning of Archaeology in Contemporary Popular Culture*, London: Routledge.

Klopfer, E., Osterweil, S., Salen, K. (2009). *Moving Learning Games Forward*, Cambridge, MA: The Education Arcade.

McGonigal, J. (2011). *Reality Is Broken: Why Games Make Us Better and How They Can Change the World*, London: Penguin.

Meyers Emery, K. and Reinhard, A. (2015). Trading shovels for controllers: A brief exploration of the portrayal of archaeology in video games. *Public Archaeology*, 14(2): 137–149.

Reinhard, A. (2018). *Archaeogaming: An Introduction to Archaeology in and of Video Games*, New York: Berghahn Books.

Rejack, B. (2007). Toward a virtual reenactment of history: Video games and the recreation of the past. *Rethinking History*, 11(3): 411–425.

Resnick, M. (2004). Edutainment? No thanks. I prefer playful learning. *Associazione Civita Report on Edutainment*, 14: 1–4.

Schell, J. (2014). *The Art of Game Design: A Book of Lenses*, Boca Raton, FL: AK Peters/CRC Press.

Rubio-Campillo, X. (2013). El pasado en tu sofá: juegos de simulación histórica en entornos computacionales portables. *Heritage & Museography*, 13: 55–62.

Salen, K., Tekinbaş, K.S. and Zimmerman, E. (2004). *Rules of Play: Game Design Fundamentals*, Cambridge, MA: MIT Press.

van der Schilden, R. and Heijltjes, B. (2017). Herald: How Wispfire used history to create fiction. In: A. Mol, C. Ariese-Vandemeulebroucke, K. Boom & A. Politopoulos, eds, *The Interactive Past: A Book on Video Games and Archaeology*, Leiden: Sidestone Press, pp. 73–82.

Sicart, M. (2008). Defining game mechanics. *Game Studies*, 8(2). [online] Available at: http://gamestudies.org/0802/articles/sicart [Accessed 6 May 2019].

Slater, M. and Wilbur, S. (1997). A framework for immersive virtual environments (FIVE): Speculations on the role of presence in virtual environments. *Presence: Teleoperators & Virtual Environments*, 6(6): 603–616.

Squire, K.D. (2008). Video games and education: Designing learning systems for an interactive age. *Educational Technology*, 48(2): 17.

Vogel, J.J., Vogel, D.S., Cannon-Bowers, J., Bowers, C.A., Muse, K. and Wright, M. (2006). Computer gaming and interactive simulations for learning: A meta-analysis. *Journal of Educational Computing Research*, 34(3): 229–243.

Wilson, K.A., Bedwell, W.L., Lazzara, E.H., Salas, E., Burke, C.S., Estock, J.L. and Conkey, C. (2009). Relationships between game attributes and learning outcomes: Review and research proposals. *Simulation & Gaming*, 40(2): 217–266.

Zilhao, J., Angelucci, D.E., Badal-Garcia, E., d'Errico, F., Daniel, F., Dayet, L. and Zapata, J. (2010). Symbolic use of marine shells and mineral pigments by Iberian Neandertals. *Proceedings of the National Academy of Sciences*, 107(3): 1023–1028.

Ludography

Ancestors: Stories of Atapuerca (2018). Murphy's Toast Games. [iOS and Android].

Assassin's Creed: Origins (2017). Ubisoft Montreal [Multiple platforms].

Herald: An Interactive Period Drama (2017). Wispfire. Wispfire. [PC, MAC and Linux].

Monster Hunter series (2004–2018). Capcom. [Multiple platforms].

Never Alone (*Kisima Inŋitchuŋa*) (2014). Upper One Games. E-Line Media. [Multiple platforms].

Red Dead Redemption 2 (2018). Rockstar Games. [Playstation 4 and Xbox One].

Tomb Raider series (1996–2018). Core Design & Crystal Dynamics. Eidos Interactive & Square Enix. [Multiple platforms].

Uncharted series (2007–2016). Naughty Dog. Sony Interactive Entertainment. [PlayStation 3 and PlayStation 4].

Learning in the museum

An Inclusive Prehistory Game by the Blind and Visually Impaired. Creating an Inclusive App Game on Prehistoric Archaeology with the BSVN e.V. for the Permanent Exhibition of the Neanderthal Museum

Anna Riethus

Federation of the Blind and Partially Sighted in Nordrhein (BSVN e.V.) in cooperation with the Foundation of the Neanderthal Museum, Germany

Abstract

Can an app game make a museum exhibition on prehistoric archaeology more accessible for guests with visual impairments? This is the research question of the NMsee project, a cooperative undertaking of BSV Nordrhein e.V. and the Neanderthal Museum in North Rhine Westphalia, Germany. Archaeological

How to cite this book chapter:
Riethus, A. 2020. An Inclusive Prehistory Game by the Blind and Visually Impaired. Creating an Inclusive App Game on Prehistoric Archaeology with the BSVN e.V. for the Permanent Exhibition of the Neanderthal Museum. In: Hageneuer, S. (ed.) *Communicating the Past in the Digital Age: Proceedings of the International Conference on Digital Methods in Teaching and Learning in Archaeology (12–13 October 2018).* Pp. 61–71. London: Ubiquity Press. DOI: https://doi.org/10.5334/bch.e. License: CC-BY 4.0

museum exhibitions focus largely on visual information transfer and work with non-inclusive underlying concepts of learning and knowledge, which lead to seemingly unbreachable difficulties for blind and visually impaired museum visitors. The approach of the NMsee project is an inclusive one: by creating an app game in the museum which communicates archaeological information in a non-visual way and which can be played independent of one's visual abilities, the project searches for inclusive ways of museum experiences. The game is created through a participatory and iterative process in order to stay in close contact with the needs and wishes of its target group. Starting in January 2019, the first prototypes and testing sessions will be launched in autumn 2019. This chapter presents the project idea, the problems leading to this research and the future goals of this undertaking.

Keywords

Games, Blindness, Archaeology, Museum, Neanderthal

Problems with being a (blind) museum visitor

The visually focused museum exhibition is not an inclusive concept. This is especially true for blind and visually impaired museum visitors, who have almost no access to the information and culture presented in archaeology museums. Exhibitions tend to encode all information in the archaeological original object, exhibition texts or their architectural qualities. Being unable to encode these informational symbols, whether due to a physical impairment, an attentiveness disorder or simply 'museum fatigue', eventually means having no or very restricted access to that valuable scientific information and culture.

To be precise, this instance alone is already *not legally compliant*. After all, public cultural institutions in Germany (such as museums, science centres and memorials) are – according to current German law (see e.g. UNO-General-versammlung 2007; Ministerium des Innern des Landes Nordrhein-Westfalen 2003; 2018, §49) and the Universal Declaration of Human Rights (see Articles 22, 26 and 27 of United Nations 1948) – obliged to make their cultural property accessible to all people, including those with physical or mental impairments.

Aside from the obvious difficulties of visitors who cannot focus on or cannot see the museum's vast visual information (both textual and figurative), most exhibitions in archaeological museums have underlying concepts which create much deeper problems by preventing the creation of other, more inclusive ways of experiencing a museum visit. The following concepts seem the most problematic to me when trying to conceptualise inclusiveness in the museum exhibition:

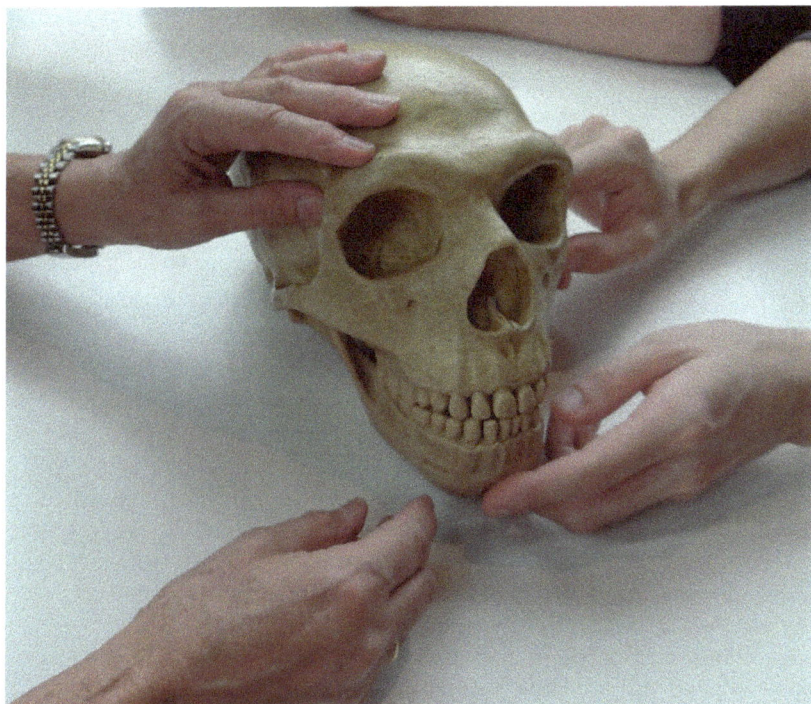

Figure 1: Museum exhibits hold valuable information encoded inside. Without wider access, such as tactile copies, this information remains restricted for guests with visual disabilities. © Neanderthal Museum.

• a positivistic conceptualisation of knowledge;
• a behaviouristic conceptualisation of learning;
• communicating knowledge as a unidirectional, linear process;
• our medical-rehabilitative explanatory model of physical and mental impairments.

Why are these concepts defined by me as exclusive or non-inclusive?

The concept of knowledge generally used in museums and their exhibitions is a *positivistic* one, which outlines knowledge as a clearly definable entity, independent of both teacher and scholar, existing outside both in an unchangeable form (Hein 1998: 18). I prefer the concept of Hein's 'constructivism' for both knowledge and learning (Hein 1998: 34), which allows for more diverse modes of learning and communicating knowledge to learners with special needs, though also making the evaluation of learning success more complex and difficult.

Hand in hand with a positivistic concept of knowledge comes a *behaviouristic concept of learning*. Learning is conceptualised as the gradual, structured accumulation of facts and information (Hooper-Greenhill 2007: 39–40). This is a passive, unidirectional form of science communication and knowledge transfer, which does not allow adapting the mode of teaching to the individual's needs. Based on these concepts, the general mode of communication in a museum exhibition is a *unidirectional, linear process*, in which predefined, encoded knowledge is handed to the passive learner (Hooper-Greenhill 1994: 69–70). This again does not allow the learner to bring in her or his individual needs, experiences and questions, which is needed when wanting to communicate knowledge to a diverse audience.

In addition to changing the underlying concepts of our museum work, our modern-day conception of physical and mental impairments is changing. The formerly valid explanatory model for impairments was a *medical-rehabilitative* one. It defined disability as a deviation of body, mind and soul from a socially recognised norm which must be eliminated, treated or avoided. Compared to this, the newer social explanatory model conceptualises disability as being disabled by a social association when conducting certain activities. From this point of view, one's disability is – in resemblance to the concept of gender – a property assigned to oneself by society (Scharringhausen 2011: 26–27, 68).

By rethinking concepts of disability, we have the chance to see the non-visuality of blind and visually impaired museum visitors as an unconventional and new approach to the archaeological content we want to provide them with. With a new toolset built from the described concepts, new inclusive modes of exhibition experience can be found.

Why research blind museum visitors?

One might ask oneself why there should be a discussion about inclusion in museums – especially archaeological ones – at all. Is the group of disabled people in Germany and Europe not a minority, unauthorised to ask for research funding and investment? The simplest argument for answering this last question with 'no' is also the answer to the latter question: together with our *demographic change and rising life expectancy*, the number of people with physical and mental impairments is ever rising – not much of a surprise, if one thinks of the correlation between advanced age and health issues (see e.g. Bertelsmann Stiftung 2015). The rising number and thus also growing political power of a former minority of people with disabilities should motivate museums and other institutions of science communication to rethink the relevance of inclusive access to the culture and information preserved by them. As mentioned earlier, the *free access to knowledge, education and lifelong learning is an essential human right*, already defined centuries ago. This is of special importance when it comes to granting or obstructing access to scientific information in museums. Additionally, the examination of the antithesis to classic visual-focused

Figure 2: Using the personal smartphone in the Neanderthal Museum is no technical problem for visually impaired guests. © Neanderthal Museum.

museum visiting – that of being 'non-seeing' – gives us a valuable starting point when searching for new museum experiences for all our visitors.

How to be a blind smartphone user

Those readers who are accustomed to gaming and smartphones might now rightly think: aren't both gaming and the use of smartphones very visual processes? How can these help blind and visually impaired museum visitors?

The smartphone is a technical innovation of the 21st century,[1] which by now defines so much of our everyday life that we interact with this medium on an hourly basis. The information technology 'smartphone' differs from the formerly described 'museum exhibition' medium in many ways, thus I will only point out the most relevant ones for this text:

- Smartphones are *created for an individual* user, not a mass of visitors.
- Smartphones *react* to the input we give them.
- On the basis of this input and their ability to react, smartphones *adapt* to their users.

---

[1] In January 2007, Steve Jobs introduced the first iPhone. In October 2008, the first Android smartphone followed (Arthur 2012).

Based on these underlying dogmata, smartphones have become a popular medium for blind and visually impaired users by helping them in everyday situations. This is possible through so-called screenreader software, which automatically reads out or describes the text or label touched on the smartphone's screen. This software has opened a wide range of new possibilities of independence and self-determination for people with visual impairments (e.g. Neffe 2019). Well-known examples of apps for visually impaired users are Barcoo, TapTapSee, BeMyEyes or Greta, which assist their users at the supermarket, in the kitchen, at the cinema or when trying to identify an unknown object.

(Inclusive) apps at the museum

Smartphones are a development which museums (could) have not ignored. Nowadays, a rising number of German museums offer their visitors their own smartphone application. According to a nationwide report from 2017, out of the 477 German museums 265 offered visitors their own app, while 214 museums provided a multimedia guide or tablet-guided tour (Institut für Museumsforschung 2018: 62). The Neanderthal Museum, for example, published its 'Neanderthal App' in 2012 and this has now been downloaded from Google Play Store more than 10,000 times. Both references illustrate the museum landscape's and the audience's rising interest in museum apps. Museum apps personalise the guests' visits and try to offer information on demand. They have the potential to introduce interactivity to the museum visit: visitors choose how to receive what kind of information, and in which media form, and can give direct feedback. Museum apps seem a more active alternative to the generally passive, unidirectional information transfer in museums and adapt to the communication form of the visitor's everyday life.

Besides the general trend in the museum landscape of adding such apps as described above, several museums have encountered the potential of smartphone applications for inclusion, especially for blind and visually impaired museum visitors. German best practice examples are the Berlinische Galerie ('Berlinische Galerie – Ein inklusiver Guide' at Google Play Store & iOS) and the SMAC, which is creating an inclusive app for its permanent exhibition. Generally speaking, these applications are accessible versions of museum audio guides and multimedia guides. These inclusive museum apps are an important step towards accessible museums indeed – but can we take the idea further?

Inclusive gaming – is that even possible?

Most questions I get asked about my work are probably based on the following underlying assumptions: blind and visually impaired people might be able to use a smartphone but cannot play a game on a digital screen-based medium.

Fortunately, accessible game design has opened the wide world of gaming to people with visual disabilities. This world is ever-growing: with 34.3 million Germans of different ages and genders playing games in 2019, every second German citizen is a 'gamer' (game – Verband der deutschen Games-Branche 2019: 6). In addition to that, the number of gamers aged 50+ is rising as well, and with 18.6 million users playing games on their smartphones, the smartphone is the favourite game platform in Germany (see ibid.: 8–9). These numbers illustrate the common use of app games in German society, as well as the potentially wide usage of app games by visually impaired players.

Accessible game design for blind and visually impaired people is a niche being filled by the gaming industry already. A both informing and enjoying list of such inclusive games can be found online on the website of the German Federation of the Blind and Partially Sighted (DBSV) (DBSV e.V. 2019). Creating these games can be done by adjusting and labelling all buttons and lines of strategy games or text adventures for screenreader software, by adding a lot of sound information to classic jump-and-run adventures or by creating something completely new based on the experience of non-visuality, as done in audio games (e.g. see *Sound of Magic*, *Blowback*, *The Nightjar*, *Papa Sangre*, *Frequency Missing*). These games do not only adapt to the special needs of their players. Instead, their whole game world and concept is based on 'not-seeing', by combining the immersive experience of a well-written audio drama with the evenly immersive concept of gameplay and game mechanics. Wilhelmsson et al. (2017) have shown us how such inclusively designed app games can provide a shared and equitable experience for users with and without visual impairments (see *Frequency Missing*, a free-to-use audio game available at Google Play Store & iOS) – and, by that, creating inclusion.

The NMsee Project

The immersion gained through games and audio drama, the accessible smartphone medium and the existing trend of museum apps are a set of potentialities which have not been combined until now. NMsee aims to fusion these potentialities in an audio-focused museum app game with accessible game design, and, in so doing, creating an inclusive and informative museum experience within the permanent exhibition of the Neanderthal Museum. The exhibition received its last update in October 2016 and currently offers many stations with touch and audio elements. On this basis, and with the support of Stiftung Wohlfahrtspflege, NRW Stiftung, LVR, Kämpgen Stiftung and NEAGES, BSV Nordrhein e.V. and the Neanderthal Museum launched the research project in January 2019.

NMsee aims to guarantee both an accessible permanent exhibition (through infrastructural factors such as a tactile guidance system, tactile labels or an indoor-navigation function within its new app) as well as a new access to the permanent exhibition's content (through a new information layer: the inclusive app game).

The current concept for our NMsee game consists of a narrative-driven adventure through a purely auditive and touchable game world within the Neanderthal Museum. This game concept is based on the outcome of two project workshops conducted in March and May 2019, in which professionals from game, exhibition and audio design worked together with museum experts and people with visual disabilities.

Inspired by audio games such as *Sound of Magic* (Everbyte GbR, 2018), tactile tours and workshops, as well as existing inclusive apps, we create a playable, walk-through audio story. When entering the museum, visitors join a selectable game character, each character having a different perspective on the museum's content. The chosen character introduces her/himself to you and gives you a short tutorial on the screenreader-like gestures for interacting with the character and the game (swiping and tapping at different speeds and different directions).

After choosing your first travel companion – e.g. a female archaeologist or a Neanderthal woman – you follow the indoor-navigation function and the tactile floor guidance system into the permanent exhibition. While walking, you listen to an audio world, representing, for example, an Ice Age Neanderthal with one ear, spotting larger animals passing by, hearing the Düssel flowing close by and eavesdropping on a few fellow Neanderthals having a chat. When approaching one of the tactile stations within the permanent exhibition, the sound landscape will change and invite you to interact with a new tactile exhibit and with your travel companion. By touching the exhibit, listening to the surrounding soundscape and communicating with your companion through given options, you explore the different character narratives, whose stories are interwoven and influence each other. By following the different narratives, you will be able to solve a mystery, which connects the different characters of the game. In some side events, you can also collect hidden gems in the game, such as bad Stone Age-related jokes.

When approaching a tactile station, your travel companion will introduce you to a new chapter of your journey. She will ask you to search for a tactile detail on the given exhibit, e.g. trepanation holes on a Stone Age skull or the nose form of a Neanderthal figure. You can ask your companion to tell you her/his life story, details about the exhibit, scientific knowledge or simple fun facts – depending on the character you chose, the information will vary.

Through this game, we aim to create an even basis for all visitors to start their museum experience on. Within an adaptive and motivating learning environment provided by the game, a both inclusive and valuable museum experience for visitors regardless of their vision becomes more and more feasible. In addition, the chosen focus on audio information and interaction with the museum's exhibits keeps the visitor's attention on the museum visit and avoids concentrating on the smartphone screen.

Figure 3: In meetings such as our first concept workshop in March 2019, we continue to improve the existing game concept together with visually impaired and seeing testers as well as with game design specialists.

This game concept is now being developed further, sharpened and prototyped together with a game design company and visually impaired as well as seeing testers. The launch of our NMsee app game is planned for autumn 2020, before which we will have several open test phases for interested gamers, archaeologists and museumgoers – both blind and seeing – to join us for a test round.

Our foci for the upcoming concept and prototype phases will be the app games' technical specifications, the usability for blind and visually impaired users and the creation of a fluent and immersive narrative. The project will be accompanied by a dissertation at the Department of History of Heidelberg University, and will conclude with a publication on the findings on what and how games like NMsee can contribute to the inclusiveness of archaeological museums.

Acknowledgements

This project could and would not exist without the patient and friendly advice, input and participation of our blind and visually impaired consultants and testers. I want to express my gratitude to this group, especially to Tamara Ströter at the BSV Mettmann, as well as Gerd Kozyk and Manfred Meyer from the BSV NRW, who contributed their valuable experience from the very start of this project idea.

References

Arthur, C. (2012). *The History of Smartphones: Timeline.* [online] *The Guardian.* Available at: www.theguardian.com/technology/2012/jan/24/smartphones-timeline [Accessed 3 September 2019].

Bertelsmann Stiftung (2015). *Demographischer Wandel 2030 – Aktualisierte Bevölkerungsvorausberechnung.* [online] Bertelsmann Stiftung. Available at: www.bertelsmann-stiftung.de [Accessed 16 April 2019].

DBSV e.V. (2019). *Smartphone- und Computerspiele.* [online] DBSV.org. Available at: www.dbsv.org/computerspiele.html [Accessed 16 April 2019].

game – Verband der deutschen Games-Branche (2019). *Jahresreport der deutschen Games-Branche 2019.* [online] Available at: www.game.de/publikationen/ jahresreport-der-deutschen-games-branche-2019 [Accessed 22 August 2019].

Hein, G.H. (1998). *Learning in the Museum,* Oxford: Routledge.

Hooper-Greenhill, E. (1994). *The Educational Role of the Museum,* New York and Abingdon: Routledge.

Hooper-Greenhill, E. (2007). *Museums and Education: Purpose, Pedagogy, Performance,* New York and Abingdon: Routledge.

Institut für Museumsforschung (2018). *Statistische Gesamterhebung an den Museen der Bundesrepublik Deutschland für das Jahr 2017,* 72, Berlin: Staatliche Museen zu Berlin.

Ministerium des Innern des Landes Nordrhein-Westfalen (2003). *Gesetz des Landes Nordrhein-Westfalen zur Gleichstellung von Menschen mit Behinderung (Behindertengleichstellungsgesetz Nordrhein-Westfalen – BGG NRW).* [online] Available at: www.recht.nrw.de/lmi/owa/br_text_anzeigen?v_ id=5420140509100636414 [Accessed 16 April 2019].

Ministerium des Innern des Landes Nordrhein-Westfalen (2018). *Bauordnung für das Land Nordrhein-Westfalen (Landesbauordnung 2018 – BauO NRW 2018).* [online] Available at: recht.nrw.de/lmi/owa/br_text_anzeigen?v_ id=74820170630142752068 [Accessed 16 April 2019].

Neffe, C. (2019). *Screenreader: Wie Menschen mit Sehbehinderung barrierefrei surfen.* [online] Available at: www.waz-online.de/Nachrichten/Medien/ Netzwelt/Screenreader-Wie-Menschen-mit-Sehbehinderung-barrierefrei-surfen [Accessed 16 April 2019].

REHADAT – Institut der deutschen Wirtschaft Köln (2019). *Blindheit und Sehbehinderung.* [online] Available at: www.rehadat-statistik.de/de/behin-derung/Behinderungsarten/Blindheit/index.html [Accessed 16 April 2019].

Scharringhausen, R. (2011). *Heilerziehungspflege Band 1 – Grundlagen und Kernkonzepte der Heilerziehungspflege*, Berlin: Cornelsen Verlag.

United Nations (1948). *Universal Declaration of Human Rights*, Paris: United Nations General Assembly. [online] Available at: www.un.org/en/udhrbook/pdf/udhr_booklet_en_web.pdf [Accessed 16 April 2019].

UNO-Generalversammlung (2007). *Convention on the Rights of Persons with Disabilities (CRPD)*. [online] United Nations. Available at: www.un.org/development/desa/disabilities/convention-on-the-rights-of-persons-with-disabilities.html [Accessed 16 April 2019].

Wilhelmsson, U., Engström, H., Brusk, J. and Östblad, P.A. (2017). Inclusive game design facilitating shared gaming experience. *Journal of Computing in Higher Education*, 29(3): 574–598.

Ludography

Blowback (2015). Carsten Busch, Deutschlandradio Kultur.

Sound of Magic (2018). Everbyte GbR.

The Nightjar (2011). Somethin' Else.

Papa Sangre (2010). Somethin' Else.

Frequency Missing (2017). University of Skövde.

Using Digital Media to Mediate Archaeology in the LVR-Archaeological Park Xanten / LVR-RömerMuseum

Stephan Quick

LVR-Archaeological Park Xanten

Abstract

For the education and mediation work of the LVR-Archaeological Park Xanten / LVR-RömerMuseum, digital media play a central role. The museum and the park preserve the foundations of the former Roman city Colonia Ulpia Traiana. The area has not been built over since late antiquity. Today only the foundations of the Roman buildings are preserved beneath the surface. Various methods are in use to visualise the dimension of the former Roman city and some of their monumental buildings to the visitors. A main feature of the museum's education service is a virtual reconstruction of the Colonia. The film is displayed on huge screens in the museum's permanent exhibition. The visitors get an impression of the Roman city from the point of view of an ancient pedestrian. The aim is to give visitors of all target groups a comprehensive and detailed impression of the city's architectural appearance and to create a realistic impression of space and atmosphere of the Colonia Ulpia Traiana, based on the archaeological evidence.

How to cite this book chapter:
Quick, S. 2020. Using Digital Media to Mediate Archaeology in the LVR-Archaeological Park Xanten / LVR-RömerMuseum. In: Hageneuer, S. (ed.) *Communicating the Past in the Digital Age: Proceedings of the International Conference on Digital Methods in Teaching and Learning in Archaeology (12–13 October 2018)*. Pp. 73–84. London: Ubiquity Press. DOI: https://doi.org/10.5334/bch.f. License: CC-BY 4.0

Keywords

Roman, Archaeology, Museum Education, Virtual Reconstruction

The Roman history of Xanten begins at around the time of the birth of Christ. At the beginning of the Augustan campaigns, Roman legions established the military camp Vetera on the Fürstenberg, south of the present city of Xanten. Just outside the legionary camp, civilians and artisans settled on a shore of the Rhine. Over time, the settlement grew in size. At the initiative of Emperor Trajan, probably around the year CE 100, it was granted the highest Roman city status. The Colonia Ulpia Traiana (CUT) was one of the most important cities in the Germanic provinces. The 73-hectare city area was crossed by streets laid out in an orthogonal grid and was surrounded by a 3.4-km-long city wall, making a total of 40 insulae. Representative public buildings such as the Forum, the Capitol Temple, the large thermal baths and the amphitheatre dominated the cityscape (Figure 1). In the heyday of the Colonia, in the mid-2nd century, there were probably more than 10,000 people of various cultural origins living in the city. In addition to Roman veterans, native Teutons, Gauls and people from other parts of the Roman Empire settled there (Heimberg, Rieche & Grote 2009; Müller 2008a; 2008b). The decline of the city began at the end of the 3rd century CE. After a destruction, the city area was reduced in size of nine insulae in the centre. In the middle of the 4th century CE, this late antiquity fortress was probably extensively destroyed by the Franks or abandoned by the inhabitants. After the end of the Roman era, the focus shifted to today's Xanten Domhügel, the area of the former Roman cemetery road. The area of the Colonia

Figure 1: Impression of the Colonia Ulpia Traiana. © H. Stelter, LVR-APX.

had not been built over since late antiquity, so the ancient stone materials were plundered, sold or reused for the construction of the medieval city (Heimberg, Rieche & Grote 2009; Otten & Ristow 2008).

Today, only the foundations of Roman buildings or their underground trenches have been preserved. The LVR-Archaeological Park Xanten (LVR-APX) has been protecting, researching and mediating these remains since 1977 as one of the most important archaeological monuments in Germany. Based on the concept of the LVR-APX, the research results are presented to the general public. In order to provide visitors with an idea of what are today mostly invisible original findings, the archaeologically excavated remains are depicted using various methods: the modern layout of the Archaeological Park corresponds to the Roman street grid. Tree-lined avenues today mark the porticoes that were once in front of the ancient residential development. Important buildings of the Roman city such as the amphitheatre or the Roman inn have been built on their original sites and at a scale of one to one, as partial or full reconstructions in the form of 'walk-in models'. The foundations of the large town baths, on the other hand, were given a protective structure and made accessible by a footbridge to visitors. Guests to the south-eastern urban area can capture an impression of inner-city space on a section of the former Decumanus VI. Here the street line is framed by the buildings of the reconstructed craftsmen's houses and the neighbouring hostel with its small baths, based on the ancient model (Müller 2011; Hilke 1994: 58).

Recent approaches and learning objectives

Since 2008, the LVR-RömerMuseum has been part of the LVR-Archaeological Park Xanten. The permanent exhibition, with around 2,500 objects, tells the story of the Xanten area chronologically, from the time immediately before the Roman conquest, at about the time of the birth of Christ, to late antiquity and the beginning of the Franconian epoch. For the education and mediation work of the museum, digital media are of central importance. As one of the most recent projects, the LVR-RömerMuseum conceived an interactive unit for the exhibition 'The Flow of Goods – Trade, Logistics and Transport in the Roman Lower Rhine Area' to visualise different transport routes via land, river and sea as well as the provenance of edibles and raw and building materials which had to be imported to the CUT. The visitors were able to buy and sell goods, to choose different types of transportation and to gain profit like a Roman trader.

In the context of informal learning, simulations and games can offer a great potential to attract visitors in order to engage them in applying knowledge and to support historical learning. The use of virtual reconstructions is widespread in museums today. The different implementations are discussed as a tightrope walk between 'abstraction' on the one hand – in support of scientific reliability – and 'immersion' on the other hand – favouring a staged lifelike atmosphere. While not every visitor can understand a purely abstract reconstruction with technical drawings, photorealistic impressions can offer a low-threshold approach to many lay persons. Rapid technical development leads to a growing hyperrealism of the reconstructions. However, since it is not always clear where knowledge is limited, this carries the danger of conveying a fictive reality as an image of historical reality (Süß & Gräf 2017: 14–16; Dreier 2010: 162; Franzmeier & Hageneuer 2017: 21; Wittur 2010: 157; Lengyel & Toulouse 2016).

The virtual reconstruction of the Colonia Ulpia Traiana

Building structures of the CUT on the surface are no longer preserved and direct access to the remaining archaeological evidence in the ground is hardly possible. In the years 2014 to 2016, the LVR-Archaeological Park Xanten / LVR-RömerMuseum, in cooperation with Faber Courtial GbR, produced a six-part virtual reconstruction of the CUT. The aim was to give the visitors a comprehensive impression of the architectural appearance in the form of an ancient city walk in the Roman town. In the following, three partial sequences of the virtual reconstruction will be discussed more in detail: the archaeological record of the Forum, the large town baths and the harbour will be examined as basis of their virtual reconstruction. At first, the technical realisation and the museum's implementation of the installation in the permanent exhibition of the LVR-RömerMuseum will be explained.

The film sequences are shown in the permanent exhibition on three large screens, which are installed above a real model of the CUT, 3 × 3 metres in size, on a scale of 1:350. The three-dimensional form of representation of the Colonia in the mid-imperial period contributes significantly to an understanding of the entire urban system. Visitors to the museum look at the extent of the Roman city from a bird's-eye view. The reduced scale representation allows the recording and conveying of large buildings such as the Forum and the amphitheatre, or infrastructural facilities such as the harbour, showing not only their location but also their proportions in the context of the city structure (Henke-Bockschatz 2016). The individual segments bounded by the grid are reversible and can be amended in the case of new scientific evidence.

Currently, about 20% of the inner-city area has been scientifically studied. A large part of this is attributable to public and religious buildings (Figure 2). These areas include insula 10, with the large town baths, insula 37, with the so-called Harbour Temple, and parts of insulae 38 and 39, with the hostel and small baths and the residential and craftsmen's houses. In the physical model these areas are characterised by special attention to detail such as a naturalistic colour scheme and tile-and-slate roof appearance. On the other hand, more than 80% of the inner-city area, including large parts of the civil buildings, has not been examined by archaeological excavations. Geo-prospecting methods that have been carried out continuously since 2006 have proven that these

Figure 2: Model of the Colonia Ulpia Traiana in the scale of 1:350. © O. Ostermann, LVR-APX.

areas were built up to a large extent. Sometimes, however, it is unclear how, for instance, the central area of individual insulae was developed and whether this served, for example, for keeping livestock, productive or working animals or was cultivated as acreage for self-supply (Kienzle 2008: 413; Müller & Zieling 2014; Babucic & Seifert 2018). In order to illustrate the different research statuses in the city model, these areas are displayed by residential and commercial buildings coloured in light grey without any architectural details.

The combination of the three-dimensional model with the virtual reconstruction not only offers the advantage of being able to convey an impression of the density of the ancient buildings but also allows the viewer to visualise the monumentality of the impressive representative buildings. The real model can be viewed from any angle, but the buildings can only be seen from the outside. The addition of the virtual reconstruction offers the possibility of a change of perspective, allowing an insight into the interiors and thus adding an ambience to the scene (Grellert 2007: 201; Lengyel & Toulouse 2016: 94). The buildings in the film sequences correspond to the archaeologically proven buildings of the ancient city at the current state of research. The findings of the buildings in the CUT generally provide detailed information on the floor plans of the buildings. In addition, researchers use structural considerations to presume the roof shape, e.g. caping or gable roofs. The findings of the areas of civilian housing that have been investigated so far by excavations have revealed a narrow perimeter block development with houses whose narrow front sides were aligned with a portico facing the street. Owing to the lack of information on the upper floors in Xanten, however, only hypothetical statements on the height development of buildings and on the design and layout of rooms on the upper floors are possible (Kienzle 2008; 2016). On the basis of the archaeological ground plan and reconstruction drawings, which building researchers have compiled over years of research and critically discussed in scientific specialist colloquia, the buildings were reconstructed three-dimensionally using computer-generated images. In order to fill the Colonia with life, people, animals, wagons and cargo barges were visually integrated in natural motion in the film. Actors were filmed against a neutral background using the so-called green screen process and then were embedded in the virtually reconstructed scenery. Only humans and animals in the background were animated. The visual implementation is supported by soundtracks, e.g. cheering or battle noise in the arena, background conversations, or ambient sounds such as footsteps, hooves or wagons.

A walk to the Forum

At the beginning of the virtual city tour, the viewers slip into the role of a Roman pedestrian, who enters the Colonia from the south through the so-called Vetera Gate. Walking on the gravelled surface of the cardo maximus, they explore the city from his point of view: most of the houses of the craftsmen's district were made up from shops and workshops at ground level and living rooms upstairs. All Roman houses had covered walkways; in some areas of the city there is evidence for paving with pebbles (Müller 2008b). The Forum was located in the city centre. We enter the site by the main entrance from the west. Here, merchants would have sold their goods in the hustle and bustle of trading. The archaeological excavations give evidence of a square paved with trachyte flagstones. On the other hand, no remnants of the statues adorning the square have yet come to light. On the north and south sides, the square was lined by approximately 21-metre-high halls with gabled roofs, which are interpreted as storage areas. The Forum basilica to the east consisted of a single-aisled hall 70 metres long, 23 metres wide and 27 metres high. Excavations in the 1990s suggested that the Forum basilica was constructed column-free and the open-span roof structure covered the building with a width of more than 20 metres (Precht 1997; Precht 2008) (Figure 3).

Inside the large town baths

The baths usually opened in the early afternoon. In the first century CE, Iuvenal (Lorenz 2017: 325) states that it was possible to visit the baths during the fifth

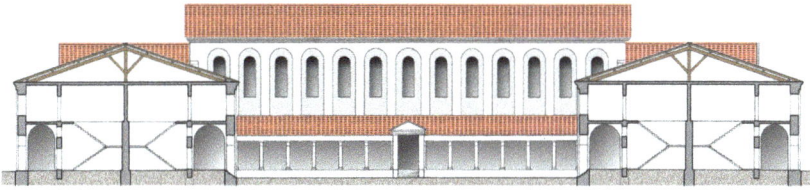

Figure 3: Reconstruction drawing of the Forum basilica with sectional view of the storage buildings. © G. Precht, LVR-APX.

Figure 4: Inside the virtual reconstructed basilica thermarum. © Faber Courtial GbR/LVR-APX.

hour, whereas Martialis (Martialis, Barié & Schindler 2002: 719) recommends going during the eighth hour of the day. For many Romans it was a matter of course or part of their daily routine to visit the baths. Most of the houses in the CUT had neither running water nor their own bathrooms. The camera movement takes us into the municipal baths built in Hadrian's time, where we first enter the large hall – the basilica thermarum. The LVR-RömerMuseum reveals both the dimensions and parts of the interior structure of the ancient building. Through the main entrance, the view opens into the hall, approximately 68 metres long and 19 metres wide (Figure 4). Excavations in the basilica revealed the foundations of a prestigious central portal and the charred remains of the floor, suggesting a flat wooden floor of oak planks. The interior of the museum incorporates these essential elements of the ancient entrance hall. In a narrow building located in the entrance area of the ancient hall, there were staircases leading to the upper galleries of the building, which was approximately

25 metres high. It is unclear whether bathers could use these probably circumferential galleries or if they were only accessible for servicing, e.g. for the cleaning of the windows. The wooden roof of the hall was probably clad in a cantilevered panelled ceiling. However, the excavated findings do not allow any specific statements on the exact use of this monumental hall. Probably there were shops or stands here, e.g. to buy bathing utensils, cosmetics or sports equipment. After leaving the basilica, the visitors enter the actual bathing area. The rooms of the frigidarium, tepidarium and caldarium were ordered in a row. From the cold through to the well-tempered room, one could finally approach the warm and the sweat baths (Zieling 2003: 27–28; Zieling 2008: 374–376; Schalles 2011: 146).

An efficient river port

Another perspective as seen through the eyes of the Roman pedestrian provides an impression of the harbour area, which in Roman times was located immediately in front of the north-eastern city walls of the Colonia. The Rhine flowed in the immediate vicinity of the city before it turned eastwards at the level of the so-called Harbour Temple. This is still evident today through the shape of the city's layout plan. Not only were raw materials and building materials scarce in the Lower Rhine area; the Romans also imported food, olive oil, wine and other products from almost every part of the empire. Last but not least, the Colonia was an important stop on the long-distance trade route to Britain. The CUT therefore needed a viable river port (Selke & Leih 2018; Selke & Franke 2018). Archaeological excavations have taken place since the 1930s and have revealed the remains of a multi-phase quay. Owing to the high groundwater level, there was a moist soil environment and thus a good state of preservation of the oak used for the construction. Consequently, dendrochronological investigations have been able to date the oldest construction phase to the Claudian period, around CE 46. The main landing stage was about 200 metres long and was located in the northern shore area of the CUT, running parallel to the city wall (Figure 5). The wooden structure on the river side consisted of a wall of five oak beams lying upon another stabilised laterally by posts. There are no archaeological remains of storage buildings or evidence of cranes, which had to be used for the loading and unloading of goods, as is shown in the virtual reconstruction. Although the total length of the quay can only be estimated, several barges, flat-bottomed ships, could certainly dock in parallel (Selke & Leih 2018: 286). In this type of ship, goods were stacked directly on deck. The draft of the 15- to 35-metre-long ships was usually hardly more than 50 centimetres (Schmidhuber-Aspöck 2018: 230). If there was no jetty, they could be driven directly onshore and the goods unloaded via the flat ramps at the bow and stern.

Figure 5: Virtual reconstruction of the Roman harbour of the CUT. © Faber Courtial GbR/LVR-APX.

Conclusions

The virtual reconstruction meets with a very positive response of visitors of all target groups. Guided tours such as school classes, but also families and individual visitors are able to visualise the cityscape in a vivid way. The combination of the three-dimensional model with the virtual reconstruction offers the unique advantage of being able not only to convey an impression of the densely built-up area in ancient times but also to enable the viewer to envision the monumentality of the representative buildings. The visitors can immerse themselves to a certain extent in the urban atmosphere. While observing these impressions, they are activated and motivated to pose questions about the everyday life of the Roman city and its inhabitants.

The question that museum visitors frequently ask – what was it really like in the Roman town? – is actually left open by the virtual presentation. The findings in the soil do not provide sufficient information for a clear reconstruction. Based on the current state of scientific research, the virtual reconstruction offers visitors, based on many different individual insights, a suggestion that shows what individual buildings in the context of the urban space of the CUT might have looked like in the middle of the 2nd century CE. However, only a small part of the complex construction history of the individual buildings is visualised in their urban planning context. The potential impact or previous demolition of older predecessors as well as possible structural changes due to reuse are not apparent in the form of this reconstructed snapshot. The ongoing on-site archaeological research will provide new scientific insights that may require a reassessment of current reconstruction designs (Kienzle 2016).

Against the background of an increasingly heterogeneous audience, the museum must in the future pursue innovative ways of education and mediation. As a digital medium, virtual reconstructions in the context of informal learning in the museum offer many opportunities for communicating complex relationships and facts in the sense of historical learning (Schwan 2006; Scheersoi 2006). It is important to prepare relevant information and content in the right balance (Lengyel & Toulouse 2016: 96), taking into account the expectations of the visitors with regard to modern viewing habits, and also to take into account the scientific requirements of a virtual reconstruction. In order to achieve a comprehensive understanding of the individual findings in the CUT, an active dialogue with the archaeological content must be possible for visitors of all target groups and learning types. An ideal further development would be an extension of the physical model and virtual reconstruction in the form of an interactive module, for example using tablets that allow visitors to gain insights into the correlation between the results of the excavations and the reconstruction plans or even to try out different options of the reconstructions virtually.

References

Babucic, N. and Seifert, M. (2018). Teaching2Go – Geophysikalische Prospektionen der Hamburger Fieldschool in der Colonia Ulpia Traiana. *Archäologie im Rheinland*, 2017: 91–93.

Dreier, C. (2010). *Forumsbasilika und Topographie der römischen Siedlung von Riegel am Kaiserstuhl*, Stuttgart: Konrad Theiss Verlag.

Franzmeier, H. and Hageneuer, S. (2017). From the Nile Delta to Karlsruhe: Or how to present mud bricks in an exhibition. *CIPEG Journal*, 1: 15–26.

Grellert, M. (2007). *Immaterielle Zeugnisse. Synagogen in Deutschland. Potentiale digitaler Technologien für das Erinnern zerstörter Architektur*, Bielefeld: transcript Verlag.

Henke-Bockschatz, G. (2016). Rekonstruktionen und Modelle. Vergangenes wiederhergestellt. *Geschichte lernen*, 171: 2–7.

Heimberg, U., Rieche, A. and Grote, U. (2009). *Colonia Ulpia Traiana. Die römische Stadt. Planung, Architektur, Ausgrabung*, Cologne and Pulheim: Rheinland-Kultur.

Hilke, M. (1994). *Bäume, Sträucher, Kräuter. Botanischer Führer durch den Archäologischen Park Xanten*, Cologne: Rheinland-Verlag GmbH.

Kienzle, P. (2008). Die zivile Wohnbebauung in der CUT. In: M. Müller, H.-J. Schalles and N. Zieling, eds, *Colonia Ulpia Traiana. Xanten und sein*

Umland in römischer Zeit. Xantener Berichte, Sonderband = Geschichte der Stadt Xanten, 1. Mainz: Philipp von Zabern, pp. 413–432.

Kienzle, P. (2016). 'Sie sollten jedoch mit großer Vorsicht ausgeführt werden . . .' . Gedanken zur Rekonstruktion antiker Architektur am Beispiel des Archäologischen Parks Xanten. In: K. Zimmer, ed., *Von der Reproduktion zur Rekonstruktion – Umgang mit Antike(n) II. Summerschool vom 16.-19. Juni 2014 in Tübingen, TAF 21*, Rhaden/Westf., pp. 25–43.

Lengyel, D. and Toulouse, C. (2016). Die digitale Visualisierung von Architektur. *Blickpunkt Archäologie*, 2/2016: 91–98.

Lorenz, S. (2017). *Juvenal. Satiren*, Berlin/Boston, MA: De Gruyter.

Martialis, M., Barié, P. and Schindler, W. (2002). *Epigramme*, Düsseldorf: Artemis & Winkler.

Müller, M. (2008a). Die städtebauliche Entwicklung von der Coloniagründung bis zur Spätantike. In: M. Müller, H.-J. Schalles and N. Zieling, eds, *Colonia Ulpia Traiana. Xanten und sein Umland in römischer Zeit. Xantener Berichte Sonderband = Geschichte der Stadt Xanten, 1*, Mainz: Philipp von Zabern, pp. 269–275.

Müller, M. (2008b). Die Stadtmauer der CUT. In: M. Müller, H.-J. Schalles and N. Zieling, eds, *Colonia Ulpia Traiana. Xanten und sein Umland in römischer Zeit. Xantener Berichte, Sonderband = Geschichte der Stadt Xanten, 1*, Mainz: Philipp von Zabern, pp. 277–290.

Müller, M. (2011). Der LVR-Archäologische Park Xanten / LVR-Römer Museum – Zur Visualisierung des Bodendenkmals. In: M. Müller, T. Otten and U. Wulf-Rheidt, eds, *Schutzbauten und Rekonstruktionen in der Archäologie. Von der Ausgrabung zur Präsentation. Xantener Berichte, 19*, Mainz: Philipp von Zabern, pp. 55–69.

Müller, M. and Zieling, N. (2014). Aktueller Stand der Geoprospektionen auf dem Gelände der Colonia Ulpia Traiana. *Archäologie im Rheinland*, 2013: 91–93.

Otten, T. and Ristow, S. (2008). Xanten in der Spätantike. In: M. Müller, H.-J. Schalles and N. Zieling, eds, *Colonia Ulpia Traiana. Xanten und sein Umland in römischer Zeit. Xantener Berichte, Sonderband = Geschichte der Stadt Xanten, 1*, Mainz: Philipp von Zabern, pp. 549–582.

Precht, G. (1997). Colonia Ulpia Traiana, Archäologische Untersuchungen im Jahre 1996. *Bonner Jahrbücher*, 197: 169–175.

Precht, G. (2008). Das Forum. In: M. Müller, H.-J. Schalles and N. Zieling, eds, *Colonia Ulpia Traiana. Xanten und sein Umland in römischer Zeit. Xantener Berichte, Sonderband = Geschichte der Stadt Xanten, 1*, Mainz: Philipp von Zabern, pp. 341–353.

Schalles, H.-J. (2011). Die Inwertsetzung eines antiken Baubefundes – Schutzbau und Museum über den Großen Thermen der Colonia Ulpia Traiana/ Xanten. In: M. Müller, T. Otten and U. Wulf-Rheidt, eds, *Schutzbauten und Rekonstruktionen in der Archäologie. Von der Ausgrabung zur Präsentation. Xantener Berichte, 19*, Mainz: Philipp von Zabern, pp. 139–148.

Schwan, S. (2006). Lernen im Museum. Die Rolle der digitalen Medien für Wissenserwerb und Wissenskommunikation. In: S. Schwan, H. Trischler and M. Prenzel, eds, *Lernen im Museum. Die Rolle von Medien. Mitteilungen und Berichte aus dem Institut für Museumsforschung, 38*, Berlin: Institut für Museumsforschung, pp. 1–10.

Scheersoi, A. (2006). Computer in Museumsausstellungen – Top oder Flop? In: S. Schwan, H. Trischler and M. Prenzel, eds, *Lernen im Museum. Die Rolle von Medien. Mitteilungen und Berichte aus dem Institut für Museumsforschung, 38*. Berlin: Institut für Museumsforschung, pp. 44–54.

Selke, V. and Franke, R. (2018). Von Claudius bis Antoninus Pius (?) – zur Baugeschichte des Xantener Hafens. *Archäologie im Rheinland*, 2017: 101–103.

Selke, V. and Leih, S. (2018). Der Hafen der Colonia Ulpia Traiana. In: C. Eger, ed., *Warenwege – Warenflüsse. Handel, Logistik und Transport am römischen Niederrhein. Xantener Berichte, 19*, Mainz: Philipp von Zabern, pp. 271–288.

Schmidhuber-Aspöck, G. (2018). Binnenschifffahrt auf dem Rhein in römischer Zeit. In: C. Eger, ed., *Warenwege – Warenflüsse. Handel, Logistik und Transport am römischen Niederrhein. Xantener Berichte, 19*, Mainz: Philipp von Zabern, pp. 229–243.

Süß, J. and Gräf, B. (2017). *Lopodunum VI. Die 3D-Rekonstruktion des römischen Forums von Ladenburg. Beschreibung und Begründung der Nachbildung*, Wiesbaden: Dr. Ludwig Reichert Verlag.

Wittur, J. (2010). Darf es noch ein bisschen mehr sein? Anwendungsmöglichkeiten und Ethik computergenerierter Visualisierungen des animierten Museumsfilms. In: *Befund und Rekonstruktion. Mitteilungen der Deutschen Gesellschaft für Archäologie des Mittelalters und der Neuzeit, 22*, pp. 157–166.

Zieling, N. (2003). *Die Grossen Thermen der Colonia Ulpia Traiana. Die öffentliche Badeanlage der römischen Stadt bei Xanten*, Cologne: Rheinland-Verlag GmbH.

Zieling, N. (2008). Die Thermen. In: M. Müller, H.-J. Schalles and N. Zieling, eds, *Colonia Ulpia Traiana. Xanten und sein Umland in römischer Zeit. Xantener Berichte, Sonderband = Geschichte der Stadt Xanten, 1*, Mainz: Philipp von Zabern, pp. 373–389.

New Storytelling for Archaeological Museums Based on Augmented Reality Glasses

Adolfo Muñoz and Ana Martí

Universitat Politècnica de València

Abstract

Museums are places where cultural heritage is preserved and, therefore, we can consider them an essential resource to understand our identity, past and future. In the last two decades, they have increased the use of information and communication technologies in a remarkable way with the intention of reaching new audiences and spreading knowledge.

With the recent advent of augmented reality devices of the 'view-through' type, perceiving and interacting with virtual contents in the form of holograms anchored to the real physical space is now possible. One of the most interesting challenges is to leave the screen aside and interact with digital data in an intuitive way, through voice commands and gestures. This offers a new scenery for experimenting with storytelling creation, a current trend in archaeological museums.

In our effort to take advantage of the new capabilities of augmented reality glasses, we have developed different applications with the Microsoft HoloLens

How to cite this book chapter:
Muñoz, A. and Martí, A. 2020. New Storytelling for Archaeological Museums Based on Augmented Reality Glasses. In: Hageneuer, S. (ed.) *Communicating the Past in the Digital Age: Proceedings of the International Conference on Digital Methods in Teaching and Learning in Archaeology (12–13 October 2018)*. Pp. 85–100. London: Ubiquity Press. DOI: https://doi.org/10.5334/bch.g. License: CC-BY 4.0

glasses. In this chapter, we explain our experiences in such developments, which have led us to create an innovative storytelling for the archaeological museum of the Almoina in Valencia (Spain), a singular project where we have experimented with a fictional holographic character that attends as a guide to present a story about the city life in Valencia during the time of the Roman Republic. The story is presented as animated sequences with video, 3D reconstructions and music. The visitor conducts the storyline interacting with the marked hotspots that appear over the ruins of the museum.

Keywords

Museum, Augmented Reality, Immersive, HoloLens, Storytelling

Introduction

Over the past five years, many articles have dealt with the future of museums, with promises of how technology will help solve some of the existing problems with audience engagement and content presentation. In fact, there are different technological improvements, like the increasing computing power in smart-phones, artificial intelligence, geolocation or big data, which lead us to think that a more communicative museum is now possible (Winesmith 2017; Mannion, Sabiescu and Robinson 2015).

Nevertheless, in the last three years a new technological development has appeared that can radically change museums' storytelling, especially when it comes to museums of history, science and archaeology. We refer to the new virtual reality and augmented reality smart glasses developed by powerful companies such as Microsoft, Facebook or Magic Leap.

On the one hand, virtual reality technology has already been used successfully in the museum context in order to introduce the audience to recreated virtual living spaces. The Back to Life project, developed by Google in collaboration with the Natural History Museum in London (Clio Awards 2017; Pavid 2016), the Modigliani experience from the Tate Museum (Taylor 2018; Tate 2017) and the permanent room dedicated to VR at the National Museum of Natural History in Paris (Tiercepartie 2018; MNHN 2018) are examples of international awarded projects where virtual reality was used as a powerful tool to present and explain complex processes by transporting visitors to new experimental scenarios where they can play an active role.

On the other hand, augmented reality allows us to mix real objects with digital information at the same perceptual level. In other words, virtual reality transports users to virtual worlds; meanwhile, augmented reality brings the digital representations to our real space.

Although augmented reality (AR) technology is still at its beginning, some recent projects demonstrate its potential for enhance exhibitions: The Musée des Plans-Reliefs presented an interactive model of Mont St Michel where it is possible to go around and explore the model of the castle with interactive information related to it (Laval Virtual 2018); the Petersen Automotive Museum (Microsoft 2017) showed an exhibition of cars with apparent motion thanks to the visual overlaying of digital models; and the Kofun Virtual Guide, made by Keuchi Laboratory of the University of Tokyo, is an AR system prepared to show parts of the ancient capital of Japan, all overlaid on the real landscape environment (Epson 2018; Koetsier 2018).

These examples have in common the use of 'view-through' AR glasses. These devices are prepared to display stereoscopic video, pictures and 3D animations according to the interests of the audience, using voice and hand gestures or even simply interacting unintentionally with their body in the space of the exhibition. This kind of experience can also be shared with other visitors, taking the visit to a new level of collaborative experience that maintains and extends the social essence of museums (Eghbal-Azar et al. 2015: 133–142).

Since VR and AR open the possibility of new ways to interact with heritage, they also require new methodologies and procedures to design successful experiences for any kind of audience.

At the Universitat Politècnica de València, our research group develops AR prototypes that test new interactive-immersive narratives for museums. Our goal is to design tests to explore whether these new immersive experiences can give a better understanding of heritage and its importance in a natural and enjoyable way.

In this chapter, we describe some of those experiences, explaining the challenges we have gathered during the last three years and some advances we have achieved in the implementation of those methodologies in a prototype for a real museum: the archaeological museum in Valencia, La Almoina.

Augmented reality gets into the museum

In the last two decades, museums and heritage sites have increased the use of information and communication technologies (ICT) in a remarkable way, investing large amounts of money and time with the intention of digitising their collections to reach new audiences and spread knowledge (Tallon & Walker 2008; Wang et al. 2008). Certainly, museums are institutions that must continually reinvent themselves if they want to prosper and attract new audiences, to remain relevant centres, and technology is an essential tool to make this happen (Horwitz-Bennett 2010; Panagiotis, Despina & Chrysanthou 2013).

After the commonly adopted integration of online digital resources in the exhibition space using smartphones, a new technological revolution is already changing museum communication. Indeed, the development of new technologies has facilitated access to information, but, beyond this achievement, the way people interact with digital data is also changing, thanks especially to AR devices.

Thanks to the investments that have been developed in the last decades, AR glasses have reached a point of optimal maturity to be inserted in society. The economic predictions of the sector forecast that the investments for the year 2020 will exceed the investment in VR (Digi Capital 2016), which will mean that new and better systems will appear in the market, with applications that will expand their use to other fields still to be discovered (Digi Capital 2017).

Some of its key features are the use of 3D stereoscopic visual systems with the ability to track some of the movements of the user (head, hands and eyes) and the space, together with the use of immersive sounds. AR systems permit the incorporation of digital data in a real environment, allowing users to perceive digital recreations without losing the perception of the physical world. When compared with VR, AR approaches are a more naturalised way to interact with data, since they allow contents to be included through layers of information adapted to the real space without overloading it, being very respectful with the original piece and the naturalised experience with the related data.

In 2016, HoloLens glasses appeared on the market to demonstrate for the first time the potential of the new 'view-through' AR devices. Unlike mobile devices – where you look at the screen of the mobile to see a mix between the capture of the camera and superimposed three-dimensional elements – the AR 'view-through' glasses inaugurate a new system of total immersion among the three-dimensional elements and our natural stereoscopic visual experience. One of their most important features is that they are prepared to scan the space continuously so that they can combine real and tangible physical elements with virtual elements while the user moves freely.

The idea of taking information and superimposing it on the real world opens a new path of possibilities that allow us to better understand the information of objects, places or history, making the real world more magical (Burdea & Coiffet 2003; Osterhout 2016).

Indeed, one of the most interesting challenges is the possibility of leaving the screen behind and interacting with digital data in a much more intuitive way, through voice commands and gestures. These devices offer a new scenery with a huge potential for experimenting with storytelling creation, a current trend particularly in archaeological museums.

Developing an immersive storytelling

One of the great advances of digital media is that they allow us to take advantage of non-linear narratives, offering multiple entries to the same topic and extending the limits of linear narration, while placing the visitor at the centre of the event, where they are allowed to take decisions (Gillam 2017). Another common feature is the convergence of media (Jenkins 2008), which applied to the storytelling context allows us to mix different media that previously worked separately, for instance placing images next to text, or even animations, or introducing a musical thread at the same time that we reproduce the discourse with different devices.

Museums are natural storytellers (Johnsson 2006) and, from the very beginning, they have used different techniques to communicate exhibitions with the intention of making objects more accessible to visitors (Roussou et al. 2015; Wong 2015). As cultural storytellers, they need to tell inclusive stories, which breaks the barriers that isolated them from society (Solari 2015).

Just as 19th-century museums made some architectural changes to accommodate a greater number of visitors who could access objects (Bennett 1995), the museums of the 21st century will have to adapt to the new needs of the information society (Witcomb 2003: 115) to include ever more attractive experiences as something necessary for their survival.

With this idea in mind, we were determined to use AR in a museum context to develop different storytelling techniques that could profit from a more natural-physical communication. In that sense, we consider that the most suitable museums for this purpose are the museums of history or archaeology. Even though, in many occasions, they include pieces of artistic value, the truth is that they are mainly constituted by heterogeneous collections that show either the greatness or the history of a country or region. Their narrative is usually associated with the possibility of developing an idea or discourse, which hooks with the possibilities of experiencing storytelling through AR.

When using AR 'view-through' glasses it is possible to reconstruct objects and contexts to better understand other historical episodes. Most societies use, and have used, physical and material objects as examples of ideas or lessons. Objects become a very powerful tool to represent past events in the present. However, with the help of holographic images, together with sound and the ability to move around and interact with the data in the exhibition space, we can create innovative storytelling that may help to engage with the youngest audiences.

Traditionally, museums and heritage sites have used reconstructions of objects together with models, graphics and audio-visual media, such as documents or maps, to maintain a chronological continuity. On many occasions, in museums of history or archaeology, objects are moved from their place of origin and are exposed, decontextualised, in the room. Very often, ruins of buildings are difficult to understand from their degraded state, making very difficult to understand the history of the people who lived there in ancient times. A better understanding of the contents and an improvement of the experience is possible by using holographic glasses, giving life to those places with virtual objects that help the reconstruction of their habitat in context.

At the same time, it is necessary to act with scientific rigour, respecting the existing information of the exhibits, so that the recreations do not introduce any historical error. Obviously, history is not an exact science, and the vision of a fact can never be pure or innocent. Methodologically digital recreations should be generated following the lead of curators and experts from the museum.

Traditionally, archaeological museums focus more on exhibiting archaeological remains and objects, with some associated data, than offering a possible interpretation from them. However, in recent years, more and more archaeological museums have tended to develop narratives that help to recreate how these objects were used and by whom. Those narratives often appear as micro events that reconstruct the interpretation that is made of a particular site (Hernández 2010: 22–23).

Designing immersive experiences

In our way to develop inclusive storytelling when using AR, we started to test different methodologies in different exhibition contexts. Our idea was to test techniques, which could use the advantages of AR, in order to determine which are more natural and effective to be implemented in museums in the near future.

Garden

In June 2016, as a first attempt, we designed an experience to explain the value of the painting *The Garden of Earthly Delights* by Bosch, using the HoloLens glasses. Our goal was to create a motivational experience to increase the interest in the details of this artwork. A sequence of video and animated graphics with a voiceover was produced to explain the artwork, using the authoring software Unity to program the application. The challenge was to create a storytelling mode that would motivate interest in the work, without diminishing the importance of the real object, by adding visual elements, videos and animations projected onto a high-definition, full-size printed reproduction of the famous painting, accompanied with explanatory audio.

However, in the development of the experiment, we had some evidence of the problematic inclusion of overlaying virtual data in part of the painting and how this was negatively affecting the perception of the original artwork. Beyond some undeniable pedagogical value, the discovery of information on the canvas was seen like a game by most of the 10 testers, showing a clear conflict between the real and the virtual that is not present in other platforms, like mobile phones or PCs, where everything is perceived as a digital representation.

Nevertheless, this test helped to dismiss an important observation: one of the first findings was that this technology is not appropriate to be applied directly to overlay works of art, since in the artistic exhibitions it is important to maintain an intimate relationship between the work of art and the viewer, and the screen of the glasses darkens the colours of the painting, together with the digital data, distracting the attention from the content, which is what really matters when speaking about art.

Indeed, museums are institutions that traditionally develop narratives linked to the authenticity of works, tradition and the universality of knowledge. Both works of art and cultural heritage are made up of unique and irreplaceable objects and buildings that, thanks to this, acquire qualitative and quantitative value (Witcomb 2003: 106–107). Including digital information in front of an artwork takes away the attention of the visitor.

Other projects that used the HoloLens to overlay information in front of paintings, like the one developed by the start-up Opuscope in 2016 (Klint 2016), brings us to the same conclusion: the information that overlays the paintings makes it difficult to have a real experience with it. HoloLens glasses have also been used to show paintings from important artists from anywhere, like in the project conducted by the culture platform Boulevard Arts Inc., together with Case Western Reserve University (Case Western Reserve University 2017), showing a way to see paintings in your home in a more attractive way than in art books. Still it cannot replace the feeling of being in front of the real object.

According to Gwyneira Isaac, the technology used to copy the pieces can be understood as something enigmatic, as if it were an enchanted technology, but it affects our relationships with objects (Isaac 2016). In her opinion, these screens not only 'hypnotize' visitors but also place them in an institutionalised atmosphere.

Nevertheless, this first experience helped to draw some conclusions about the usability of the voice commands and gestures when reproducing contents, as well as to start developing the design of the interactive posters and labels together with the experimentation of the video, which we included in later developments.

Since no other universities or companies had presented research on that period on how using gestures or commands with smart glasses in the museum context, we considered this field of research of great interest.

Therefore, we began to consider a general exhibition context to test and experiment with the HoloLens glasses and AR interaction models. In February 2017, we presented an AR application called Holomuseum at the biannual Inventions Fair at the Universitat Politècnica de València, aimed at testing many of the new possibilities that AR glasses open for different exhibition contexts.

Holomuseum

Holomuseum was an application designed to facilitate the creation and maintenance of many multimedia experiences in any exhibition hall (Muñoz 2017).

The system came to solve several important problems: on the one hand, those arising from the current limits of technology – the management and

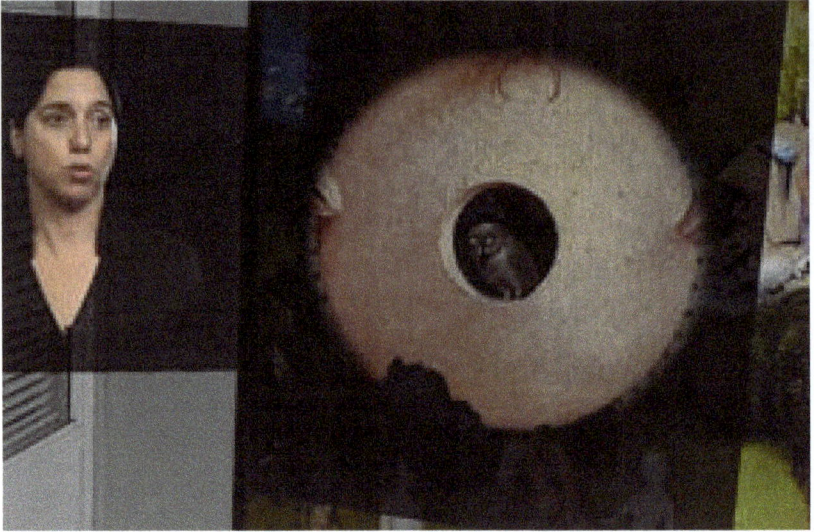

Figure 1: Example of Garden storytelling. © Universitat Politècnica de València.

maintenance of a collection of virtual contents in real space, and its location in one or several rooms – and, on the other hand, those generated by the absence of a consensus language for the management of AR contents with holographic glasses.

The application was created to be used by designers and curators when creating exhibitions, and by visitors, in the mode of visualisation: on the one hand, it has an editing mode, in which curators can manage the list of three-dimensional objects to be displayed, and decide exactly which part of the room will be presented when activated. The items list pointed to data held from the internet containing individual interactive contents ready to be downloaded. On the other hand, the system has a default mode for visits, showing the list of contents like virtual boxes hung on a real wall of the exhibition space, ready to be opened at the visitors' request. The activation and downloading of each item were made by simple voice commands or by a pinch gesture (air tap) on the virtual boxes (Muñoz & Martí 2018).

One of the main challenges of this project was creating a permanent link between the digital contents and their pertinence to a physical space. In the same way, maintaining a visual coherence between the actions of the visitors and the digital states was crucial to blend the digital and the real without conflict. In Holomuseum the audience could remember where they could trigger each content because they were marked with posters in the walls. The real posters acted as anchors for the virtual boxes floating in front of them, helping to understand them as a kind of persistent mixed-reality label. Furthermore, each box was animated when activated to show this action in a way that was easy to

Figure 2: Example curator view for editing, and visitor view for visualising. © Universitat Politècnica de València.

identify, and remained on the wall, opened until the visitor decided to close it with the voice command 'close box', or just by air-tapping the box again with their fingers.

With the intention of making a sample of the usability of the system, and testing it with different users in an exhibition hall, we designed different models suitable for different types of museums: on the one hand, we made prototypes of scientific and technological style, and, on the other hand, we created others of a more artistic or historical nature.

Figure 3: Example of Holomuseum exhibition. © Universitat Politècnica de València.

To expose these contents, some panels were printed to serve as physical posters or labels for each element. These panels explained each object. The holographic cubes were physically placed on these posters, which, once activated, were loaded from the internet and flew to the different areas of the room previously selected by the curator. At the centre of the room, a pedestal was placed to serve as a physical support to place digital contents.

Later on, in 2018, the company Holograph also presented an authoring tool to create augmented exhibitions in museums (Surur 2018), but it uses the simple modes of a traditional museum, like labels, without really exploring new ways to interact with digital data.

The development of Holomuseum helped to clarify the acceptance of AR exhibitions and the expectations of visitors when experimenting with the new media for the first time. After getting very positive reactions of the audience, we tried to go one step further with the creation of interactive storytelling specially dedicated to show the potential of AR in a real museum.

Almoina AR

Since archaeological museums usually require recreations of lost items, places or even traditions, they are one of the most suitable kind of museum for experimenting with AR. Although HoloLens have been already used in an archaeological context, the experiences were dedicated just to underline single pieces of the collection, like in Holoforge, where the glasses overlay a polychromic restitution of a bust of Akhenaton (Goguel 2017), in contrast with our more general approach.

Thanks to the collaboration with the archaeological museum of the Almoina in Valencia (Spain), we could design an experience to cover the first steps of the history of this old city, taking on the challenge of engaging the audience with AR figures and recreations of the lost buildings over the remains of the ruins.

The project was conceived around the idea of intimacy, naturality and magic, to appeal to any kind of audience.

The most natural way to attend a guided tour is with the company of a person as a guide, therefore the experience was designed to be conducted by a fictional video character, named Clelia, acting as a personal historical guide. The experience with Garden taught us that making characters from video recordings of actors is more effective than using 3D animated recreations, since the expressions of a real person makes the character more engaging, alive and empathetic. To make her presence similar to a natural one, it was decided to program the AR application in a way that the visitor did not have to do things they do not normally do when communicating with real people, like pressing buttons or typing words. At the same time, the size, staging and look of Clelia had to mimic the attributes of a person in a real space, like staring into the visitors' eyes all the time while maintaining a regular distance. The figure was always displayed from two or three metres away from the viewer, as a flat video layer that is continuously pointing towards the visitor. The videos of Clelia were produced using the chroma key technique to make possible the integration of 3D figures flying around her while preserving spatial overlaying coherence.

Following these rules, at the beginning of the experience, when the visitor wears the glasses with the application running for the first time, Clelia asks to get closer before she can start telling the story of the place. That is one of the biggest advantages of programming AR applications for this platform: knowing the position of the user facilitates the creation of patterns that help to simulate human behaviours like asking the visitor to pay attention if they are not looking at the proper place.

Once the visitor is in the correct position, Clelia's first mission is to introduce herself and teach the visitor the way to interact with the content.

In our previous experiences we discovered that to use the common gestures to interact with the digital data designed for the HoloLens 1 – the air tap – was inappropriate since less than 50% of testers were comfortable with this option.[1] Hence, the challenge was to design the interaction system to avoid the use of gestures, in favour of a system just based on the position of the visitor in the room and the direction of the head. Clelia achieved this in less than three minutes. She taught the audience that pointing their heads towards some 3D plates in the space of the room activates small parts of the story. The system was programmed to check whether the visitor learned to interact with the head or do

---

[1] The HoloLens 2 was announced in March 2019 with a big improvement for natural interaction, changing the input system from the 'air tap' model to a more intuitive system based on the tracking of both hands and eyes.

not, in which case Clelia would repeat the instructions until the 'correct body response of the visitor' was produced.

Then the visitor was invited to discover and activate the items that conformed the full storyline located in different parts of the ruins. Each plate, or coin, triggered animated synchronised sequences of video, 3D reconstructions and music, presenting part of the story that explained the history of Valencia during the time of the Roman Republic.

For the application prototype of Almoina AR, the scene named 'Sanctuary' (composed of four individual items) was just produced and tested from the five scenes scripted in the preproduction, as an example of a methodology for future developments. 'Sanctuary' was marked over the rectangular space of an antique pool in an important part of the ruins. When activated, Clelia appeared, wearing different customs to reveal the possible use of the water of the lost pool to cure people with the help of the god Asclepios.

In 'Sanctuary', Clelia invited the visitor to explore the space to discover the four items placed around the ruin of the pool. Four coins marked these spots, each one containing two-minute stories about sacrifices, the end of the original city during a civil war, or an explanation about the link of the water with gods.

During the narration, and as a part of the 'magic' strategy, a digital pool appeared, filled with water, and two figures emerged at the side, depicting medical treatment. Because all these virtual representations are perceived over the real place, the comprehension and value of the ruins change completely in the

Figure 4: Preview of the virtual architecture and character in the Almoina. © Universitat Politècnica de València.

eyes of the visitors. Some comments like 'I understand now the explanation of the brochures' from early testers seem to demonstrate the huge pedagogic potential of this storytelling based on the 3D location of digital assets in real places.

In this process, we discovered that the duration and cadence of transitions of the digital assets – appearing and disappearing – and the introduction of music or sound effects – like the sound of water when the pool is discovered – are very important in order to give enough time for visitors to understand the correspondence of the real space with the digital reconstructions. At the same time, careful, small animations in lighting, materials and objects helped to emphasise the wonder of the experience.

Conclusions

The prototype for the Almoina demonstrates that AR will become a disruptive medium in the future of museums and exhibitions, especially for educational purposes, since AR is demonstrating that it has a very high pedagogical value in explaining not only how lost archaeological items were once situated in the real space but also how they worked and were used in the past. It is certainly possible with AR to create adapted storytelling that respects heritage sites while engaging new audiences. Holograms are capable of constructing the layers of history so that visitors can better understand what ruin belonged to which building.

We can determine that most of the testers of Almoina AR enjoyed the contents, interacting in a natural and intuitive way with almost no training.

The choice to portray Clelia in video, in contrast with other approaches like 3D avatars or cartoons, was a success, since none of the testers complained about the lack of three-dimensionality – Clelia was just a video projected on a flat 3D surface facing the glasses dynamically. Furthermore, they were amused by the fact that she seemed to look them directly in the eyes all the time, and even waited for the actions she needed them to make.

Although we have tested the potential of AR glasses to shape the future of storytelling in exhibits, it is necessary to underline that this technology is still too expensive and immature to be fully integrated as part of the main offering of museums. The budget and professionals to produce new AR media are still difficult to quantify, considering the extended number of professionals needed to produce this media, composed – as in the case of Almoina AR – of a mix of audio-visual production, video game programming and 3D reconstructions. Other unresolved issues will arise as well, like the time that these experiences will take for the average museum visitor or the adaptation to different languages.

Nevertheless, the development of closed prototypes and trial tests in real museums, like Almoina AR, will be necessary for convincing institutions to take a chance on this technology and be prepared to implement it in the near future.

Surely, as AR technology improves towards a more advanced input system based on the tracking of the eyes and individual fingers on space – like the second version of the HoloLens, announced for the end of 2019 – it will be even easier to implement the 'natural' interaction approach that we have described as the core of any AR storytelling for museums.

References

Bennett, T. (1995). *The Birth of the Museum*, New York: Routledge.

Burdea, G.C. and Coiffet, P. (2003). *Virtual Reality Technology*, New York: John Wiley & Sons.

Case Western Reserve University (2017). *New Microsoft HoloLens app lets users examine renowned British art collections from anywhere in the world.* [online] Cleveland. Available at: https://thedaily.case.edu/new-microsoft-hololens-app-lets-users-examine-renowned-british-art-collections-anywhere-world [Accessed 2 September 2019].

Clio Awards (2017). *Back to Life in Virtual Reality: Rhomaleosaurus & Giraffatitan.* [online] Clio Awards. Available at: https://clios.com/awards/winner/branded-entertainment/google-arts-culture/back-to-life-in-virtual-reality-rhomaleo-saurus-gir-19572 [Accessed 2 September 2019].

Digi Capital (2016). *Augmented/Virtual Reality Revenue Forecast Revised to Hit $120 Billion by 2020.* [online] Digi Capital. Available at: https://www.digi-capital.com/news/2016/01/augmentedvirtual-reality-revenue-forecast-revised-to-hit-120-billion-by-2020 [Accessed 3 December 2017].

Digi Capital (2017). *After Mixed Year, Mobile AR to Drive $108 Billion VR/AR Market by 2021.* [online] Digi Capital. Available at: https://www.digi-capital.com/news/2017/01/after-mixed-year-mobile-ar-to-drive-108-billion-vrar-market-by-2021/#more-1617 [Accessed 3 December 2017].

Eghbal-Azar, K., Merkt, M., Bahnmueller, J. and Schwan, S. (2015). Use of digital guides in museum galleries: Determinants of information selection. *Computers in Human Behavior*, 57: 133–142.

Epson. (2018). *Bring Your Exhibition to Life.* [online] Epson. Available at: https://www.epson.co.uk/viewcon/corporatesite/cms/index/11938 [Accessed 2 September 2019].

Gillam, S. (2017). *Spotlight VR/AR: Innovation in Transformative Storytelling.* MW17. [online] Museums and the Web. Available at: https://mw17.mwconf.org/paper/spotlight-vrar-innovation-in-transformative-storytelling [Accessed 6 May 2019].

Goguel, O. (2017). *HoloLens Bringing the Past Back to Life.* [online] Holoforge. Available at: http://www.holoforge.io/work/hololens-and-archeology [Accessed 29 March 2019].

Hernández, F.H. (2010). *Los museos arqueológicos y su museografía*, Gijón: Trea.

Horwitz-Bennett, B. (2010). *High-Tech Museums: The Future is Now.* [online] Interiors + sources. Available at: https://www.interiorsandsources.com/

article-details/articleid/9931/title/high-tech-museums-the-future-is-now [Accessed 6 May 2019].

Isaac, G. (2016). Technology becomes the object. The use of electronic media at the National Museum of American Indian. In: B.M. Carbonell, *Museum Studies. An Anthology of Contexts*, Oxford: Blackwell, pp. 533–546.

Jenkins, H. (2008). *Convergence Culture: La cultura del a convergencia de los medios de comunicación*, Barcelona: Paidós comunicación.

Johnsson, E. (2006). *Telling Tales, A Guide to Developing Effective Storytelling Programmes for Museums*, London: Claire Adler.

Klint, L. (2016). *HoloLens könnte in Museen bald Wirklichkeit werden.* [online] Windows United. Available at: https://windowsunited.de/hololens-in-museen-koennte-bald-wirklichkeit-werden [Accessed 2 September 2019].

Koetsier, J. (2018). 500K people have used these augmented reality smartglasses that you've never heard of. [online] *Forbes*. Available at: https://www.forbes.com/sites/johnkoetsier/2018/02/01/500k-people-have-used-these-augmented-reality-smartglasses-that-youve-never-heard-of/#67c0ebd16a31 [Accessed 19 February 2018].

Laval Virtual (2018). *Award Winners VR/AR for a Cause.* [online] Laval Virtual. Available at: https://www.laval-virtual.com/award-winners [Accessed 2 September 2019].

Mannion, S., Sabiescu, A. and Robinson, W. (2015). *An Audio State of Mind: Understanding Behaviour around Audio Guides and Visitor Media*. MW15. [online] Museums and the Web. Available at: https://mw2015.museumsandtheweb.com/paper/an-audio-state-of-mind-understanding-behviour-around-audio-guides-and-visitor-media [Accessed 17 January 2018].

Microsoft (2017). *Mixed Reality Brings Ford GT Supercars to Life.* [online] Microsoft. Available at: https://www.microsoft.com/inculture/arts/petersen-automotive-museum [Accessed 2 September 2019].

MNHN (2018). *Cabinet de Réalité virtuelle.* [online] Muséum national d'histoire naturelle. Available at: https://www.mnhn.fr/en/visit/lieux/cabinet-realite-virtuelle-cabinet-virtual-reality [Accessed 2 September 2019].

Muñoz, A. (2017). *Web de Holomuseum.* [online] Private Blog. Available at: https://goo.gl/bf5XNd [Accessed 10 March 2019].

Muñoz, A. and Martí, A. (2018). Holomuseum: A Hololens Application for Creating Extensible and Customizable Holographic Exhibitions. In: L. Gómez Chova, A. López Martínez and I. Candel Torres, eds, *EDULEARN18 Proceedings*, Valencia: IATED Academy, pp. 2303–2310.

Osterhout, R. (2016). *AWE Annual AR versus VR debate* [Interview] (8 June 2016).

Panagiotis, Z., Despina, M.-G. and Chrysanthou, Y. (2013). Learning through multi-touch interfaces in museum exhibits: An empirical investigation. *Educational Technology & Society*, 16(3): 374–384.

Pavid, K. (2016). *How to Resurrect a Sea Dragon.* [online] National History Museum. Available at: http://www.nhm.ac.uk/discover/how-to-resurrect-a-sea-dragon.html [Accessed 19 February 2018].

Roussou, M., Pujol, L., Katifori A., Chrysanthi, A., Perry, S. and Vayanou, M. (2015). *The Museum as Digital Storyteller: Collaborative Participatory Creation of Interactive Digital Experiences.* [online] Museums and the Web. Available at: https://mw2015.museumsandtheweb.com/paper/the-museum-as-digital-storyteller-collaborative-participatory-creation-of-interactive-digital-experiences [Accessed 6 May 2019].

Solari, M. (2015). *Creating the Inclusive Museum through Storytelling.* [online] MuseumNext. Available at: https://www.museumnext.com/insight/creating-the-inclusive-museum-through-storytelling [Accessed 11 February 2018].

Surur (2018). *MR Guide Is the HoloLens Tour Authoring Tool Your Local Museum Has Been Waiting For.* [online] MSPoweruser. Available at: https://mspoweruser.com/mr-guide-hololens-tour-authoring-tool-local-museum-waiting [Accessed 2 September 2019].

Tallon, L. and Walker, K. (2008). *Digital Technologies and the Museum Experience: Handheld Guides and Other Media,* Lanham, MD: Altamira Press.

Tate (2017). *Behind the Scenes. Modigliani VR. The Ochre Atelier.* [online] Tate. Available at: https://www.tate.org.uk/whats-on/tate-modern/exhibition/modigliani/modigliani-vr-ochre-atelier [Accessed 2 September 2019].

Taylor, J. (2018). *Modigliani VR wins D&AD Award.* [online] Preloaded. Available at: https://preloaded.com/modigliani-vr-wins-dandad [Accessed 2 September 2019].

Tiercepartie (2018). *Voyage au cœur de l'Évolution, application de réalité virtuelle.* [online] Tiercepartie. Available at: https://www.tiercepartie.fr/portfolio-item/voyageaucoeurdelevolution [Accessed 2 September 2019].

Wang, Y.; Stash, N.; Aroyo, L.; Gorgels, P.; Rutledge, L.; Schreiber, G. (2008). Recommendations based on semantically enriched museum collections. [Report] *Web Semantics: Science, Services and Agents on the World Wide Web,* 6(4): 283(8).

Winesmith, K. (2017). *How SFMOMA Made Its Audio-First, Location Aware App,* Melbourne: MuseumNext.

Witcomb, A. (2003). *Re-Imagining the Museum. Beyond the Mausoleum,* New York: Routledge.

Wong, A. (2015). *The Whole Story, and Then Some: 'Digital Storytelling' in Evolving Museum Practice.* [online] Museums and the Web. Available at: https://mw2015.museumsandtheweb.com/paper/the-whole-story-and-then-some-digital-storytelling-in-evolving-museum-practice [Accessed 6 May 2019].

The Challenges of Archaeological Reconstruction: Back Then, Now and Tomorrow

Sebastian Hageneuer
University of Cologne

Abstract

Archaeological reconstruction has been part of archaeology since its beginnings. From rudimental sketches to elaborated artwork, from pages in a notebook to immersive three-dimensional worlds, from detailed scientific research to mere fantasy, the spectrum of quality, media and reliability of archaeological reconstructions is broad and shows a wide variety. In most cases, however, we are not able to see that variety in the visualisation itself and are misled in believing what the past looked like. Reconstructions are a popular way of communicating the past to a broader audience, as can be observed in museums, magazines, documentaries or even video games. The effect of an elaborated reconstruction is however often preferred over the truthfulness of the underlying sources. Although there are guidelines and charters promoting a good way of documenting and presenting, they are often ignored. This chapter aims to sum up the development of reconstructions from the very beginning to today and give a glimpse into the future.

How to cite this book chapter:
Hageneuer, S. 2020. The Challenges of Archaeological Reconstruction: Back Then, Now and Tomorrow. In: Hageneuer, S. (ed.) *Communicating the Past in the Digital Age: Proceedings of the International Conference on Digital Methods in Teaching and Learning in Archaeology (12–13 October 2018).* Pp. 101–112. London: Ubiquity Press. DOI: https://doi.org/10.5334/bch.h. License: CC-BY 4.0

Keywords

Reconstruction, Museum, Communication, Documentation, Heritage

Introduction

In 1717, William Stuckeley, British antiquarian and member of the Royal Society, said: 'Without drawing or designing the Study of Antiquities or any other Science is lame and imperfect' (Piggott 1978: 7). Since its beginnings, archaeology has always been accompanied by visual media, and rightly so. Visual media help to convey information non-verbally and at a glance, whether plans, sections, photos, sketches or – for the purpose of this chapter – reconstructions. Reconstructions try to re-visualise artefacts, a landscape or architecture, which does not exist anymore. The latter in particular are often used within archaeology, a good example being images by Jean-Claude Golvin, as they show the different ways in which reimagination of the ancient past can take place (Golvin 2019). Although often described as such, visual representations of reconstructions are far more then pretty pictures.

Reconstructions grab the attention of the viewer, as visual media do in general. Well-made visualisations have the power to convey authenticity (Bahrani 2001: 16), which makes them credible to a point that we even today turn back to them as a valid reference of the past (Micale 2010). In this respect, they can be a dangerous source of misinformation, if communicated wrongly. The question therefore remains: what can we actually learn from reconstructions? We also need to ask ourselves how much of the reconstructions we can believe (Simon 1997: 25). As they are always influenced by the state of knowledge as well as assumptions and agendas, we can be sure at least that they will tell us something about the time they were created: 'Such reconstructions are fantasies that tell us more about the period of reconstruction than about the ancient past' (Bahrani 2001: 17).

However, as they do inform us about the state of our knowledge, reconstruction drawings can function as a kind of visualised theory (Bator, van Ess & Hageneuer 2013; Hageneuer 2014), helping as a reference for argumentation to be discussed like any other scientific paper. The question remains whether they are also suitable for conveying information in a museum setting. In the field of a museum exhibition, in particular, reconstruction images or animations are often used to convey information about the past. In this regard, I have pointed to the danger of blindly accepting reconstructions as such (Hageneuer 2016a) and offered possibilities to counter that problem (Hageneuer 2016b; Franzmeier & Hageneuer 2017). In this chapter, however, I want to submit a very condensed overview of reconstruction drawings in the museum with one example from the past, one from today and a glimpse into the future. In this way, I hope to showcase what we can learn from the past and what we need to improve for the future. My examples will focus on the region of the Near East and Egypt, although this overview could be done for any other archaeological discipline as well.

Reconstructions of and from the past

As mentioned before, reconstructions in archaeology are as old as the discipline itself. Since its beginnings, archaeologists have used reconstruction drawings to illustrate their findings and interpretations. As an example, I want to take a closer look at one of the first archaeological reconstruction drawings of the ancient Near East. Sir Austen Henry Layard (1817–1894) was on his way from London to Ceylon (modern-day Sri Lanka) to become a lawyer, but lost interest in this during his travels through Mesopotamia. After abandoning his plans to go to Ceylon, he quickly became the assistant to Sir Stratford Canning, the British ambassador in Constantinople, for whom he started the excavations in Nimrud, near modern-day Mosul in Iraq. Finding the remains of two Neo-Assyrian palaces on his first day (Larsen 2010: 101–103), his work lasted from 1845 to 1847 and in a second campaign from 1849 to 1851 he also excavated Tell Kuyunjik (ancient Nineveh). He published his results in different editions but mainly in the form of widely available travelogues (for example Layard 1849a; 1853a) or expensive large folio publications intended for a more scientific audience (Layard 1849b; 1853b). In his 1853 large folio publication *A Second Series of the Monuments of Nineveh*, the first plate consisted of a reconstruction drawing of the western side of the palaces of Nimrud (Figure 1).

In the scope of this chapter, I do not want to discuss the contents of the drawing (Layard 1853b: 1), the scientific value of the reconstruction itself (Reade 2008) or even the Orientalist message behind it (Bahrani 2001), but rather its popularisation and distribution. Layard's publication was what we would call today a limited edition, with only a couple of hundred copies distributed anywhere in the world. By that time, however, Layard and his excavations were what everyone was talking about. His popularity combined with a good sense of public engagement made sure his (and James Fergusson's) thoughts about the visual representation of ancient Assyria remained popular. Today, the image is still frequently used as a cover image for various scientific and non-scientific publications worldwide (for example, Parpola & Whiting 1997; Adkins 2003; Faiella 2006; *Der Spiegel* 2016), which should not be surprising considering its artistic beauty.

Zainab Bahrani correctly points to the problem of the general authority in elaborate reconstruction drawings (Bahrani 2001: 16), a problem that is also discussed with the newer medium of 3D models today (Buccellati 2015;

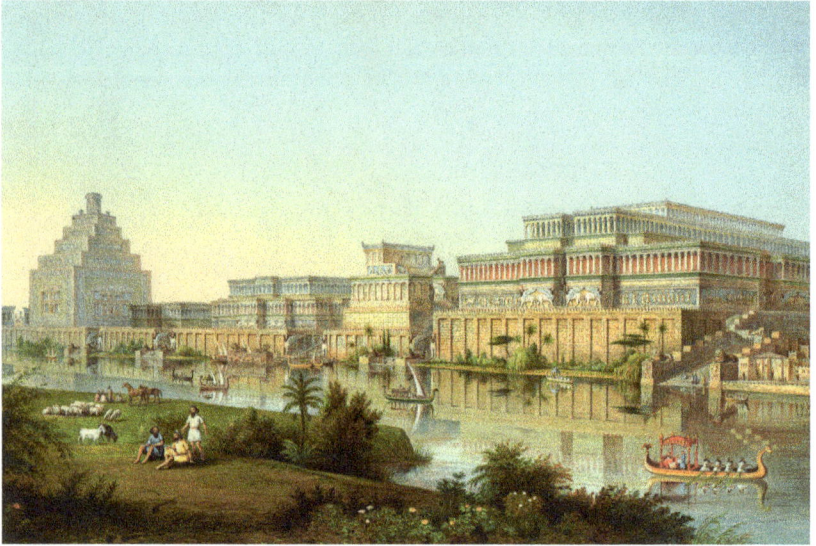

Figure 1: A proposal of the western side of the palaces of Nimrud. Drawn by Thomas Mann Baynes under instructions of James Fergusson for Sir Austen Henry Layard, published in 1853.

Lanjouw 2016: 3–4). With the older medium of drawings, however, we already can see the longevity of beautiful reconstructions, despite their problems. In a recent exhibition at the British Museum in London ('I am Ashurbanipal, king of the world, king of Assyria', 8 November 2018–24 February 2019), Layard's reconstruction was used in its promotional video[1] as the basis for a three-dimensional reconstruction of a city during the narrative of the clip. Besides the already-mentioned archaeological problems with this reconstruction and the widely known discussion around it, the creators of the video failed to mention that Ashurbanipal's palace was located in Nineveh and not in Nimrud, as suggested by the reconstruction. Nevertheless, as this image is one of the more elaborate ones depicting the Neo-Assyrian Empire, it never lost its authority, even to scholars of ancient Near Eastern archaeology.

I am no exception and use the reconstruction frequently in class or in articles (for example Hageneuer 2016c; 2019) to show an example of one of the first reconstruction drawings made. Nevertheless, I believe it is important to highlight the problematic parts of the image or (like in this chapter) its discourse. The communication of these images needs to reflect our current understanding of it.

---

[1] [online] YouTube. Available at: https://youtu.be/0OZe-y5tk9Q [Accessed 13 May 2019].

Reconstructions today

We should expect that reconstructions made today are more thoroughly researched and better communicated than in the past, but, as the example of the British Museum has shown, this often is not the case. Of course, we have to differentiate commercial from scientific work, but (1) these categories do not need to be mutually exclusive and (2) both should live up to a certain standard.

As an example of a reconstruction made in the last few years ('the present'), I want to discuss a reconstruction made by myself in 2016. Up to that point, I was a freelancer specialising in creating 3D reconstructions for archaeological projects from around the world. Similar to the reconstruction before, this also shows a whole complex of buildings, in fact a whole city (Figure 2). The city of Pi-Ramesse ('House of Ramesses') was founded by King Ramesses II at the beginning of his 67-year reign in the early 13th century BCE in the north-eastern Nile Delta, about 120 kilometres north-east of modern Cairo.[2] Between 17 December 2016 and 18 June 2017 the Badisches Landesmuseum Karlsruhe hosted an exhibition called 'Ramesses – Divine Ruler of the Nile'.[3] Beside Ramesses himself and his life, one part of the exhibition was dedicated to his capital city. In an animation (Artefacts 2016), I was assigned to give an insight into the results of over 35 years of excavation and the daily life in Pi-Ramesse in under seven minutes.

I do not want to get into either the details of the content (Franzmeier & Hageneuer 2017: 23) or the popularisation or distribution (which we cannot analyse at this point). Instead, in continuation of the argument before, I want to talk about the communication of archaeological knowledge. In order to do so, I would like to start with an insight into the communication process with the client, which in this case was the Badisches Landesmuseum Karlsruhe (as host of the exhibition), the Roemer- und Pelizaeus Museum in Hildesheim (as the current partner of the excavation) and the excavation project itself (providing the necessary data). All three partners (and I) were excited about creating a 3D visualisation of the ancient capital of Ramesses II, although everyone had individual expectations. For the museum partners, a visually pleasing result with animated flyovers of the reconstructed city were important. Also, the animation should not be too long, as visitors needed to pass by constantly. The excavation project on the other hand was more focused on presenting as much data as possible and showcasing the newest and best results. Also, a potential continuation of the created 3D model was intended or at least wished for. I, as the

---

[2] For more information See: Franzmeier and Pusch 2016; Franzmeier and Hageneuer 2017; Hageneuer 2016b; Pusch and Herold 2001.

[3] For more information about the exhibition see: [online] Landesmuseum Karlsruhe. Available at: https://www.landesmuseum.de/website/Deutsch/Sonderausstellungen/Rueckblick/2017/Ramses.htm [Accessed 16 May 2019].

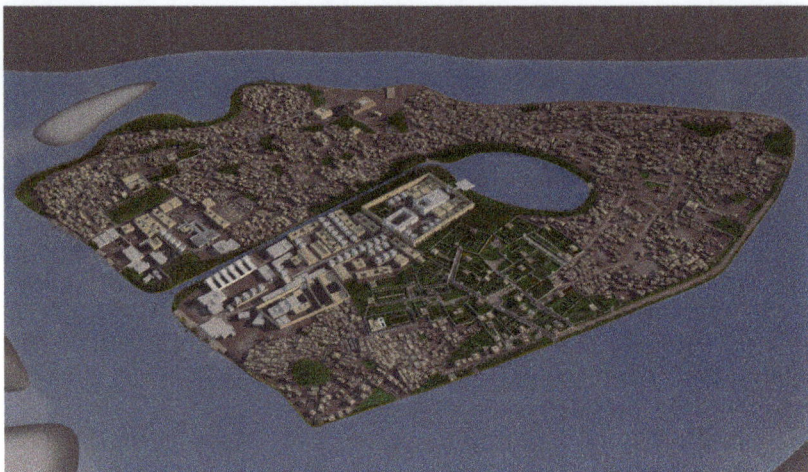

Figure 2: Reconstruction of the city of Pi-Ramesse in the early 13th century BCE, 2016. © artefacts-berlin.de.

contractor, was concerned with the timeline and amount of work (in relation to the compensation), as the opening of the exhibition was only nine months away. We therefore had to find a way to create and document the animation rather quickly in order to be able to communicate it properly for a broader as well as scientific audience.

The reconstruction process was a mixture of different methods. Where the excavations had produced sufficient results, the reconstruction was based upon these results and intense discussions with Edgar B. Pusch, the former excavator and walking encyclopaedia of information about the site. Former reconstruction attempts were available and incorporated whenever possible and the whole discussion and all decisions, mostly done via e-mail, were archived for later publication. One example of a more detailed reconstruction can be seen with the royal stables near the end of the animation (Artefacts 2016: 4:10–6:19). Where there was no excavation but geomagnetic prospection, the reconstruction process relied heavily on other sites, for example where private houses had already been found and reconstructed (e.g. Endruweit 1994; Aufrère, Golvin & Goyon 1991–1997; Tietze 2008). These were recreated in close discussion with the head of the excavation project in Pi-Ramesse, Henning Franzmeier, and put accordingly on the outlines provided by the geomagnetic prospection plan. For the third area, the area neither excavated nor surveyed and mostly built over by the modern-day village of Qantir, another approach was necessary. By analysing the already-reconstructed parts of the city based on the excavation and geomagnetic prospection, we jointly discussed possible ways of filling the gaps, by copying existing reconstructions and creating new ones based on assumptions of architecture that was not found but was most probably

Figure 3: Reconstruction of the royal stables in the city of Pi-Ramesse in the early 13th century BCE, 2016. © artefacts-berlin.de.

in existence (like the royal palaces, now probably found where expected, see Franzmeier, forthcoming).

In order to give the audience a way to understand this underlying thought process, the decision was made to present, before showing a whole recon-structed city, the sources used. After introducing the site, a 3D view shows the empty island in the Nile where Pi-Ramesse was located. On a first layer, the excavated areas of the city are mapped, which comprises only 0.25% of the whole estimated city area. On a second layer, the extensive geomagnetic prospection is shown, which comprises at least 10% of the whole area. Only then does the animation show the reconstruction in these introduced parts, areas that owing to the excavation and geomagnetic prospection can be recon-structed to a certain degree of certainty. The image speaks for itself, as only a small fraction of the city area is actually reconstructed (less than 10%, as not all of the magnetic survey detected remains). Only as a last layer, the anima-tion shows a full reconstruction (with flyovers!) of the city of Pi-Ramesse, as we presume it to have been, and then continues in displaying certain details of the city (Figure 3). All steps in the animation are accompanied by explanatory texts showing the museum visitor the sources used and openly discussing the uncertainty of the reconstruction.

The animation is now part of the permanent exhibition at the Roemer-und Pelizaeus Museum in Hildesheim, where artefacts of the excavation in Pi-Ramesse are also displayed. Additionally, the animation was presented in another exhibition in 2019 at the Cincinnati Museum Centre in Ohio, USA, titled 'Egypt: The Time of Pharaohs', a touring exhibition through North Amer-ica. Images of the reconstruction were used in various popular special-interest magazines (e.g. *Antike Welt* 2019; *Welt der Wunder* 2019). The result of this project is therefore used for scientific as well as popular science communication in various ways.

This example shows what is already in discussion today: thorough documentation, presentation and communication of archaeological reconstructions (Hageneuer 2019). In reconstructing for a broader audience in particular, we as archaeologists need to take on the responsibility of communicating our work correctly without creating an image of the past that is accepted without discussion. In the archaeological community, at least since the theoretical discussions of post-processualism, we are quite aware of not blindly accepting the results as they are presented. We need to bring this critical thinking into the museum as well and engage visitors by enabling them to evaluate the knowledge presented to them.

Challenges of the future

We can never predict what will happen in the future, but upcoming technologies like virtual or augmented reality are already finding their way into museums today (see Muñoz/Martí in this volume). The same holds true for reconstructions as presented in this chapter (as well as Quick in this volume) or interactive games and apps (Riethus in this volume). As technologies will get cheaper and more easily usable, I am expecting an increase of these technologies inside museums, not to mention the invention of new technologies. The question I am concerned with here, however, is not what technologies to expect (see Ch'ng 2009) but rather to reflect on the future methods of communicating the past in museums to not repeat the mistakes already made.

We should ask ourselves the question: are these new technologies that will improve in hyperrealism, immersion and usability a good way of communicating the past or not? In increasing the realism of reconstructions we also increase their potential for evoking authority and therefore misinformation. This does not necessarily mean we should not create sophisticated reconstructions or pursue the development of virtual environments for archaeology and for archaeological communication, but we have to use guidelines to do so and to communicate them correctly. Guidelines that already exist, like the London Charter (2009) or the Seville Principles (2011) are very useful documents in that regard, but they are in no way binding to archaeological projects or museums.

The responsibility lies therefore with the creators and the contracting clients (e.g. archaeological projects or museums) to invest the extra effort in creating reconstructions following these guidelines and afterwards ensuring that the communication is done in a way which is informing and not misleading the visitor. This is also dependent on the thoughtful selection of available technologies and possible realism in these works. I would also argue that most of the time this is even intended by the creating authors, but the responsibility does not end there. As copyright holders of reconstructions, we have the possibility to make sure our visualisations get communicated the right way even in the future. We can for example demand a clear declaration of the image or animation as a 'reconstruction' or 'proposal' when used by third parties. It is more difficult, though, when the copyright does not exist anymore, as in the case of Layard's reconstruction.[4] In this case, the third party has the responsibility to correct communication, but as experience shows this is not always the case.

In my opinion, the communication of the past is in fact the most important part of our field. The example of Layard shows us that the longevity and authority of these images exist and are not revoked easily. Owing to developments in our field and cheaper technologies, images like these are not restricted to artists or even archaeologists anymore. The creation of hyper-real reconstructions is getter easier year by year and their number will therefore increase. This leads me to the importance of correct documentation and especially communication, as I have shown in my own example. This is of course in need of improvement and the level of showing uncertainty has to get significantly higher. Here, creators and contractors need to take on the responsibility, especially in the future. We already have two guidelines that are concerned with authority (London Charter 2009: 3.3), documentation (London Charter 2009: 4.1–4.12; Seville Principles 2011: 7.1) and communication (Seville Principles 2011: 4.1–4.3), but they are not binding in any way. I would argue that, if contracting clients or funding organisations persist on using these guidelines, the communication of archaeological reconstructions will get more transparent and in fact more communicative, as people outside the reconstruction project will be able to take part on the discussion and interpretation. Museum visitors can get involved in the thinking process instead of absorbing a prepared image in an exhibition and can get a better communicated past in the future.

References

Adkins, L. (2003). *Empires of the Plain: Henry Rawlinson and the Lost Languages of Babylon*, New York: Harper.

Antike Welt (2019). *Auferstehung der Antike. Archäologische Stätten digital rekonstruiert*. Special Issue. Darmstadt: Zabern.

Artefacts (2016). *The Reconstruction of Pi-Ramesse*. [online] Artefacts. Available at: http://piramesse.artefacts-berlin.de/ [Accessed 16 May 2019].

Aufrère, S., Golvin, J.-C. and Goyon, J.-C. (1991–1997). *L'Égypte restituée*. 3 volumes. Paris: Errance.

---

[4] Depending on the country and whether we are talking about a person or a company as the copyright holder, the copyright expires 70–95 years after the death of the creator.

Bahrani, Z. (2001). History in reverse: Archaeological illustration and the invention of Assyria. In: T. Abusch, P.-A. Beaulieu, J. Huehnergard, P. Machinist, P. Steinkeller and C. Noyes, eds, *Historiography in the Cuneiform World: Proceedings of the XLV Rencontre assyriologique international*. Bethesda, MD: CDL Press, pp. 15–28.

Bator, S., van Ess, M. and Hageneuer, S. (2013). Visualisierung der Architektur von Uruk. In: N. Crüsemann, M. van Ess, M. Hilgert and B. Salje, eds, *Uruk – 5000 Jahre Megacity*. Exhibition Catalogue. Petersburg: Imhof, pp. 365–371.

Buccellati, F. (2015). What might a field archaeologist want from an architectural 3D model? In: M.G. Micale and D. Nadali, eds, *How Do We Want the Past to Be? On Methods and Instruments of Visualizing Ancient Reality*. Piscataway, NJ: Gorgias Press, pp. 157–169.

Ch'ng, E. (2009). Experiential archaeology: Is virtual time travel possible? *Journal of Cultural Heritage*, 10(4): 458–470.

Der Spiegel (2016). *Mesopotamien. Aufbruch in die Zivilisation*, Der Spiegel Geschichte 2/2016, Hamburg: Spiegel.

Endruweit, A. (1994). *Städtischer Wohnbau in Ägypten. Klimagerechte Lehmarchitektur in Amarna*, Berlin.

Faiella, G. (2006). *The Technology of Mesopotamia*, New York: Rosen.

Franzmeier, H. (forthcoming). Qantir-Pi-Ramesse – Preliminary Report on the 2016 and 2017 seasons (site Q VIII). In: *Proceedings of the Sixth Delta Survey Workshop, held at the University of Mansoura, 11–12 April 2019*, Special Edition of the *Journal of Research*, Mansoura University, 2020.

Franzmeier, H. and Hageneuer, S. (2017). From the Nile Delta to Karlsruhe: Or how to present mud bricks in an exhibition. *CIPEG Journal*, 1: 15–26, DOI: https://doi.org/10.11588/cipeg.2017.1.40326.

Franzmeier, H. and Pusch, E.B. (2016). 'Pi-Ramesse'. In: M. Bauks and K. Koenen, eds, *Das wissenschaftliche Bibellexikon im Internet*, [online] Available at: http://www.bibelwissenschaft.de/stichwort/32607 [Accessed 16 May 2019].

Golvin, J.-C. (2019). *Jean-Claude Golvin*. [online] Jean-Claude Golvin. Available at: https://jeanclaudegolvin.com [Accessed 20 May 2019].

Hageneuer, S. (2014). The visualisation of Uruk – First impressions of the first metropolis in the world. In: W. Börner and S. Uhlirz, eds, *Proceedings of the 18th International Conference on Cultural Heritage and New Technologies 2013 (CHNT 18, 2013)*. [pdf] Wien: Museen der Stadt Wien. Available at: https://www.chnt.at/chnt-18-2013-proceedings [Accessed 16 April 2019].

Hageneuer, S. (2016a). The influence of early architectural reconstruction drawings in Near Eastern archaeology. In: R.A. Stucky, ed., *Proceedings of the 9th International Congress on the Archaeology of the Ancient Near East*, Wiesbaden: Harrassowitz, pp. 359–370.

Hageneuer, S. (2016b). Die virtuelle Rekonstruktion von Pi-Ramesse. In: Badisches Landesmuseum Karlsruhe, ed., *Ramses. Göttlicher Herrscher am Nil*, Petersburg: Imhof, pp. 268–272.

Hageneuer, S. (2016c). *Archaeological Reconstructions*. [online] Smarthistory. Available at: https://smarthistory.org/archaeological-reconstructions [Accessed 9 May 2019].

Hageneuer, S. (2019). 'Without drawing the study of antiquities is lame!' – Architektur-Rekonstruktion als wissenschaftliches Tool? In: P. Kuroczynski, M. Pfarr-Harfst and S. Münster, eds, *Der Modelle Tugend 2.0*, Heidelberg: arthistoricum.net, pp. 203–212.

Lanjouw, T. (2016). Discussing the obvious or defending the contested: Why are we still discussing the 'scientific value' of 3D applications in archaeology? In: H. Kamermans, W. de Neef, C. Piccoli, A.G. Posluschny and R. Scopigno, eds, *The Three Dimensions of Archaeology, Proceedings of the XVII UISPP World Congress (1-7 September 2014, Burgos, Spain)*, Volume 7/Sessions A4b and A12, Oxford: Archaeopress, pp. 1–11.

Larsen, M.T. (2010). *Versunkene Paläste – Wie Europa den Orient entdeckte*, Berlin: Osburg.

Layard, A.H. (1849a). *Nineveh and Its Remains: With an Account of a Visit to the Chaldean Christians of Kurdistan, and the Yezidis, or Devil-Worshippers; and an Enquiry into the Manners and Arts of the Ancient Assyrians*, London: John Murray.

Layard, A.H. (1849b). *The Monuments of Nineveh. From Drawings Made on the Spot*, London: John Murray.

Layard, A.H. (1853a). *Discoveries among the Ruins of Nineveh and Babylon; with Travels in Armenia, Kurdistan and the Desert: Being the Result of a Second Expedition Undertaken for the Trustees of the British Museum*, New York: Harper & Brothers.

Layard, A.H. (1853b). *A Second Series of the Monuments of Nineveh*, London: John Murray.

London Charter (2009). *The London Charter for the Computer-Based Visualisation of Cultural Heritage*, Draft 2.1. [pdf] London Charter. Available at: http://www.londoncharter.org/fileadmin/templates/main/docs/london_charter_2_1_en.pdf [Accessed 18 May 2019].

Micale, M.G. (2010). Designing architecture, building identities. The discovery and use of Mesopotamian features in modern architecture between Orientalism and the definition of contemporary identities. In: P. Matthiae, ed., *Proceedings of the 6th International Congress on the Archaeology of the Ancient Near East (Rome, May 5–10 2008)*, Wiesbaden: Harrassowitz, pp. 93–112.

Parpola, S. and Whiting, R. (1997). *Assyria 1995. Proceedings of the 10th Anniversary Symposium of the Neo-Assyrian Text Corpus Project, Helsinki, September 7–11, 1995*. Helsinki: Neo-Assyrian Text Corpus Project.

Piggott, A. (1978). *Antiquity Depicted: Aspects of Archaeological Illustration*, London: Thames and Hudson.

Pusch, E.B. and Herold, A. (2001). 'Piramesse'. In: D.B. Redford, ed., *The Oxford Encyclopedia of Ancient Egypt*, 3, Oxford: Oxford University Press, pp. 48–50.

Reade, J. (2008). Nineteenth-century Nimrud: Motivation, orientation, conservation. In: J.E. Curtis, H. McHall, D. Collon and L. al-Gailani Werr, eds, *New Light on Nimrud. Proceedings of the Nimrud Conference 11th–13th March 2002*, London: British Institute for the Study of Iraq, pp. 1–21.

Seville Principles (2011). *The Seville Principles. International Principles of Virtual Archaeology*, final draft. [pdf] Seville Principles. Available at: http://smartheritage.com/wp-content/uploads/2015/03/FINAL-DRAFT.pdf [Accessed 18 May 2019].

Simon, J. (1997). Drawing inferences. Visual reconstruction in theory and practice. In: B.L. Molyneaux, ed., *Cultural Life of Images. Visual Representation in Archaeology*, Abingdon: Routledge, pp. 22–48.

Tietze, C. (2008). *Amarna: Lebensräume – Lebensbilder – Weltbilder*. Potsdam: Universitätsverlag Potsdam.

Welt der Wunder (2019). *Das unglaubliche Leben der Bienen*, 19(5), Hamburg: Bauer Media.

Digital tools in the classroom

Re-coding Collaborative Archaeology: Digital Teaching and Learning for a Decolonised Future

Katherine Cook

University of Montreal

Abstract

What does it mean to decolonise archaeology in teaching and learning today? What role can (or should) digital technology and approaches play in transforming training and practice? This chapter will use case studies developing hybrid interventions in museum exhibits through collaborations between the University of Victoria, the Royal BC Museum (RBCM), descendant communities and diverse publics in Victoria, BC, to examine how digital media and platforms can be used to extend and reshape existing archaeology and decolonisation measures and spark relevant and much needed dialogues about heritage, education and practice in an increasingly digital era.

Keywords

Digital Archaeology, Public Archaeology, Collaborative Research, Decolonisation, Inclusivity

How to cite this book chapter:
Cook, K. 2020. Re-coding Collaborative Archaeology: Digital Teaching and Learning for a Decolonised Future. In: Hageneuer, S. (ed.) *Communicating the Past in the Digital Age: Proceedings of the International Conference on Digital Methods in Teaching and Learning in Archaeology (12–13 October 2018)*. Pp. 115–126. London: Ubiquity Press. DOI: https://doi.org/10.5334/bch.i. License: CC-BY 4.0

Teaching collaborative archaeology is a bit like writing knitting or weaving manuals. In the effort to distil complex processes and networks of people, knowledge and narratives, one ends up either with a curated and overly stylised Pinterest-style explanation, or assembly instructions for flat-pack furniture, complex to the point of confusion. In either case, the multidimensional ethical, political, economic and social implications and realities always seem reduced down to a one-dimensional message that community-engaged scholarship is valuable, even essential today but difficult to achieve.

This is certainly true for the contexts in which the case study presented here developed. With sincere respect for the Lkwungen-speaking peoples on whose traditional territory this research and teaching was conducted, and the Songhees, Esquimalt and WSÁNEĆ peoples whose historical relationships with the land continue to this day, understanding the position of collaborative archaeology in Canada entails recognising the complexity of heritage practice on land that is unceded but where colonisation and related institutions, policies and attitudes continue to exclude and to isolate. When I first arrived in British Columbia, Canada, as a settler and an archaeologist recently returned from a doctoral programme in Europe, the conflict, tension and momentum of change was palpable; although the colonial history of Canada and even the discipline of archaeology was a familiar one, the urgency and intensity had shifted recently and archaeologists in universities, museums and private companies were at last beginning to respond.

And, while there seemed to be something unique happening at that time and place, ultimately this is the challenge for *all* archaeological and heritage practice today. Geographic isolation from the ongoing legacies of colonialism has perhaps insulated certain places, particularly Europe, from addressing the colonial barriers and limitations that remain deeply rooted in archaeology. However, it does not in fact matter where in the world you are working: archaeology and heritage practice bring systems of oppression, in the structures of research and of collections, and in dissemination (Figure 1). It is therefore the responsibility of *all of us* to find ways to decolonise the discipline.

Teaching and learning play a huge role in transforming archaeology; part of the problem is that most archaeologists (or perhaps all archaeologists) still do not know wholly how to achieve a globally ethical, inclusive, equitable and decolonised discipline. This is in part because it is a multifaceted and extremely messy problem, intersecting diverse and contextual histories and cultures. However, it is also because we were taught to see, to approach, to understand archaeology in a certain way. Unseeing it and unlearning it is a long process. Despite a sea change of attitudes and recognition of these interconnected issues, higher education has not been substantially changed in much of the world, and therefore it will continue to reinforce the problematic systems of archaeology and heritage and reproduce structures of oppression in the minds and works of new generations of archaeologists.

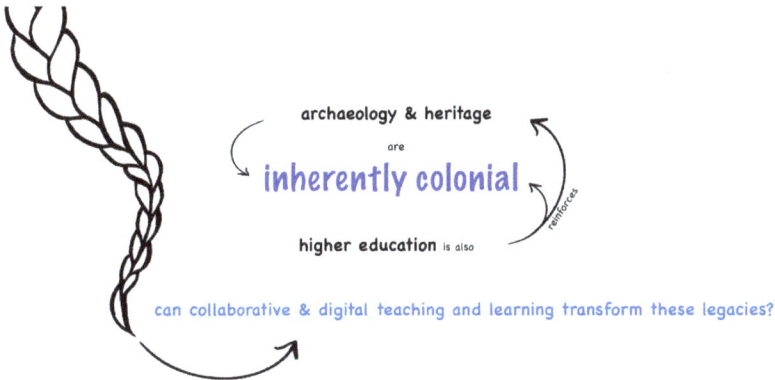

archaeology & heritage
are
inherently colonial
higher education is also
reinforces

can collaborative & digital teaching and learning transform these legacies?

Figure 1: The relationship between archaeology, colonialism and training is complicated and still highly problematic.

What does it mean to *decolonise* archaeology in teaching and learning today (see also Battiste 2016; Battiste, Bell & Findlay 2002; Cote-Meek 2014)? What role can (or should) digital technology and approaches play in transforming training? This chapter will use case studies developing hybrid interventions in museum exhibits through collaborations between the University of Victoria, the Royal BC Museum (RBCM), descendant communities and diverse publics in Victoria, BC, utilising digital media and platforms to extend and reshape existing public archaeology and decolonisation measures in Canadian heritage settings (see also Cook & Hill 2019). The experiences, ongoing challenges and future directions, however, offer thoughtful avenues for considering the future of teaching and learning in archaeology more globally.

Archaeology and decolonisation: a digital perspective

Increasingly urgent calls to reform archaeology, recognising systems of colonialism, exclusivity and inequity bound within the structures of research and scholarship, but also heritage curation and exhibition (Kreps 2011; Wintle 2013), have triggered pioneering inclusion and diversity work. In particular, projects challenging traditional perceptions of authority and unidirectional dissemination or outreach to truly integrate and honour diverse knowledge systems through collaborative practice (Chalifoux & St-Pierre 2017; Lynch 2011) are transforming archaeology, particularly in former colonies, such as Canada, the United States and Australia. An incredibly powerful and ever-growing body of work, particularly developed by indigenous, black, queer and feminist scholars, has started to build a framework for re-envisioning archaeology *and* higher education.

Building on Susan Dion's (2009) use of the term 'braiding histories', one of the most profound contributions has come from Sonya Atalay and the concept of braiding knowledge, to reflect the potential for diverse sources and forms of knowledge to be valued, reworked and combined in community-based archaeology projects. Rather than thinking of archaeology as being fundamentally at odds with indigenous knowledge, Atalay and others have since discussed the ways in which analogue media (like graphic novels) and digital media (including animation and virtual reality) can be used to partner indigenous and archaeological ways of knowing to 'mobilise knowledge', weaving it together and moving it into places where it is accessible by multiple public audiences (Atalay 2012; Lyons et al. 2016).

Digital technologies offer obvious opportunities for transforming access to and authorship of the past but the complex ethical and political frameworks for digital applications in postcolonial archaeology and heritage practice with descendant communities has been increasingly a concern. However, many of the elements of knowledge braiding also overlap with concepts from maker, coder and hacker culture. Advocating for the value of pooled, reworked and recirculated code, resources, software, tools, skills and knowledge could teach us a lot about how to encourage sharing, modifying and recording/citing co-authorship or co-production, designing hives, communities and spaces for shared teaching and learning, and the true value of creative collective processes of production (see also Compton, Martin & Hunt 2017). It is often the integration of maker and coder cultures through cultural institutions like museums, galleries, libraries and universities that has created new barriers and structures of exclusion in these traditionally grass-roots movements, once again dominating the narratives with heterosexual, white, cis-male perspectives and voices (see also Martin 2017; Taylor, Hurley & Connolly 2016). New approaches to inclusion, interdisciplinarity and active participation must be mobilised to truly engage in cultural criticism, meaning making, and transformation of models of knowledge production in archaeology.

Nevertheless, the paradigmatic frameworks of knowledge braiding and maker models for sharing tools, skills and knowledge offer up collectivised approaches with the potential to transform archaeology and heritage. From a teaching and learning perspective, this is all rather fitting because pedagogical literature highlights the value and impact of learning through doing (experiential, problem-based and constructivist literature), and through teaching (i.e. public outreach). In particular, teaching digital literacy contributes to new tools for collaborating, layering voices and interpretations (Watrall 2017), engaging diverse audiences and increasing access and participation (Rothberg & Reich 2014; Roussou et al. 2015), while developing transferrable and professional skills, heightening and complicating ethical responsibilities and the sense of accountability to communities, and learning through hands-on practice. In theory, then, teaching archaeology students digital public archaeology by working in museum environments, with communities and the public, provides opportunities to introduce and reinforce critical skills to collaborative research in the digital era. Beyond pedagogical relevance, there is also the opportunity to use these frameworks to change the perspective of the next generations of archaeologists so that collaboration, ethics and multi-vocality are not after-thoughts or PR stunts but the starting point for every research project, reshaping the skewed relationship between archaeologists and communities.

Bridging communities: two sequential case studies

Borne out of an interest in redeveloping collaborations between the University of Victoria and the RBCM and engaging communities in protecting and valorising local archaeology sites and collections, the first archaeology pop-up exhibit was organised with approximately 12 students from the Department of Anthropology and staff from the RBCM Human History and Learning departments in the winter/spring of 2017. The result was the Excavating Royal Jubilee pop-up, which explored a never-before-exhibited museum collection relating to a local hospital in a free public event complemented by long-term, open-access, web-based resources.

Reflecting on these experiences, a second, expanded pop-up was undertaken the following autumn, involving roughly 30 students from two separate courses from the University of Victoria, one focused on public archaeology and the other focused on digital archaeology. The resulting Bridging Victoria pop-up explored three never-before-exhibited collections again through public events and a range of open-access digital media and resources. These two case studies provided the opportunity to examine the complex relationship between technology, classrooms, and communities in re-envisioning higher education, and archaeology more broadly.

Objectives and approaches

These projects were predominantly stimulated by both academic and museum efforts to decolonise archaeology on the west coast of Canada, reflecting the perspectives and demands of diverse First Nations communities as well as the recommendations of the Truth and Reconciliation Commission (Kapyrka & Migizi 2016; Supernant 2018). It was therefore important to find ways to share that process and the outcomes not only among students, professionals and descendant communities but also the general public.[1] It should also be noted that, while each of these projects was undertaken over a span of two to four

---

[1] Recognising that these categories (student, professional, descendant community, public etc.) are not necessarily mutually exclusive but rather deeply entangled and individuals may identify with one, several or all of these groups.

months, they benefitted greatly from previous work, particularly undertaken by the RBCM and local descendant communities to redevelop relationships and establish better codes of practice. The projects were therefore directed by goals and policies that had already been established over the course of a much longer period of collaboration by the museum and their indigenous advisory board. These objectives included layering existing exhibits with more dynamic representations of the past and to address accessibility. Part of this related to the provincial museum's position on a small island in a much larger province and country; digital media were already being mobilised to answer this problem; however, policy and regulations on digitisation were still under development.

Fortuitously, these objectives fundamentally complemented the University of Victoria's emphasis on community-engaged scholarship and decolonisation of higher education. On another level, the discipline-specific coursework developed in these two cases also sought to address the lack of substantial change to education and training reflecting transformations in digital and public archaeological practice, with the interest of improving employability, ethical practice and global citizenship. In particular, the courses sought to:

- gain in-depth, multifaceted knowledge of particular peoples, processes, places and histories to appreciate the past and present diversity of human life;
- understand and employ ethical principles, relationships and practice and foster respectful, reciprocal and collaborative partnerships through work with local museums and heritage sites;
- build communication skills, including writing effectively for diverse audiences and genres and communicating digitally, through respectful and creative dialogue;
- build project management skills, including managing time and data, demonstrating accountability, and working collaboratively in teams.[2]

Although the learning objectives remained largely unchanged in their values and attitudes, the two sequential versions of this project represent substantial changes reflecting experiences, barriers and problems that emerged during the first project. During the first version, for instance, public and digital skills were separated into two courses that unfolded in isolation. However, with the exception of one student who had an immense background in heritage practice, most students in the digital course struggled to apply digital technology to real-world needs (it largely fitted the tech for tech's sake doctrine) without a strong commitment to ethical responsibilities and respectful practice. On the other hand, students in the parallel historical archaeology course proved to be exceptional narrators with a keen sense of ethics but often lacked the digital

---

[2] Building on University of Victoria's semi-scripted learning outcomes (2016/2017).

Figure 2: Workflow and examples of projects that were produced throughout the process.

skills to support the projects they imagined. In the second year, the two courses were interconnected to allow students to focus on developing specialised sets of skills (reflecting the complexity of each branch of practice) but also to partner with other students that might have complementary knowledge and vision. All of these students were then integrated to varying degrees with the partnerships between the museum, descendant communities and the public(s).

Process and products

The initial workflow sought to reproduce organisational structures in museum or heritage environments, including liaisons between archaeologists/curators/researchers, educators, digital professionals/freelancers and descendant communities (Figure 2). Approaches to collaborative/community archaeology were primarily defined by the abovementioned museum policies and advisory boards. Although experimentation and development created variations between the two projects, both started with a period of consultation and familiarisation bringing everyone together, designed largely to introduce students to the partnerships (as the partnerships themselves predated these projects). Following the drafting of objectives, policies, methods and schedules, a phase of individual and small group research mobilised knowledge, (re)interpreted collections and designed museum interventions and web-based components, which often organically brought satellite groups back together towards completion, weaving together divergent threads of objects, narratives and resources. The intensively collective launch of the in-person event and web-based initiatives was followed by a range of debriefing sessions with different groups and individuals. This phase was extended during the second project because of the value that this reflection and feedback process brought to the finessing of resources.

The products crafted through these processes were as diverse as the individuals and communities involved, but also the target audiences, with the intention of engaging a range of ages, cultural backgrounds and abilities. This includes 'in-person' physical applications, such as interactive maps with 3D printed objects, MakeyMakey and electrical components (Heckadon et al. 2017) and augmented reality, but also analogue media (illustration etc.). These media were supplemented by web-based resources, including soundscapes and audio guides (Fletcher, McPherson & Ran 2017), timelines and more (Cook 2017; Kroeger 2017a), thoughtfully crafted to create similarly immersive experiences for in-person visitors and those using the web to access the museum from a distance. More general documentation and long-term content was also produced and curated on the RBCM's learning portal (Kroeger 2017b), motivated by the need to centralise web-based media created and housed on different platforms, and to share the pop-up 'experience', and for the long-term preservation of the research produced through these collaborations. Each component was designed to work on its own but also to contribute to a network of digital and analogue, public and private resources that complement each other, creating a collective but diverse vision of the local area's history. The combination of analogue and digital media was viewed as important to engaging the diverse audiences participating in the event, but also reflecting policies defined by descendant communities about digitisation and where it was appropriate. United in their commitment to immersive and meaningful storytelling and to encouraging interaction between visitors, students and professionals, every imaginative and innovative choice of digital or analogue formats was balanced with questions about logistics (access to electricity, appropriate lighting, available technology, accessibility for the public) and ethics (digitisation or reproduction of objects, impact or message).

Inputs and outcomes

The outcomes of these projects, beyond the projects, resources and events produced, most notably included the opportunities for learning and engagement between academic, professional, descendant and 'general public' communities (Figure 3). Students in particular identified with the sense of accountability and respect for communities and a resolute commitment to them as the primary outcome of these experiences, which drove them to develop digital and public archaeology skills and professionalism while also reinforcing project management, deadlines and ethical responsibilities (see also Cook and Hill (2019) for more discussion of students' feedback and debriefing). The experience of doing this work, feedback from course evaluations and additional evaluation/

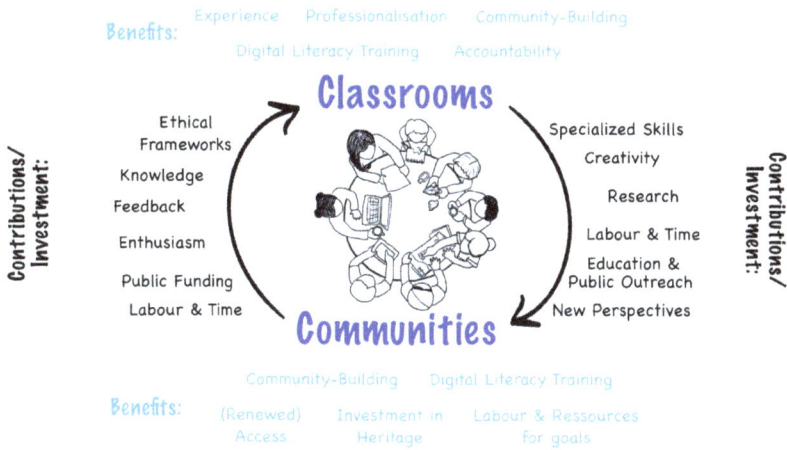

Figure 3: Visualisation of the possible contributions or investments of partnered classrooms and communities, and potential benefits or advantages for each group.

debriefing formats, as well as comparing the level of student work, critical thinking and employment following this course and more 'traditional' courses demonstrate the ways in which these projects shaped not only student but professional and community experiences, understandings and future practices. However, this was largely achieved by transforming archaeological teaching and learning from classroom-focused to expanding who is included and where it takes place. The point at which these diverse communities converged created new opportunities to cultivate different understandings and narratives, but also to share skills, knowledge and vision. Blurring the boundaries between groups, between 'teachers' and 'learners', and between publicness and true openness, also recognises the complexities of decolonising archaeology by confronting authority and access and making contemporary heritage experiences cooperative, inclusive and sustainable.

On a more practical digital level, both the collaboration process and the resources and events produced created an opportunity for broader digital literacy training too, beyond just student skills development. Students ended up spending time at the in-person events and online, explaining how to use the digital technology, which often led to discussions about how it worked, why they had chosen to do use specific tools or applications, and any ethical or policy-based decisions that they made. This developed an unexpected level of transparency and critical engagement with the public that proved exceedingly valuable. Some visitors even ended up reflecting on other digital applications that they had seen at museums or heritage sites around the world, asking questions or extrapolating from discussions about whether or not they were ethical, useful or even necessary. If we want to create a public that is critically engaged in the evaluation of 'good' or 'ethical' archaeology (and in turn challenging pseudoarchaeology, unethical approaches, looting etc.), which I would argue is critical as a step towards decolonising archaeology (and society more broadly), these discussions are invaluable and should continue to be fostered and supported.

Conclusion

Bringing together students, instructors, researchers, heritage professionals, descendant communities and the public is both a pedagogical and epistemological starting point to transforming a discipline that was built on inequity, exclusion and discriminatory practice. Collaborative applications of digital technology offer the opportunity in these contexts to produce accessible and meaningful heritage narratives but also to layer diverse perspectives and voices in powerful ways. More importantly, however, these collaborative archaeologies, when they emerge out of the open and deconstructed classrooms described above, can utilise digital practice to stimulate and respond to complex ethical, practical, political and epistemological questions, enhancing and expanding contexts of teaching and learning in archaeological training and public education. Future avenues for development should include experimentation with these same digital media, and other digital applications for interactivity, to extend and expand the opportunities and timelines for collaboration, learning, and the critical evaluation of digital heritage products and resources. It should also be recognised that these processes, valuable as they might be, are in desperate need of external support in the form of funding and modifications to career structures (to enhance job security etc.); training and research in public digital archaeology cannot transform long-standing traditions and legacies of exclusion, control and applications of technology for technology's sake without stable and reliable systems of support, clear expectations of ethical practice, and new structures of training and education. Digital practice, however, does offer new (and truly global) paths to taking responsibility for past traumas and conflicts and braiding digital and analogue narratives and dialogues that restructure and renew communities of practice.

References

Atalay, S. (2012). *Community-Based Archaeology: Research with, by and for Indigenous and Local Communities*, Berkeley, CA: University of California Press.

Battiste, M. (2016). *Decolonizing Education: Nourishing the Learning Spirit*, Saskatoon, SK: Purich Publishing.

Battiste, M., Bell, L. and Findlay, L.M. (2002). Decolonizing Education in Canadian Universities: An Interdisciplinary, International, Indigenous Research Project. *Canadian Journal of Native Education*, 26: 82–95.

Chalifoux, E. and Gates St-Pierre, C. (2017). *Décolonisation de l'archéologie: émergence d'une archéologie collaborative*. [online] Salons. Available at: https://salons.erudit.org/2017/08/01/decolonisation-de-larcheologie [Accessed 16 May 2019].

Compton, M.E., Martin, K. and Hunt, R. (2017). Where do we go from here? Innovative technologies and heritage engagement with the MakerBus. *Digital Applications in Archaeology and Cultural Heritage*, 6: 49–53.

Cook, K. (2017). *Excavating Royal Jubilee*. [online] Royal BC Museum Learning Portal. Available at: https://learning.royalbcmuseum.bc.ca/playlist/excavating-royal-jubilee [Accessed 16 May 2019].

Cook, K. and Hill, G. (2019). Digital heritage as collaborative process: Fostering partnerships, engagement and inclusivity. *Digital Heritage Studies*, 3(1): 83–99.

Cote-Meek, S. (2014). *Colonized Classrooms: Racism, Trauma and Resistance in Post-Secondary Education*, Halifax, NS: Fernwood Publishing.

Dion, S.D. (2009). *Braiding Histories: Learning from Aboriginal Peoples' Experiences and Perspectives*, Vancouver: UBC Press.

Fletcher, R., McPherson, K. and Ran, V. (2017). *Bridging Victoria*. [online] Sound-cloud. Available at: https://soundcloud.com/user-842052864-784784360 [Accessed 16 May 2019].

Heckadon, A.E., Sparks, K., Hartemink, K., van Muijlwijk, Y., Chater, M. and Nicole, T. (2017). *Interactive Mapping of Archaeological Sites in Victoria*. [online] Epoiesen. Available at: https://epoiesen.library.carleton.ca/2018/04/17/interactive-mapping-archae-victoria-response2 [Accessed 16 May 2019].

Kapyrka, J. and Migizi, G. (2016). Truth and Reconciliation in Archaeology: Dismantling the Kingdom. *Arch Notes* 21(4): 3-9.

Kreps, C. (2011). Changing the rules of the road: Post-colonialism and the new ethics of museum anthropology. In: J. Marstine, ed., *The Routledge Companion to Museum Ethics: Redefining Ethics for the Twenty-First-Century Museum*, London/New York: Routledge, pp. 70–84.

Kroeger, S. (2017a). *Bridging Victoria: Experiencing the Exhibit*. [online] Royal BC Museum Learning Portal. Available at: https://learning.royalbcmuseum.bc.ca/playlist/bridging-victoria-experiencing-the-exhibit [Accessed 16 May 2019].

Kroeger, S. (2017b). *Bridging Victoria: Stories from the Archaeological Past*. [online] Royal BC Museum Learning Portal. Available at: https://learning.royalbcmuseum.bc.ca/playlist/bridging-victoria [Accessed 16 May 2019].

Lynch, B. (2011). Collaboration, contestation, and creative conflict: On the efficacy of museum/community partnerships. In: J. Marstine, ed., *The Routledge Companion to Museum Ethics: Redefining Ethics for the Twenty-First-Century Museum*, London/New York: Routledge, pp. 146–163.

Lyons, N., Schaepe, D.M., Hennessy, K., Blake, M., Pennier, C., Welch, J.R., McIntosh, K., Phillips, A., Charlie, B., Hall, C., Hall, L., Kadir, A., Point, A., Pennier, V., Phillips, R., Muntean, R., Williams, J. Jr., Williams, J. Sr., Chapman, J., and Pennier, C. (2016). Sharing deep history as digital knowledge: An ontology of the Sq'éwlets website project. *Journal of Social Archaeology*, 16: 359–384.

Martin, K. (2017). *Centering Gender: A Feminist Analysis of Makerspaces and Digital Humanities Centers*. Paper presented at Institute for Digital Arts and Humanities Speaker Series. [online] Indiana University. Available at: http://hdl.handle.net/2022/21827 [Accessed 27 August 2019].

Rothberg, M. and Reich, C. (2014). *Making Museum Exhibits Accessible for All: Approaches to Multi-Modal Exhibit Personalization*. [pdf] Available at: https://openexhibits.org/wp-content/uploads/papers/MakingMuseum ExhibitsAccessibleForAll.pdf [Accessed 14 March 2019].

Roussou, M., Pujol, L., Katifori, A., Chrysanthi, A., Perry, S. and Vayanou, M. (2015). *The Museum as Digital Storyteller: Collaborative Participatory Creation of Interactive Digital Experiences*. [online] MW2015: Museums and the Web 2015. Available at: https://mw2015.museumsandtheweb.com/paper/the-museum-as-digital-storyteller-collaborative-participatory-creation-of-interactive-digital-experiences [Accessed 16 May 2019].

Supernant, K. (2018). Reconciling the Past for the Future: The Next 50 Years of Canadian Archaeology in the Post-TRC Era. *Canadian Journal of Archaeology* 42: 144-153.

Taylor, N., Hurley, U. and Connolly, P. (2016). *Making Community: The Wider Role of Makerspaces in Public Life*. Conference on Human Factors in Computing Systems, San Jose, CA, USA, 7–12 May.

Watrall, E. (2017). Public heritage at scale: Building tools for authoring mobile digital heritage and archaeology experiences. *Journal of Community Archaeology & Heritage*, 5: 114–127.

Wintle, C. (2013). Decolonising the Museum: The Case of the Imperial and Commonwealth Institutes. *Museum & Society*, 11(2): 185–201.

The X Marks the Spot – Using Geo-games in Teaching Archaeology

Michael Remmy

University of Cologne

Abstract

Digital media have influenced the viewing and learning habits of students for the past decades. At the same time, teaching habits in archaeology have not changed to the same extent.

A popular approach of digital teaching/learning is the use of e-learning portals and gamification methods. The University of Cologne tested this teaching/learning method of geo/educaching in a seminar course at the Archaeological Institute in cooperation with Humanities Computer Science. The main goal of the course was to design virtual geocaching quests that students had to solve by using mobile devices with the setting of Roman Cologne. On the one hand, the development of geo-games allowed the students to use their expertise in digital media while learning archaeological facts. On the other hand, new impulses were given through the change of learning environment.

How to cite this book chapter:
Remmy, M. 2020. The X Marks the Spot – Using Geo-games in Teaching Archaeology.
In: Hageneuer, S. (ed.) *Communicating the Past in the Digital Age: Proceedings
of the International Conference on Digital Methods in Teaching and Learning in
Archaeology (12–13 October 2018).* Pp. 127–140. London: Ubiquity Press. DOI:
https://doi.org/10.5334/bch.j. License: CC-BY 4.0

After this first test seminar the need for a modular system that could be not only used for archaeological topics but referred to other subjects such as art history, politics or history was seen. The state-funded system Biparcours and the related application Actionbound could be a possible solution and was tested as teaching and learning tool for an archaeological excursion.

This chapter describes the seminars held, the requirements and outcome as well as a future perspective of this method for teaching and learning. The usefulness of this method for excursion seminars will be discussed in particular.

Keywords

Educaching, Geocaching, Teaching, Gamification, E-learning

Introduction

Digital media have influenced the viewing and learning habits of students for the past decades. At the same time, teaching habits in archaeology have not changed to the same extent: frontal teaching and lectures are often still seen as best practice (Kelly 2019). The state of the art in didactical methodology is often developed in schools[1] and finds its way to universities through teachers' seminars and appliance in disciplines of the humanities. This leads to the questions: why is archaeology still dependent on conservative teaching methods and how can geo-games break up this status quo?

Requirements in teaching/learning archaeology

The public interest in archaeology is as old as the discipline itself. Artists have systematically reproduced ancient art since the 16th century (Vorster et al. 2018a; Vorster 2018b). J.J. Winckelmann, who is seen as the founder of archaeology as a scientific discipline, wanted to broadcast his thesis not only in scientific circles but also to the interested public (Winckelmann 1756; Winckelmann 1760). Famous excavations around the Mediterranean also found their echoes in the collective memories of society and are sometimes manifested in museums (Bernau 2011).

For centuries the education of archaeologists in universities was influenced by documents of archaeological finds and objects such as drawings, etchings, plaster casts and finally photography (Scheding & Remmy 2014). The general public on the other hand made trips to ancient places. The 'grand tour' of

---

[1] See e.g. Ihamäki (2014) with outdoor learning projects in schools.

English gentlemen in the 18th and 19th centuries was seen as the ultimate way of getting to know ancient cultures and art (Chaney 2000).

The visual aspect of archaeological education is crucial. For decades this information was spread by teachers in archaeology through seminars with frontal teaching and talks.

In particular, the reorganisation of universities' curriculums through the Bologna process prevented interest-oriented teaching and learning: courses have to fit into the curriculum of both teachers and students and the time for studying is regulated (Bloch 2006). This organisational corset is surely one reason for the slow development of archaeological teaching. However, the influence of social changes requires a paradigm shift from teachers as knowledge providers to students as the knowledge and skill acquirer. The student becomes an active part in the application of knowledge and is no longer just a recipient (Mocinic 2012).

E-learning and gamification

A popular approach to digital teaching/learning is the use of e-learning portals and gamification methods. E-learning portals are currently a 'must have' for organising and teaching in universities. The platforms provide material as well as tasks to successfully pass classes. It is an asset for students to get information whenever and wherever they want. Additionally, the portals support innovative teaching methods like flipped classrooms (Bergmann & Sams 2012), MOOCs (massive open online courses) (Van Treeck, Himpsl-Gutermann & Robes 2013) or blended learning (Buchegger et al. 2006), approaches that can have an interactive note. This interaction is supported by the up- and download concepts of tasks, homework etc. However, this flexibility in learning sometimes contradicts the need for contact time between teacher and students within seminars and lectures.

In higher education, a tendency to use gamification approaches in teaching is visible. In this case the broader definition of gamification – 'the application of typical elements of gameplaying (e.g. point scoring, competition with others, rules of play) to other areas of activity, typically as an online marketing technique to encourage engagement with a product or service' (Oxford Dictionaries 2019) – is defined as the teaching/learning method. These methods are strongly influenced by the gaming industry, which invests big money in new developments and techniques.

A part of the creative learning aspect that can be achieved with gamification – the motivation and interest of students in these methods – is seen as a big pro. Unfortunately, ineffective use of gamification can lead to the opposite and might trivialise important topics and issues (Hand 2016; Kyriakova, Angelova & Yordanova 2017).

In almost all of these cases students learn in a closed environment such as auditoriums or their private rooms. However, researchers from the geographical disciplines started to stress the benefits of learning outside the classrooms while using e-learning approaches (Schleicher 2006).

Geocaching as 'missing link'

An approach that uses parts of e-learning portals as well as gamification and therefore can be seen as the 'missing link' is geo- or in a specific way educaching. Geocaching originally is an activity that uses a GPS (Curlie 2018) receiver to locate and hide small containers (caches) all over the world. This game was established in the year 2000, when location via GPS became accurate and open for private use. The first cache was placed in Oregon, USA, in May 2000 (Geocaching 2000) and from this moment on the geocaching movement started to spread. With the establishment of smartphones as main communication tool in society the originally analogue activity was transferred into the digital world. The caches are received via smartphones and can represent either different kinds of hints for the next cache or the final point of a quest (Cacher-Reisen 2019). The recreational focus of geocaching was expanded by the educational facet of the game. This emphasis led to the neologism 'educaching' (Brombach 2010; Educaching 2012). This method was tested, evaluated and used successfully in teaching series in schools (Kissinger, Naumann & Siegmund 2016).

Here especially the outdoor education as an experiential learning approach (Ihamäki 2014: 356–357) has to be seen – the change of learning environments and methods can be a positive impulse for the learning outcome of the user.

Documentation of the use of educaching in universities is rather short.[2] In a compilation for the *Hochschulforum Digitalisierung* the whole variety of digital teaching methods in Germany was published with short examples (Wannemacher et al. 2016). Educaching is discussed very briefly, with a small example from the University of Bochum (Wannemacher et al. 2016: 23).

Case studies at Cologne University[3]

At Cologne University, the educaching method was tested at the Archaeological Institute in cooperation with Humanities Computer Science in two lectures. The main goal of the course was to design virtual geocaching quests that the user had to solve by using mobile devices on an archaeological site. The showcase

---

[2] For one of good example of a course documentation using geocaching see Robison (2011).

[3] Special thanks to Dr Jan Wieners for the joint conduct of the seminar and the students for their openness and feedback.

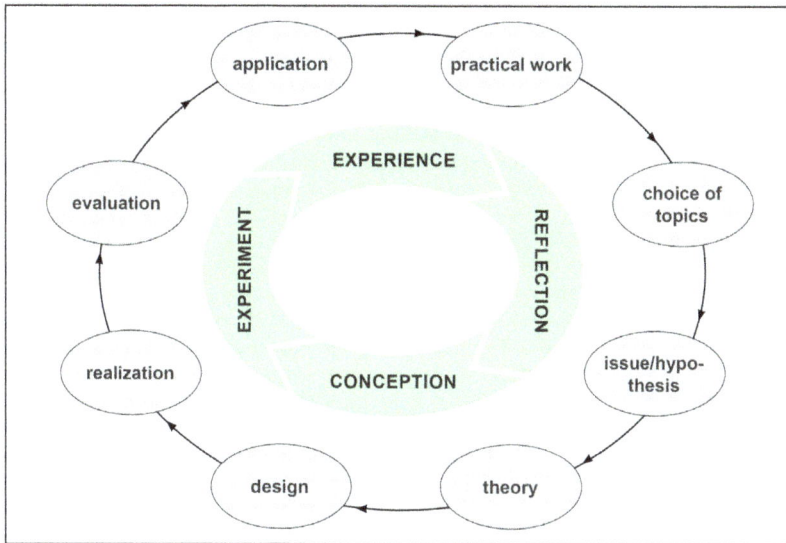

Figure 1: Learning circle of explorative/research-based learning (after Wildt 2009).

was the Roman city of Cologne (Fischer & Trier 2013). However, the teachers predefined neither the story nor the content.

The composition of the student group was quite heterogeneous. Aside from archaeologists, there was a high percentage (40%) of computer science students attending the class.

To get the best possible work and learning outcomes for the students the class was divided into groups that represented both disciplines. Working in groups needs not only discipline from students but also micromanagement by teachers. The seminar was structured in input and working phases (sprints) that led to a sprint report. Each member of the group had to report on the progress and the strong/weak points of the sprint. This helps to hold the group together and also to get the students to reflect on their own work.

The didactical concept of explorative or research-based learning (Wildt 2009) was chosen to give the students the most open and creative framework to solve their tasks and represents a learning circle that can be used for further seminars as well (Figure 1).

From the teacher's point of view, five objectives were defined that ideally helped the students to work in the seminar:

- Students should be able to work together with colleagues of other disciplines in order to solve problems and create a product – teamwork.
- Students should be able to use different tools while working on the developments of the product (e.g. Leaflet (Leaflet 2017), GeoJson (GeoJson 2016)) – application. These tools should be open source.

- Students should be able to organise their own study time and working hours – organisation (Figure 2).
- Students should be able to gather information on Roman life in the city of Cologne – research (Figure 3).
- Students should be able to present their workflow and final product in different media – reflection/presentation.

Within 15 lessons the groups were taught the use of different tools and programs they should use while working on the realisation of their project. On the other hand, there was enough free space for the students to be creative and deal with the execution of the regular sprint tasks.

Outcome

After the first sprint reports, the different approaches of the three groups emerged.

'Life of Julius' puts the user into the position of a Roman citizen who can climb the cursus honorum (Brennan Carrey 2015) after answering questions on ancient buildings in Cologne (Figure 4). The avatar, called Julius, lives in the city of Cologne and wonders what great achievements the Romans brought into the city. In particular, infrastructure such as the city wall or the temples come into his mind while thinking of this golden age of Cologne. Multiple-choice

Figure 2: Learning about Roman Cologne at one of the city wall towers. Photo: M. Remmy.

Figure 3: Getting organised. Photo: M. Remmy.

questions to these buildings have to be answered and the price is the climbing of the cursus honorum steps.

'Agrippina op Jöck' focuses on Cologne's founder, Agrippina, who has to successfully play mini games in order to refurbish the city (Figure 5). Agrippina walks through her city and visits Cologne's important landmarks. In order to re-erect or refurbish buildings or city quarters she has to answer questions or play mini games (e.g. jigsaws). The walk through the city within this game is pre-set by the developers. After the last task Agrippina gets an overall view of the buildings that were successfully renewed.

'Mission Barbaricus' leads a retired Roman legionary into the city of Cologne. Unfortunately, he has lost his army diploma and has to ask people for the way to the Roman administration. Right answers bring him closer to the goal; wrong answers make him suspected of being a spy (Figure 6). The walk through the city is also pre-set by the developers. This helps to control the degree of difficulty of the questions. The user is informed of the game's progress by a 'suspicion bar' on the upper rim of the screen.

All games were developed as walks through the city. The desktop versions of the games were the foundation for a later mobile version that would lead the user directly to the Roman remains of Cologne.

On the one hand, the development of geo-games allowed the students to use their expertise in digital media while learning archaeological facts. On the other hand, new impulses were given through the change of learning environment and the use of self-organised learning. Topics such as storytelling, app design and project steering were as important as the archaeological knowledge. Teaching methods such as clustering, project learning and the evaluation of different project sections were used to get the best possible learning outcome. An

Figure 4: Screenshot 'Life of Julius'.

Figure 5: Screenshot 'Agrippina op Jöck'.

accompanying website documented the progress of the seminar and backed up all results, including the code for the tool.

Not all these methods and topics were seen as 'l'art pour l'art'. They were chosen to help the students to get a different perspective on the material that they are learning within the curriculum of archaeological or computer science

Figure 6: Poster 'Mission Barbaricus'.

subjects. The most important objective was to create a real case scenario for a future job. One future possibility to link a university course to the labour market would be a service-learning offer (Remmy 2016). Of course, with this, the laboratory conditions of our held seminar would make an even bigger impact on the students.

The feedback of the students who attended the seminars was very positive. 'Better motivation', 'learning in an open environment outside the classroom' and 'practical experience usable for later jobs' were the most stated advantages. On the other hand, students wanted 'a seminar over two semesters in order to get more basic knowledge in programming'. Also the 'missing time for the creation of a really satisfying product' was demanded. The feedback show that the development of a course like this requires a lot of preparation and experience in teaching. For future courses a questionnaire would be helpful to get feedback on the learning objectives, methods and also the actual outcome of the seminar.

Excursion approach

The already-stressed paradigm shift from a passive to an active learner can also be transferred to the educational format of excursions. One definition stresses the major goals of excursions: excursion is a form of teaching with the goal of a real encounter with the spatial reality outside the classroom. The purpose of the excursion is to enable the student to directly record geographic phenomena, structures, functions and processes on site (Rinschede 1997: 7–10). Within the excursion didactics the classification of overview excursion, working excursion and tracking excursion shows a significant differentiation (Hemmer & Uphues 2009) (Figure 7). Educaching approaches can be related to the more active, flexible and reflected excursions.

In our case the students reflected on their work at the end of the seminar and articulated a possible field of use in excursions. The need for a modular system that could be not only used for archaeological topics but referred to other subjects such as art history, politics or history was seen as real asset to the teaching in archaeology.

In a brainstorming session at the end of the seminar, requirements for a future geocaching tool were fixed. The students stressed that a modular system could help to create flexible and non-static tools for teaching and learning. This also leads to an open and possible interdisciplinary approach.

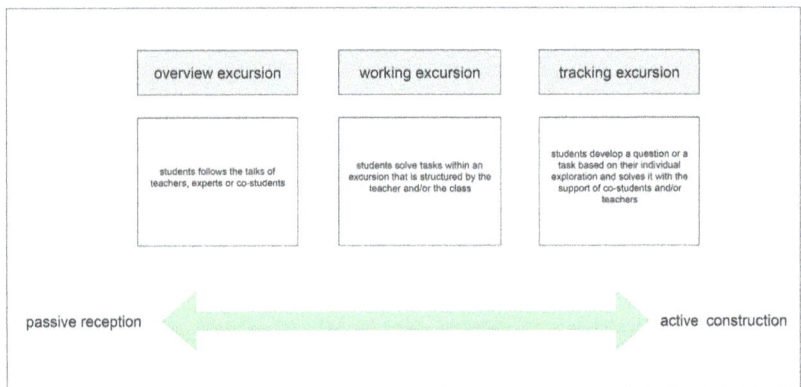

Figure 7: Classification of excursions (after Hemmer & Uphues 2009).

An important issue for the students was usability. Intuitive handling at both the front and back end are the key for wider use in university context. Furthermore, ideas of open source and sustainability show the students' providence.

Unfortunately, there was not enough time to create first mock-ups or codes for such a tool. Therefore, we evaluated available systems. In our case, the two related systems Actionbound (Actionbound 2019) and Biparcours (Biparcours 2019) came quite close to the students' requirements. Actionbound is an interactive app-based game approach for smartphones and tablets: players are invited to accomplish tasks, which can be defined through the Bound-Creator on the website actionbound.com, in order to playfully discover their environment by learning more about its history, politics and culture. In contrast to a geocache or a scavenger hunt, Actionbound requires the players to create their own content (Actionbound 2019). Unfortunately, the licences for universities are not free.

Biparcours is funded by the Ministry of North Rhine Westphalia. The app is an interactive learning tool that allows users to perform exciting tasks that need to be solved at certain waypoints: from finding specific points and answering quiz questions to taking your own photos and videos. Since the app is state-funded, it is not possible to use this app outside North Rhine Westphalia.

A proof of concept project was established within a student excursion of the Archaeological Institute to Greece in 2018.[4] In order to see how stable the system is and how students react to this gamification approach on knowledge sharing, one simple quest in the sanctuary of Olympia (Mallwitz 1972) was developed with the Actionbound application. After minor problems with the GPS signals, all students had the opportunity to try the game and give feedback. Negative aspects were the connection problems and deficiencies in usability. Positive comments refer to the motivation factor as well as the learning environment as key aspects that lead to better learning. In this case the students used their own mobile devices. For future attempts to integrate mobile devices into courses, the support of the university or a foundation is mandatory in order to provide the devices with a similar operating system to all students and create technical and social equality.

Outlook

As a proof of concept, the seminar showed that an educaching approach in teaching archaeology can be very fruitful. The students' feedback as well as the experience from the teacher's perspective were very positive. However, the integration in the curriculum of archaeological teaching at universities has still to

---

[4] Special thanks to Prof. Thoralf Schröder and Dr Frank Hulek for the support and Felix Kußmaul for the development of the quests and the support on site.

be tackled. If there were more test runs with using geocaching in this teaching area, implementation would be easier. The usefulness of this method, especially for excursion seminars, is evident but it is also obvious that the geo-game approach is not sensible for all kinds of seminars or topics but instead has to be seen as tool to set stimuli and get students and teachers engaged. A very important task of teachers and students is the publication of the course's outcomes. This will especially help with the research on this topic, for which compilations of courses held in different universities are very important. However, the field of application surely does not end in the context of higher education at universities. There is more room for experimenting with these methods and this should lead to knowledge transfer in the cultural heritage sector (Rowland 2013) (e.g. museums or landscape or city archaeology) to get the general public involved and attached.

References

Actionbound (2019). [online] *Actionbound Official Website*. Available at: https://www.actionbound.com [Accessed 1 April 2019].

Bergmann, J. and Sams, A. (2012). *Flip Your Classroom*, Washington, DC: ISTE.

Bernau, N. (2011). Das Pergamonmuseum und seine vier Museen als Lehrinstrumente einer anderen Moderne. In: R. Grüßinger, V. Kästner and A. Scholl, eds, *Pergamon. Panorama der antiken Metropole*, Berlin: Imhof, pp. 388–392.

Biparcours (2019). [online] *Biparcours Official Website*. Available at: http://biparcours.de [Accessed 1 April 2019].

Bloch, R. (2006). Schwerpunkte gegenwärtiger Entwicklung in der Hochschulbildung. In: P. Pasternak, R. Bloch and C. Gallert, eds, *Die Trends der Hochschulbildung und ihre Konsequenzen*, Wittenberg: Institut für Hochschulfoschung, pp. 47–100.

Brennan Carrey, T. (2015). *cursus honorum*. [pdf] Oxford Classical Dictionary. Available at: https://oxfordre.com/classics/view/10.1093/acrefore/9780199381135.001.0001/acrefore-9780199381135-e-1965 [Accessed 1 April 2019].

Brombach, G. (2010). Vom Geo- zum Educaching. Das Web 2.0 bietet neue didaktische Chancen. [online] dotcomblog. Available at: https://www.dotcomblog.de/wp-content/uploads/downloads/2010/05/educache_ppB.pdf [Accessed 1 April 2019].

Buchegger, B., Krisper-Ullyett, L., Michl, J. and Ortner, J. (2006). Collaborative blended learning. Eine Orientierung für Lehrende, ModeratorInnen und TutorInnen zum Thema: Wie kann ich das E-Medium für Lernprozesse in der Erwachsenenbildung nutzen? Vienna: facultas.

Cacher-Reisen (2019). *Cacher-Reisen Official Website*. [online] Available at: http://www.cacher-reisen.de/cachearten [Accessed 1 April 2019].

Chaney, E. (2000). *The Evolution of the Grand Tour: Anglo-Italian Cultural Relations since the Renaissance*, London: Routledge.

Curlie (2018). [online] *Curlie Official Website*. Available at: https://curlie.org/Science/Earth_Sciences/Geomatics/Global_Positioning_System [Accessed 1 April 2019].

Educaching (2012). [online] *Educaching Official Website*. Available at http://www.educaching.com [Accessed 1 April 2019].

Fischer, Th. and Trier, M. (2013). *Das römische Köln*. Cologne: Bachem.

Geocaching (2000). [online] *Geocaching Official Website*. Available at: https://www.geocaching.com/about/history.aspx [Accessed 1 April 2019].

GeoJson (2016). [online] *GeoJson Official Website*. Available at: https://geojson.org [Accessed 1 April 2019].

Hand, B. (2016). *Designing Successful Gamification Practices in Higher Education*. [online] GettingSmart. Available at: http://www.gettingsmart.com/2016/12/gamification-successes-and-failures-higher-education [Accessed 1 April 2019].

Hemmer, M. and Uphues, R. (2009). Zwischen passiver Rezeption und aktiver Konstruktion – Varianten der Standortarbeit am Beispiel der Großwohnsiedlung Berlin-Marzahn. In: M. Nickel and G. Glasze, eds, *Vielperspektivität und Teilnehmerzentrierung – Richtungsweiser der Exkursionsdidaktik*, Vienna: LIT, pp. 39–50.

Ihamäki, P. (2014). Evolving letterboxing game on Pori Cultural Heritage Road: Emerging challenges for teachers. *International Journal of Teaching and Case Studies*, 4(4): 354–366.

Kelly, M. (2019). *Lectures in Schools – Pros and Cons*. [online] ThoughtCo. Available at: https://www.thoughtco.com/lecture-pros-and-cons-8037 [Accessed 1 April 2019].

Kissinger, T., Naumann, S. and Siegmund, A. (2016). Vom Geocaching zum Educaching. Potential und Nutzen von digitalen Geomedien im Rahmen von Outdoor Education. In: J. von Au and U. Gade, eds, *Raus aus dem Klassenzimmer: Outdoor Education als Unterrichtskonzept*, Weinheim/Basel: Beltz, pp. 111–118.

Kyriakova, G., Angelova, N. and Yordanova, L. (2017). *Gamification in Education*. [pdf] Stellenbosch University. Available at: https://www.sun.ac.za/english/learning-teaching/ctl/Documents/Gamification%20in%20education.pdf [Accessed 1 April 2019].

Leaflet (2017). [online] *Leaflet Official Website*. Available at: https://leafletjs.com [Accessed 1 April 2019].

Mallwitz, A. (1972). *Olympia und seine Bauten*, Darmstadt: WBG.

Mocinic, S.N. (2012). *Active teaching strategies in higher education*, [pdf] Available at: https://hrcak.srce.hr/file/124604 [Accessed 1 April 2019].

Oxford Dictionaries (2019). [online] *Oxford Dictionary Official Website*. Available at: https://en.oxforddictionaries.com/definition/gamification [Accessed 1 April 2019].

Remmy, M. (2016). Manus manum lavat – the idea of service learning and research-based-learning in archaeology. In: I. Pinto, ed., *Entre ciência e cultura: da interdisciplinaridade à transversalidade da arqueologia, Actas das VIII Jornadas de Jovens em Investigação Arqueológica*, Lisbon, pp. 529–546.

Rinschede, G. (1997). Schülerexkursionen im Erdkundeunterricht - Ergebnisse einer empirischen Erhebung bei Lehrern und Stellung der Exkursionen in der fachdidaktischen Ausbildung. In: *Regensburger Beiträge zur Didaktik der Geographie II*, Regensburg: University Regensburg. pp. 7–80.

Robison, D. (2011). Geocache adventures: Ubiquitous handheld computing as an aid to promote environmental awareness amongst students. *International Journal of Innovation and Leadership in the Teaching of Humanities*, 1(2): 47–56.

Rowland, M. (2013). Geocaching and cultural heritage. *The Artefact: Journal of the Archaeological and Anthropological Society of Victoria*, 36: 3–9.

Scheding, P. and Remmy, M. (2014). Antike Plastik 5.0://. 50 Jahre Forschungsarchiv für Antike Plastik in Köln, Berlin: LIT, pp. 182–221.

Schleicher, Y. (2006). Digitale Medien und E-Learning motivierend einsetzen. In: H. Haubrich, ed., Geographie unterrichten lernen. Die neue Didaktik der Geographie konkret, Munich: Oldenbourg Schulbuchverlag, pp. 207–222.

van Treeck, T., Himpsl-Gutermann, K. and Robes, J. (2013). Offene und partizipative Lernkonzepte. E-Portfolios, MOOCs und Flipped Classrooms. In: M. Ebner and S. Schön, eds, *Lehrbuch für Lernen und Lehren mit Technologien (L3T)*. [pdf] Available at: http://l3t.eu/homepage/das-buch/ebook-2013/kapitel/o/id/149/name/offene-und-partizipative-lernkonzepte [Accessed 1 April 2019].

Vorster, C., Satzinger, G., Luckhardt, J. and Döring, T. (2018a). *Die Antikenalben des Alphons Ciacconius in Braunschweig, Rom und Pesaro*, Braunschweig: Herzog Anton-Ulrich- Museum und Autoren, pp. 8–276.

Vorster, C. (2018b). Die Zeichnungsalben des Alphons Ciacconius und ihr Zeugniswert für Antikensammlungen des 16. Jahrhunderts. *Kölner Jahrbuch*, 51: 463–481.

Wannemacher, K., Jungermann, I., Scholz, J., Tercanli, H., von Villiez, A. (2016). Digitale Lernszenarien im Hochschulbereich. In: K. Wannemacher, ed. *Hochschulforum Digitalisierung Arbeitspapier*, 15. [pdf] Hochschulforum Digitalisierung. Available at: https://hochschulforumdigitalisierung.de/sites/default/files/dateien/HFD%20AP%20Nr%2015_Digitale%20Lernszenarien.pdf [Accessed 1 April 2019].

Wildt, J. (2009). Forschendes Lernen: Lernen im 'Format' der Forschung. *journal hochschuldidaktik*, 20(2): 4–7.

Winckelmann, J.J. (1756). *Gedanken über die Nachahmung der griechischen Werke in der Malerey und Bildhauerkunst*, Dresden/Leipzig: Walther.

Winckelmann, J.J. (1760). *Description des pierres gravées de feu Baron de Stosch*, Florenz.

How to be a 'Good' Anglo-Saxon: Designing and Using Historical Video Games in Primary Schools

Juan Hiriart

University of Salford

Abstract

Over the last decades, digital games have become an important form of historical engagement, with a great potential to influence popular conceptions about the past (Uricchio 2005; Chapman 2012). In spite of the growing academic interest in harnessing this power for historical education, many questions remain unclear with regard to the representational appropriateness of the medium and the theoretical and practical problems involved in designing and using historical computer games in school classrooms. In this chapter, I would like to give an overview of a PhD research set to analyse the potential of digital games for historical education. Adopting a practice-based approach, this research was led by the iterative development of a series of historical game prototypes, designed to explore everyday life in early Anglo-Saxon Britain. At different stages of design,

How to cite this book chapter:
Hiriart, J. 2020. How to be a 'Good' Anglo-Saxon: Designing and Using Historical Video Games in Primary Schools. In: Hageneuer, S. (ed.) *Communicating the Past in the Digital Age: Proceedings of the International Conference on Digital Methods in Teaching and Learning in Archaeology (12–13 October 2018)*. Pp. 141–151. London: Ubiquity Press. DOI: https://doi.org/10.5334/bch.k. License: CC-BY 4.0

the prototypes were evaluated by historians, archaeologists and educators, moving at a later stage to their implementation and testing within the history curriculum of a key stage 2 school classroom (eight to 11 years old). In this phase, qualitative and quantitative data was collected following a pre-post test methodology. This methodology provided valuable insights into children's previous assumptions and naive theories about the past, which were interrogated and in many instances challenged by their experiences within the game. Drawing from this process, this research has contributed to gain a better understanding of the theoretical issues involved in the design and implementation of historical game-based learning methodologies, making empirical connections between educational theory, historical learning, and game design.

Keywords

Digital Games, Games and Learning, Historical Games, Historical Simulation Games, History Education, History Teaching, Historical game-based Learning, Game Design, Virtual Environments

Introduction

Digital historical games made their appearance in school classrooms at an early stage in the adoption of educational technology. One of the earlier examples of such experiences is *The Oregon Trail* (*The Oregon Trail* 1971), a now-classic educational game simulating the epic westward migration of covered wagons throughout 2,000 miles of the 19th-century US. Since then, many experiences followed but their documentation in academic literature is scattered (McCall 2016). Most of the applications discussed in literature concentrate on secondary education, with the integration of commercial game titles into school curriculums. Among these, Taylor's (2003) implementation of *Civilization I* and *II* into the modern history course of a secondary school yielded interesting insights. For this author, games' main potential as historical media resides on three main characteristics: games are interactive, capable of representing complex historical processes in a visual and integrated manner, and can present the past as experienced by those who live it.

A year later, scholars Squire and Barab (2004) explored the pedagogical utilisation of *Civilization III* (*Civilization III*, 2001) in formal learning environments. Through three case studies, these authors examined how game engagement, social interactions and understanding evolved in the classroom, drawing conclusions about the role of the game's mediation in the development of the students' understanding. Among many interesting insights, Squire and Barab found that the game itself was not the most important aspect in the learning experience, but rather the social dynamics that surrounded or emerged from its implementation in the classroom. The game became a central element of a community of learning, where its educational value heightened as students and teachers played, discussed, analysed, critiqued and expanded the original game.

While both Taylor and Squire and Barab used different versions of *Sid Meier's Civilization*, the game's complexity and steep learning curve make it challenging to use in primary schools. In this context, the more recent and sandbox game *Minecraft*, developed by Mojang, has made its way into classrooms of this age group, being used to teach a range of topics while also being adopted for educational research (Nebel, Schneider & Rey 2016). With an intuitive interaction in an environment entirely made out of textured cubes, this game is simple enough to be learned in one or two hours (Brand & Kinash 2013), while offering multiple possibilities for the creative exploration and transformation of the game space. By removing and adding blocks with different appearance and properties, players can reconstruct historical places, buildings and artefacts, also becoming part of a community of practice actively sharing their work, process and knowledge through different social media.

While all these experiences and research projects have certainly contributed to the understanding of the potential of digital games for historical education, I would argue that to further the comprehension of this research area it is necessary to expand the study of historical games beyond existing commercial titles, creatively exploring new game mechanics, narrative systems and forms of educational use. To this end, the experimental development of new game forms designed to respond to the specific requirements of teaching history in formal educational settings appears advantageous, or at least complementary to the study of the educational potential of published titles.

In this chapter, my intention is to give an overview of a research project led by the development of a digital game designed with the goal of teaching Anglo-Saxon history in primary schools. In a first phase, the game was iteratively developed with the participation of historians, archaeologists and history educators, who critically analysed the game prototype at different stages of design. In a second phase, the game was tested in a primary school classroom, where it was evaluated in a real context of use. In the following sections, I will explain some of the key ideas that guided the game's design process, along with the most relevant conclusions that raised from its contextual implementation.

Designing a historical game for the primary school curriculum

Despite the medieval period of British history forming part of the history curriculum of primary schools in England and Wales, it is often not very well covered, resulting in many pupils finishing their formal education with little or no knowledge of this period. Houghton (2016) in this regard remarks how, for many undergrad students of ancient and medieval history, their university courses are in fact their first encounter with the medieval period of British history.

Following the directives of the Department of Education in the United Kingdom, historical education at primary school level should be capable of inspiring the 'pupil's curiosity to know more about the past', think critically and 'understand the complexity of people's lives, the process of change, the diversity of societies and relationships between different groups, as well as their own identity and the challenges of their time' (2013: 1). Can games be used to foster pupils' understanding of life in Anglo-Saxon times, with an acquired sense of the differences and similitudes with our modern lives?

The Anglo-Saxon era can be marked as the time when Germanic tribes – Angles, Saxons and Jutes – arrived and settled in Britain after the departure of the Romans around CE 410. This was a time of great change, where the Romano-British cultural and social identity was radically transformed. According to historical and archaeological sources, the finding of the means to survive in the challenging environment of post-Roman Britain was hard and time-consuming. To sustain themselves, early Anglo-Saxons had to dedicate most of their time to finding and/or producing food and drink, an occupation that determined their lives 'both at the basic level of survival and at the level of everyday social interaction' (Crawford 2009: 93). A key part of surviving at this time was the intimate understanding of how the landscape worked: where to find vital resources, how to identify the best soils, where the land would not support farming and where the best hunting was.

Arguably, owing to their interactive and participatory nature, digital games are better equipped to convey these meanings than more traditional forms of historical mediation are. In games, players are not just limited to be external observers of a historical representation but are imbued with the agency of 'doing stuff' with immediate and long-terms effects. This added capacity is given by the simulation of environmental processes and relationships through computer code. The encoding of these processes, however, always implies a certain degree of simplification. How can the intricate relationships between people and environment be translated into computing algorithms while preserving its essential meanings? For Ingold (2000), the livelihood in a natural environment can be abstracted into two distinct processes, conventionally denoted by the terms of collection and production. In most games, the collection of objects from the environment is denoted by their remotion from the game environment, translating their properties to the abstract space of a player's inventory. With regard to the production of new things, Ingold differentiates between the making of things and the processes involved in the growing of things, where humans assist 'in the reproduction of nature, and derivatively of their own kind' (Ingold 2000: 81).

Conceiving the relationship between early Anglo-Saxons and their environment under Ingold's analytical framework, the game's core mechanics implemented the processes of collecting, making and growing of things. To translate

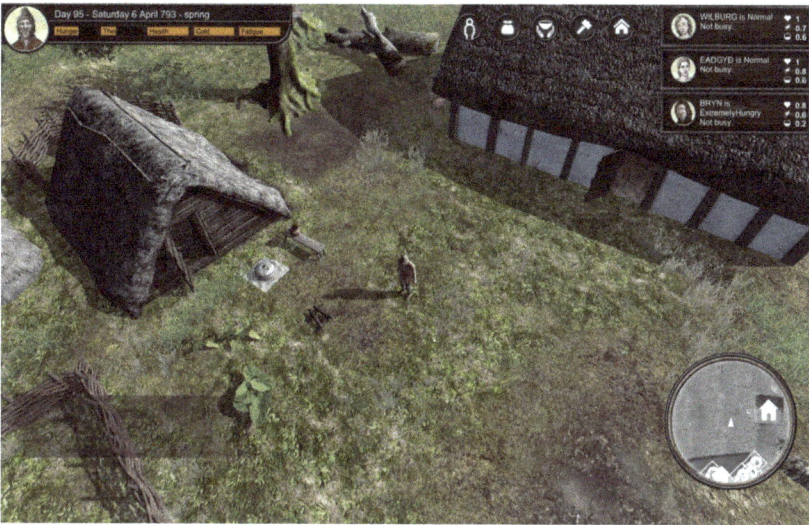

Figure 1: Final Anglo-Saxon game prototype.

these processes into game form, the popular Unity3D engine and editor tools were chosen. With its component-based design approach, this development platform greatly facilitated the translation of Anglo-Saxon everyday life into polygonal computer graphics and computer code. Within the game, players adopted the identity of a free peasant who had to find the means to survive in a simulated post-Roman world. Surviving in this environment demanded the incessant undertaking of a flow of tasks, the 'constitutive acts of dwelling' (Ingold 2000: 195) that make possible to understand the complex processes of human inhabitation. In this sense, the game can be conceptualised as a 'playable taskscape', in reference to the conceptual layer proposed by Ingold to further the understanding of human inhabitation of and intervention in the landscape. To communicate these meanings in game form, however, tasks require to be more than mere survival acts. They need to be also designed to convey cultural and social meanings, communicating how identities, roles and social interactions were defined by divisions of work.

For this, it seemed necessary to incorporate a social level of interaction into the game. This was resolved by the addition of virtual 'family members': non-player agents with whom the player interacted primarily through text-based graphic interfaces. Along with providing the opportunity for the player to delegate tasks to the virtual agents, reducing in this way the tediousness of repetitive labouring, these agents also brought the possibility of exploring relevant topics of Anglo-Saxon culture and way of life. Through text-based interactions, children engaged in dialogues designed to foreground the differences between modern and past ways of thinking and living.

Figure 2: Eadgyð and Wilburg, the characters designed to act as family members within the game.

Testing the game in a primary school classroom

When the Anglo-Saxon game prototype reached a playable state, the investigation moved to the context of a primary school, where it was implemented and evaluated as part of their history curriculum. This contextual evaluation had a number of goals. Firstly, it sought to explore the ways in which the game could be used in the formal environment of a school classroom in integration with other learning activities. Secondly, it attempted to assess the potential of the game's ludic and narrative systems to communicate how Anglo-Saxons went through their lives. Finally, it sought to evaluate the extent to which the game was able to challenge children's preconceptions about this period.

To this end, the research adopted a pre-post test design. In the first sessions, children were asked to draw how they imagined life in Anglo-Saxon times. In the sessions that followed, children were asked to play the game in a free form, and their playing actions were recorded by the system in a data file stored on each computer. After playing the game, children were asked to draw once more their ideas about the Anglo-Saxon age. In both the first and last drawing sessions, children were informally interviewed, using their drawings as 'conversation drivers' to gain a better understanding of their historical assumptions and playing experiences.

The combination of drawings and mini-interviews proved to be revealing. Through their drawings, children were able to express ideas, emotions and experiences often difficult to articulate in verbal language at their age. In

Figure 3: Drawing of a child-imagined Anglo-Saxon world done in a pre-test session.

most cases, these ideas were expressed in the form of vivid narratives, with the drawing's author taking an active role within the representation. In this sense, the historical engagements of drawing and gameplaying with the past shared similar traits. In both activities, children did not just create or interact with historical representations as external observers but situated themselves as active agents within imagined worlds. In these narrative engagements, their interactions revealed as much about their personal identities, lives and world views in the present as about their conceptions about the past. A close study of these visual recounts revealed that children's previous assumptions and naive theories about the Anglo-Saxon age became interrogated and in many instances challenged by their gaming experiences, resulting in dissonances that were later productively addressed in post-play discussions with the teacher and peers.

Through their drawings and comments, children evidenced assumptions about the hardships of everyday life ('life was very hard'), violence ('they used to fight a lot, and people got hurt a lot') and social life ('sometimes they met on campfires to sing songs and tell stories') in Anglo-Saxon times. While playing the game, these assumptions were very much present, coinciding or being at odds with their interpretation of game experiences. These two processes can be analysed through the lens of Piaget's (1973) learning theory. When coinciding, the game narratives were assimilated, reinforcing the previous ideas that children had before interacting with the game. However, when the game experiences and previous ideas were at odds, the internal contradiction had to be resolved through a process of accommodation, leading to a subsequent reorganisation and complexification of the children's existing structures of knowledge.

For children to resolve the emerging discrepancies between their historical assumptions and their game experiences, however, the game worked at its best when it was able to engage children empathetically with the dramatic situations presented to their fictional selves. As different authors have pointed out, owing to their capacity to drive players to inhabit the roles and perspectives of their avatars and experience the consequences of their actions and decisions, games are distinctly well suited to support educational activities or programmes where empathy is a key method or goal (Belman & Flanagan 2009; Isbister 2016). In the next paragraphs, I will centre the attention on some of these situations, reflecting on the ways in which they can be used as triggers of productive teachable moments.

History as conflict and empathy

According to the evaluation of the game in the school classroom, children interacted with it in contrasting ways. Following Fine (1983), these interactions can be categorised in three different patterns. Firstly, children inhabited the game space through the identity of their avatar, an Anglo-Saxon free peasant with the goal of settling and making a living in a new land. However, while embodying this fictional identity, children did not entirely disconnect from their personal aspirations and modes of thinking in the real world. Rather, their personal identities were very much part of their actions and decisions as they inhabited the goals of their avatars. Finally, children also interacted with the game as players; their motivations and strategies following a progressive under-standing of the game's rules, which had to be mastered in order to 'win' or prove themselves better than their peers.

Perhaps nowhere the interplay between these identities became more evi-dent than in the children's interactions with their virtual 'family members'. Despite these agents being designed with a practical function – children could delegate tasks to them, improving their chances of survival – some children deemed them as a burden and refused to feed them or to engage at all with their text-based dialogues. In these cases, it can be said that children engaged with the game primarily as players, a form of consciousness that took precedence over the fictional drivers of the game. In sharp contrast, in other cases chil-dren made a significant effort in taking care of the virtual agents, evidencing an engagement with the game's fictional situations as experienced by their avatars. While playing the game in this way, certain narratives set children's fictional and personal identities in conflict, triggering strong emotional responses. This was the case of a particular dialogue in which Wilburg, the player's son, facing the uncertainty and possible failure of the farmed land to yield enough food to survive, begs not to be sold as a slave. After interacting with this narrative, many children demanded the teacher to confirm whether a situation of this sort might have happened in medieval times, as well as to know more about what slavery would entail for a child like Wilburg in Anglo-Saxon times.

This observation begs the following questions: to what extent do we wish emotion to become part of historical understanding? What do we gain by letting ourselves feel for or empathise immediately and deeply with particular people, events or situations from the past? These questions have no simple answer. Inasmuch as we can see a defined purpose in engaging empathetically with the past, the proposition does not go without detractors. One of the most important sources of criticism to this kind of engagement involves the 'sins of presentism': the de facto impossibility to divorce ourselves from our present values, beliefs and experiences when looking at the past. I would argue, however, that it is precisely this ability to draw connections between our personal experiences and the particular circumstances affecting historical agents that makes history engaging and motivates us to learn more about the past. After being confronted with Wilbur's drama, children demanded to know more about childhood and slavery in medieval Britain because they cared about the possible fate of this fictional character, with whom they identified at a personal level.

From this line of analysis, I would argue that the most important learning situations triggered by the game were those in which children engaged empathetically and affectively with the circumstances affecting the lives of their avatar or family members. Devoid of this affective plane, the engagement with the game simulation of everyday life through representative tasks had limited educational value. As Robinson remarks, 'one can learn to play simulation games quite well without acquiring much knowledge at all of real history' (2013: 578). 'Real history' is the level of understanding that can only be achieved by empathising with people's lives and experiences. Ultimately, it is only through emotional involvement that students' preconceptions and naive forms of understanding can be challenged and changed. For this to happen, a willingness from the learner's part to enter the liminal space, where the security of the knowledge already known is left behind, is necessary. Commonly, this step is not taken without a good reason. Care provides the reason and purpose to enter the uncomfortable space where learning takes place.

One of the main motivations of this project was the exploration of the ways in which the experimental development of a historical game could inform the research field of historical game-based learning. Reaching the end of this project, and after having iteratively produced and testing an experimental historical game, it is possible to say that this process triggered interesting questions and paths for further exploration. Undoubtedly, the most important outcomes coming from this investigation emerged from the evaluation sessions with archaeologists, historians and history educators, where the design and pedagogical use of the game were extensively discussed. This serves as an eloquent indicator of the potential of *making* as a research method, which is certainly amplified when multiple disciplinary perspectives are integrated into the design process.

References

Belman, J. and Flanagan, M. (2009). Designing games to foster empathy. *International Journal of Cognitive Technology*, [online] 14(2): 5–15. Available at: http://www.maryflanagan.com/wp-content/uploads/cog-tech-si-g4g-article-1-belman-and-flanagan-designing-games-to-foster-empathy.pdf [Accessed 6 May 2019].

Brand, J.E. and Kinash, S. (2013). Crafting minds in Minecraft. *Education Technology Solutions*, [online] 55(2013): 56–58. Available at: https://pure.bond.edu.au/ws/portalfiles/portal/27949355/Crafting_minds_in_Minecraft.pdf [Accessed 6 May 2019].

Chapman, A. (2012). Privileging form over content: Analysing historical videogames. *Journal of Digital Humanities*, 1(2): 1–5.

Crawford, S. (2009). *Daily Life in Anglo-Saxon England*, Wesport: Greenwood World Publishing.

Department of Education (2013). *History Programmes of Study: Key Stages 1 and 2 National Curriculum in England*. [online] Available at: https://assets.publishing.service.gov.uk/government/uploads/system/uploads/attachment_data/file/239035/PRIMARY_national_curriculum_-_History.pdf [Accessed 6 May 2019].

Fine, G.A. (1983). *Shared Fantasy: Role-Playing Games as Social Worlds*, London and Chicago, IL: University of Chicago Press.

Houghton, R. (2016). Where did you learn that? The self-perceived educational impact of historical computer games on undergraduates, *Gamevironments*, 5: 8–45.

Isbister, K. (2016). *How Games Move Us: Emotion by Design*, London and Cambridge, MA: MIT Press.

Ingold, T. (2000). *The Perception of the Environment*. London and New York: Routledge.

McCall, J. (2016). Teaching history with digital historical games. *Simulation & Gaming*, 47(4): 517–542.

Nebel, S., Schneider, S. and Rey, G.D. (2016). Mining learning and crafting scientific experiments: A literature review on the use of Minecraft in education and research. *Educational Technology and Society*, 19(2): 355–366.

Piaget, J. (1973). *The Future of Education*, New York: Grossman Publishers.

Robinson, W.B. (2013). Stimulation, not simulation: An alternate approach to history teaching games. *The History Teacher*, [online] 46(4): 577–588. Available at: http://www.jstor.org/stable/43264159 [Accessed 6 May 2019].

Squire, K. and Barab, S. (2004). *Replaying History: Learning World History through Playing Civilization III*. Indiana University. [online] Available at: http://website.education.wisc.edu/kdsquire/REPLAYING   HISTORY.doc [Accessed 6 May 2019].

Taylor, T. (2003). Historical simulations and the future of the historical narrative. *Journal of the Association for History and Computing*, [online] 6(2). Available at: https://quod.lib.umich.edu/cgi/t/text/text-idx?c=jahc;view=text;rgn=main;idno=3310410.0006.203 [Accessed 6 May 2019].

Uricchio, W. (2005). Simulation, history, and computer games. In: J. Raessens and J. Goldstein, eds, *Handbook of Computer Game Studies*, Cambridge, MA: MIT Press, pp. 327–338.

Ludography

Civilization III (2001). Firaxis Games. [Multiple platforms].

The Oregon Trail (1971). Minnesota Educational Computing Consortium & The Learning Company. [Multiple platforms].

Digital learning environments

Mobile Technology and Science Outreach in Archaeology: Integrating Didactics

David Frederik Hölscher

KiSOC – Kiel Science Outreach Campus a joint venture of Kiel University (Institute of Pre- and Protohistoric Archaeology) and the IPN – Leibniz Institute for Science and Mathematics Education

Abstract

This contribution outlines approaches to the integration of didactic principles and educational research into science outreach in archaeology and cultural heritage. The focus lies on the target group's conceptions prior to involvement with the outreach programme and the development of learning objectives. The chapter gives insights into the author's PhD project at Kiel Science Outreach Campus, a joint venture of Kiel University and Leibniz Gemeinschaft. The project combines an educational research agenda with the development of a mobile learning environment including elements of spatial games on basis of didactic principles. The chapter concludes with a demand for a more frequent application of didactic principles by those who are involved in the planning and implementation of public outreach in archaeology and cultural heritage as well as for the consideration of the boundaries of scientific knowledge in connection with outreach activities.

How to cite this book chapter:
Hölscher, D. F. 2020. Mobile Technology and Science Outreach in Archaeology: Integrating Didactics. In: Hageneuer, S. (ed.) *Communicating the Past in the Digital Age: Proceedings of the International Conference on Digital Methods in Teaching and Learning in Archaeology (12–13 October 2018)*. Pp. 155–166. London: Ubiquity Press. DOI: https://doi.org/10.5334/bch.l. License: CC-BY 4.0

Keywords

Science Outreach, Human–Environment Interaction, Public Archaeology, Educational Research, Outdoor Learning

Introduction: digital science outreach and didactics in European archaeology today

Archaeological topics and research are brought to the public's attention by many formats. Among the most important are exhibitions and educational programmes in museums as well as radio and television broadcasts (see Bonacchi 2014). As – in Central Europe at least – archaeology is almost absent from school education, informal learning opportunities are the most significant way of gaining archaeological knowledge outside higher education. In the course of rapid technological development, especially in the digital sector, multimedia formats have been included in informal learning settings. In recent years, a vast number of multimedia guides and especially mobile applications have been developed concerning cultural heritage in general and in some cases archaeological topics in particular.[1] Examples are the offline mobile app 'Limes Mittelfranken Mobil' from southern Germany, which deals with the Roman Limes in Franconia (Bavaria) (Flügel & Schmidt 2013; edufilm und medien GmbH 2019); the multimedia-augmented reality app 'England's Historic Cities App' | 'England Originals', providing information about selected historical sites in several English cities (England's Historic Cities 2019; Hex Digital Ltd. n.d.; VisitBritain 2019); and the Danish multimedia app 'Digitale Tråde over landskapet' | 'Digital Threads across the Landscape', about archaeological sites and finds from Jutland, which contained augmented reality elements as well (Andersen & Møbjerg 2013; Møbjerg 2019).[2] Among the museums in northern Germany, Hamburg Archaeological Museum is exceptionally active in the field of digital outreach programmes, having set up, among others, several mobile exhibition guide applications, a digital 'archaeological window' (showcase) and digital exhibitions (Archäologisches Museum Hamburg 2019). As an international benchmark the British Museum could be named, which – in cooperation with a leading technological brand – has integrated a digital 'discovery centre' for learning in the exhibitions and exploring them with help of digital media (British Museum 2019). Thus, digital and mobile outreach is becoming a key element in the communication of our field.

---

[1] For a review see Malegiannaki and Daradoumis (2017).
[2] Discontinued in 2018 (ibid.).

Yet, the actual didactic benefits of formats like these are seldom evaluated, at least on the basis of didactical research questions or within the framework of educational research (see Degenkolb 2012; Hasberg 2012; Lautzas 2012; Malegiannaki & Daradoumis 2017). Malegiannaki and Daradoumis published a list of publications (2003–2015) in their review concerning 34 heritage-related mobile spatial games, only seven of which did not report outcomes of user experience or learning (Malegiannaki & Daradoumis 2017, Appendix C).

However, relative to their vast quantity, very little information about the designing process or the development of outreach programmes in our field of interest is published at all. It is not common to investigate the user's learning outcome. Educational research and publication of evaluation results is necessary, though, in order to:

1. analyse whether the concept of outreach on which a specific outreach programme or its set-up is based actually fulfils the planners' expectations;
2. judge which kind of educational approaches, mediation strategies and media (e.g. videos, audios, texts, pictures, animations, VR, AR) are especially well suited for education with mobile technology – in general and in specific contexts.

Although, for example, download numbers might give insight into the popularity of an application, they do not tell us anything about learning outcome, the users' relationship to the topics mediated and this relationship's development during the use of an outreach format. This is aggravated by the fact that there is no existing theoretical didactical framework for archaeology as opposed to, for example, history (Hasberg 2012; Lautzas 2012; Samida 2010). Even though hints about good practice and didactical frameworks can be derived from other disciplines and fields of research, namely didactics of history and environmental education, it is stated here that the specific nature of archaeological research and sources, of cultural heritage, its remains and management, require educational inquiry in their own right.

Filling the gap – outlines for the integration of didactics

The deficit outlined so far is not one of technological development but one of communicative and didactic principles. It is caused by developments in research and disciplinary traditions. The obvious, yet not simple, solution is to integrate didactics and findings of educational research into archaeology- and heritage-related educational work. But, as stated before, it is also necessary to implement educational research on these learning opportunities. This can only be successful, though, if experts in archaeology or heritage, respectively, work together with experts in educational research and didactics.

The educational opportunities discussed here are forms of scientific or public outreach. In order to set up any kind of outreach format several decisions have to be made (see American Association for the Advancement of Science 2019; Könneker 2012: 2–12).

Probably the most important ones – leaving aside monetary questions – concern:

- topics that are to be communicated or communication goals (disciplinary information or political agendas);
- target groups or audience;
- the environment in which communication is to take place;
- the communication tool(s) or means of communication (technology, media, strategies for engagement, didactic approaches).

Even though one format might be suited for communication of a wide range of topics, in most cases the topic – be it results of current archaeological research or a socio-political aim, such as acceptance for heritage protection within the public – determines many of the other aspects (see American Association for the Advancement of Science 2019). Some topics for example might concern only a special audience (e.g. political decision makers) or could not be communicated as well in one place or space as in another. The topic thus stands at the core of our communication. Yet, it is not the key element that facilitates comprehension and thus learning. Educational research has shown that, in order to aid the learning process, it is important to understand the learners' (i.e. the audience's) knowledge and conceptions of the topic in question prior to the communication process (Bell et al. 2009: e.g. 297; Duit et al. 2012; Holfelder 2018; Kattmann et al. 1997; Wehen-Behrens 2014).[3] This is a prerequisite for the transformation of the scientific or disciplinary information to a level of information comprehensible for the non-expert audience (ibid.). Thus, when developing an outreach or educational programme, we should not ask, 'what do we want to tell our audience?' but 'what is it we want them to understand and how can we approach them?' (see also American Association for the Advancement of Science 2019; Könneker 2012: 5). This forces us to set up explicit learning objectives and to analyse the target group of the planned programme. The learning process can furthermore be facilitated by connections to learners' lived-in world (Bell et al. 2009: e.g. 297; Duit et al. 2012; Holfelder 2018; Kattmann et al. 1997; Wehen-Behrens 2014).

---

[3] This research was mainly conducted in school contexts but its fundamental results are transferred here to a broader sphere of learning (cf. National Research Council 2000: 10–12, 14ff).

'Knowledge transfer in archaeology': science outreach in landscape archaeology

The approach to science outreach and learning environments outlined so far has been developed as part the author's PhD project. This project will be described on the following pages as an example for the connection of science outreach, didactic findings, and educational research. Named 'Knowledge transfer in archaeology. A study on the communication of current research content through multimedia learning environments' (working title), it also connects archaeological outreach and digital learning. The project is part of Kiel Science Outreach Campus (KiSOC), a joint project of Kiel University and the Leibniz Institute for Science and Mathematics Education (IPN). Within KiSOC, several researchers from different disciplines are concerned with questions of the principles, effects, development and improvement of science outreach programmes (KiSOC – Kiel Science Outreach Campus 2019). The trans- and interdisciplinary connections of KiSOC provide an important framework enabling a crucial exchange of expertise.

Being rooted in archaeology, the author's project is associated with the Institute of Pre- and Protohistoric Archaeology and the Graduate School 'Human Development in Landscapes' at Kiel University (Kiel University 2019a; 2019b). Fostered by both institutions, archaeological research at Kiel University has been focusing on matters of human–environment interaction and related societal or cultural developments in different periods for more than 10 years. As a consequence, the general topic pursued in the project 'Knowledge transfer in archaeology' was derived from the scope of these institutions' research. It aims to communicate dimensions of human–environment interactions from an archaeological perspective to the public. This focus concerns fundamental issues of human existence, but also ties in well with discussions about environmental issues and sustainability over approximately the last three decades. It therefore inherently bears connections to the lived-in world of present audiences. A second major topic chosen for the project is the character of knowledge dealt with and produced in archaeology. While the question of human–environment interactions lies on a level of disciplinary knowledge and concepts about processes in the past, this second major aspect concerns the ambiguous and imperfect nature of sources as well as the preliminary nature and different levels of certainty of interpretations (see Clark 2004; Clarke 1973; Eggert & Samida 2013: 50–59; Fulbrook 2002; Trautwein et al. 2017: 15–16).[4] This second topic thus deals with the very core of production and judgement of

---

[4]   It seems to the author that the theoretical debate about the epistemology of the past and history, strongly kindled by constructivist and postmodern thought, has been much more accounted for in history than in archaeology, even though this debate's basic implications also apply to the latter – which leads to the quotation of several works of historical theoretical literature here.

scientific knowledge,[5] and is connected to epistemological theories of research on the past and history.

In practice, these general topics could be addressed in relation to one single archaeological site and/or period. However, the project introduced here follows a diachronic approach in order to explain the heterogeneous development and chronological depths of humans' relationships with their (natural) environment. The audience will follow individual examples from different places and periods, yet within one region in northern Germany. These examples are connected via different sub-topics covering different times and cultures such as food production, the use of natural resources, settlement patterns and burial rites. These 'case studies' also allow for the consideration of challenges or uncertainties connected to the archaeological record and its interpretation.

To take human–environment interactions to a tangible level, landscape constitutes a key concept in the project. This chapter is not the place to define or discuss landscape as a concept – nor environment or nature – but on a local and regional level landscape provides a spatial and cognitive framework in which human interaction with the environment can be placed (see Förster et al. 2012; Kolen, Renes & Hermans 2015). At the same time the local landscape serves as a link connecting past development, present state and the audience's lived-in world. This is strengthened by the mediation strategy and set-up. As in many other examples (see introduction) an explorative, on-site approach is taken: information will be conveyed in the landscape at places where significant archaeological remains and traces of human or natural impacts on landscape development can be traced. To achieve this, an offline mobile app will be used for the project, which provides the users with GPS-guided cycling tours. While cycling tours (of approximately 25 kilometres) offer an easy way to experience a greater area in short time, mobile app technology forms an up-to-date as well as very flexible tool for communication. Several studies have shown positive effects of outdoor activities on motivation, learning, and general wellbeing (Alon & Tal 2017; Crawford, Holder & O'Connor 2017). Crawford, Holder and O'Connor (2017) could, for example, show that mobile applications and personal guided tours are potentially equally effective, at the same time exceeding information boards (interpretive signage). A further argument in favour of the use of mobile technology in outside conditions can be added: it fits the communication habits of young people and has shown positive effects on their motivation in educational contexts (Crawford, Holder & O'Connor 2017; Medienpädagogischer Forschungsverbund Südwest 2018: 77–80; Molitor 2014). This is of high importance as the main target group defined for the project are children and adolescents between 10 and 15 years. To maintain interest

---

[5] Compare discussions of the 'nature of science' in the natural sciences (Lederman 2007).

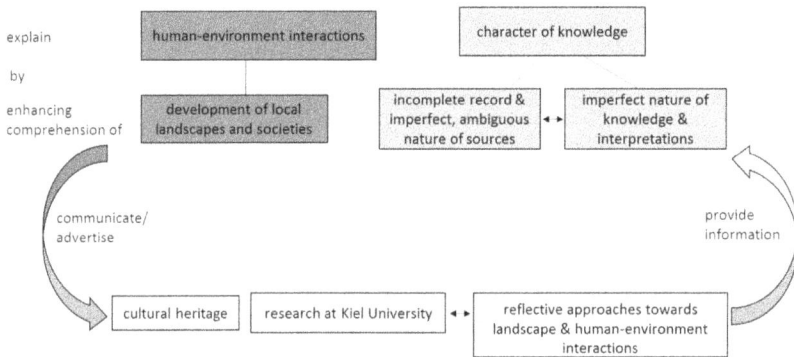

Learning Objectives

Figure 1: Learning objectives in the project 'Knowledge transfer in archaeology. A study on the communication of current research content through multimedia learning environments' (working title).

and facilitate inquiry-based learning experiences, game elements composed as tasks and challenges will be integrated into the mediation process.

In conclusion, all major decisions in the project 'Knowledge transfer in archaeology' are not only based on disciplinary, technological and practical considerations but rooted in didactic premises. To further strengthen the didactic aspect and to meet the requirements outlined above, the author uses data from semi-structured interviews to discern potential users' conceptions of archaeology and human–environment relations. To enable a systematic selection and transformation of the disciplinary information in accordance with the users' level(s) of knowledge, represented by their conceptions, learning objectives have been developed (Figure 1). They constitute a constant guideline for the development of content. This approach draws on considerations from the 'Model of Educational Reconstruction', developed by Kattmann et al. (1997) and Duit et al. (2012).

From the connection of disciplinary information, users' (or learners') conceptions, learning objectives, practical considerations and communication strategies follow the scheme for content development in the project shown in Figure 2.

In respect of overall methodology, this outreach as well as research project uses design-based research. It integrates theory, development, practice and evaluation and via an iterative design and development process leaves room for adjustments 'on the run' (Raatz 2016; Reinmann 2005). Even though didactic principles and findings from educational research are incorporated into the planning and designing process, the question of effects on the users'

Developing Content

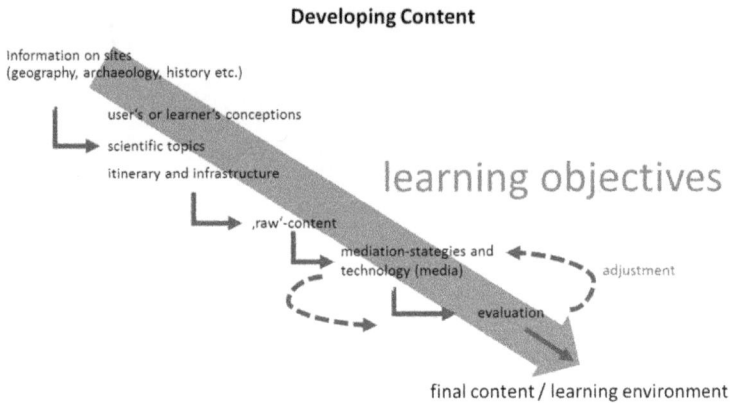

Information on sites
(geography, archaeology, history etc.)

user's or learner's conceptions

scientific topics

itinerary and infrastructure

learning objectives

,raw'-content

mediation-stategies and
technology (media)

adjustment

evaluation

final content / learning environment

Figure 2: Scheme for the development of content during archaeological outreach outdoors.

learning remains. To actually be able to judge the success of this outreach project, learning achievement will be examined using qualitative methods. Unlike quantitative approaches, they are well suited for an explorative and design-based approach, as qualitative methods leave more room for 'unexpected' findings or ad hoc adjustments and in-depth investigation (Bortz & Döring 2006: 308–336; Wider 2018: 72). In the framework of design-based research this also means that certain parts of the learning environment might be evaluated before the overall evaluation of learning achievements caused by use of the completed mobile app. Again, learning objectives play a vital part in the research design, as they constitute the standard of comparison. The effectiveness of mobile applications as learning environments should be ensured before they are launched. And, as the research interest thus lies on the effectiveness of this certain type of tool, a design comparing learning achievement with set learning objectives or communication goals seems much more reasonable than test group–control group designs. For a comparison with other media or types of learning environments (e.g. personal guides tours or display boards), on the other hand, other approaches might be more adequate.

Concluding remarks

This chapter does not aim at marginalising the achievements of practitioners in museum pedagogy, nor those of planners or designers of outreach activities in archaeology and cultural heritage. But if we as archaeologists or heritage managers want to get serious with (science) outreach and (science) education, we have to incorporate didactic principles and results of educational research when designing and developing instruments for outreach and science communication. Two important elements are:

1. to set clear/explicit learning objectives;
2. to take the target group's conceptions and prior knowledge into account.

From a disciplinary perspective, a third aspect that should not be neglected is to stay true to the archaeological results and the boundaries of insight in archaeological research. While this should go without saying, in practice there has been a tendency towards too much simplification and overstatement in order to gain public attention. However, as the past cannot be recreated, all our attempts to work out its course and nature are approximations (e.g. Clark 2004; Clarke 1973; Winiwarter & Knoll 2007: 19–21). Thus, uncertainty stands at the centre of interpretations in our discipline; gaps in our knowledge of the past and the attempts to fill them play a major role in scientific work about the past. These vital circumstances should not be neglected in our public communication but be prominently dealt with – at least as far as time and occasion allow. Marking uncertain parts or levels of uncertainty (of interpretations) and missing information should be able to provoke curiosity, activate learning processes and help non-experts comprehend the nature of our trade.

Furthermore, we have to evaluate our tools of mediation, not only in museum surveys being kept unpublished (as is common practice in Germany), and not only in respect of usability and user satisfaction, but on an empirical, scientific basis considering the learning process. This needs exchange beyond disciplinary borders, including experts from archaeology or cultural heritage, educational research, didactics and educational practice.

References

Alon, N.L. and Tal, T. (2017). Field trips to natural environments: how outdoor educators use the physical environment. *International Journal of Science Education, Part B*, 7(3): 237–252.

American Association for the Advancement of Science (2019). *Communication Fundamentals*. [online] American Association for the Advancement of Science. Available at: https://www.aaas.org/resources/communication-toolkit/communication-fundamentals [Accessed 22 February 2019].

Andersen, L.R. and Møbjerg, T. (2013). 'Digital Threads across the Landscape' – a smartphone application co-developed by users. *Archäologische Informationen*, 36: 45–53.

Archäologisches Museum Hamburg (2019). *Digital Supply*. [online] Archäologisches Museum Hamburg. Available at: https://amh.de/en/digital-supply [Accessed 22 February 2019].

Bell, P., Lewenstein, B., Shouse, A.W. and Feder, M.A. (2009). *Learning Science in Informal Environments: People, Places, and Pursuits*, Washington, DC: National Academies Press.

Bonacchi, C. (2014). Understanding the public experience of archaeology in the UK and Italy: a call for a 'sociological movement' in public Archaeology. *European Journal of Post-Classical Archaeologies*, 4: 377–400.

Bortz, J. and Döring, N. (2006). *Forschungsmethoden und Evaluation: für Human- und Sozialwissenschaftler*, Heidelberg: Springer-Medizin-Verlag.

British Museum (2019). *Samsung Digital Discovery Centre*. [online] British Museum. Available at: https://www.britishmuseum.org/learning/samsung_centre.aspx [Accessed 22 February 2019].

Clark, E.A. (2004). *History, Theory, Text: Historians and the Linguistic Turn*. Cambridge, MA: Harvard University Press.

Clarke, D. (1973). Archaeology: the loss of innocence. *Antiquity*, 47: 6–18.

Crawford, M.R., Holder, M.D. and O'Connor, B.P. (2017). Using mobile technology to engage children with nature. *Environment and Behavior*, 49(9): 959–984.

Degenkolb, P. (2012). Archäologie, Schule und Museum im Spannungsfeld kultureller Bildung: Einführung in das Tagungsthema. *Archäologische Informationen*, 35: 89–92.

Duit, R., Gropengießer, H., Kattmann, U., Komorek, M. and Parchmann, I. (2012). The model of educational reconstruction – a framework for improving teaching and learning science. In: D. Jorde and J. Dillon, eds, *Science Education Research and Practice in Europe: Retrospective and Prospective*, Rotterdam: Sense Publishers, pp. 13–37.

Eggert, M.K.H. and Samida, S. (2013). *Ur- und Frühgeschichtliche Archäologie*, Tübingen: Francke.

England's Historic Cities (2019). *England's Historic Cities*. [online] Heritage Cities. Available at: http://www.heritagecities.com/stories/explore [Accessed 22 February 2019].

Flügel, C. and Schmidt, R. (2013). Auf neuen Wegen unterwegs am Limes – Die Smartphone-App 'Limes Mittelfranken Mobil'. *Der Limes*, 2(7): 36–37.

Förster, F., Großmann, R., Iwe, K., Kinkel, H., Larsen, A., Lungershausen, U., Matarese, C., Meurer, P., Nelle, O., Robin, V., Teichmann, M. (2012). What is landscape? Towards a common concept within an interdisciplinary research environment. *eTopoi. Journal for Ancient Studies*, [online] 3: 169–179. Available at: http://journal.topoi.org/index.php/etopoi/article/view/124 [Accessed 19 March 2019].

Fulbrook, M. (2002). *Historical Theory*, London: Routledge.

Hasberg, W. (2012). Kultur – Bildung – Archäologie. Anmerkungen zum Verhältnis von Archäologie und historischem Lernen. *Archäologische Informationen*, 35: 125–132.

Holfelder, A.-K. (2018). *Orientierungen von Jugendlichen zu Nachhaltigkeitsthemen: Zur didaktischen Bedeutung von implizitem Wissen im Kontext BNE*, Wiesbaden: Springer Fachmedien Wiesbaden.

Kattmann, U., Duit, R., Gropengießer, H. and Komorek, M. (1997). Das Modell der Didaktischen Rekonstruktion – Ein Rahmen für naturwissenschafts-didaktische Forschung und Entwicklung. *Zeitschrift für Didaktik der Naturwissenschaften*, 3(3): 3–18.

Kiel University. (2019a). *Human Development in Landscapes*. [online] Graduierten Schule. Available at: http://www.gshdl.uni-kiel.de/de [Accessed 24 September 2018].

Kiel University. (2019b). *Institute of Pre- and Protohistoric Archaeology*. [online] Institut für Ur- und Frühgeschichte. Available at: https://www.ufg.uni-kiel.de/en [Accessed 19 March 2019].

KiSOC – Kiel Science Outreach Campus (2019). *KiSOC – Kiel Science Outreach Campus*. [online] Available at: http://www.kisoc.de/en [Accessed 22 February 2019].

Kolen, J., Renes, H. and Hermans, R. (eds) (2015). *Landscape Biographies: Geographical, Historical and Archaeological Perspectives on the Production and Transmission of Landscapes*, Amsterdam: Amsterdam University Press.

Könneker, C. (2012). *Wissenschaft kommunizieren: ein Handbuch mit vielen praktischen Beispielen*, Weinheim: Wiley-VCH.

Lautzas, P. (2012). Die Archäologie im Bildungswesen in Deutschland. Fragen und Wünsche an die Archäologie aus der Praxis. *Archäologische Informationen*, 35: 235–236.

Lederman, N. (2007). Nature of science: Past, present, and future. In: S.K. Abell and N.G. Lederman, eds, *Handbook of Research on Science Education*, London: Routledge, pp. 831–879.

Malegiannaki, I. and Daradoumis, T. (2017). Analyzing the educational design, use and effect of spatial games for cultural heritage: A literature review. *Computers & Education*, 108: 1–10.

Medienpädagogischer Forschungsverbund Südwest (2018). [pdf] Available at: https://www.mpfs.de/fileadmin/files/Studien/JIM/2018/Studie/JIM_2018_Gesamt.pdf [Accessed 19 March 2019].

Møbjerg, T. (2019). 'Digital threads across the Landscape' – a smartphone application involving co-creators. In: T. Møbjerg, L. Ræder Knudsen, H. Rostholm and U. Mannering, eds, *The Hammerum Burial site. Customs and Clothing in the Roman Iron Age*, Aarhus: Jysk Arkæologisk Selskab & Aarhus Universitetsforlag.

Molitor, H. (2014). Bildung durch digitale Medien? In: U. Michel, A. Siegmund, W. Ehlers, W. Jahn and A. Bittner, eds, *Digitale Medien in der Bildung für nachhaltige Entwicklung: Potenziale und Grenzen*, Munich: Oekom Verlag, pp. 25–32.

National Research Council (2000). *How People Learn: Brain, Mind, Experience, and School: Expanded Edition*. Washington, DC: National Academies Press.

Raatz, S. (2016). Design-based research – Innovation für Bildungswissenschaft und -praxis. In: S. Raatz, ed., *Entwicklung von Einstellungen gegenüber verantwortungsvoller Führung: Eine Design-based Research Studie in der Executive Education*, Wiesbaden: Springer Fachmedien, pp. 37–61.

Reinmann, G. (2005). Innovation ohne Forschung? Ein Plädoyer für den Design-Based Research-Ansatz in der Lehr-Lernforschung. *Unterrichtswissenschaft*, 33(1): 52–69.

Samida, S. (2010). Was ist und warum brauchen wir eine Archäologiedidaktik? *Zeitschrift für Geschichtsdidaktik*, 9: 215–226.

Trautwein, U., Bertram, C., von Borries, B., Brauch, N., Hirsch, M., Klausmeier, K., Körber, A., Kühberger, C., Meyer-Hamme, J., Merkt, M., Neureiter, H., Schwan, S., Schreiber, W., Wagner, W., Waldis, M., Werner, M., Ziegler, B., Zuckowski, A. (2017). *Kompetenzen historischen Denkens erfassen: Konzeption, Operationalisierung und Befunde des Projekts 'Historical Thinking – Competencies in History' (HiTCH)*, Münster: Waxmann.

VisitBritain (2019). *England's Originals – Discover England Fund Project*. [online] VisitBritain. Available at: https://trade.visitbritain.com/destination-uk/discover-england-fund/englands-originals [Accessed 22 February 2019].

Wehen-Behrens, B. (2014). 'Früher hat man mit der Umwelt gelebt, heute lebt man über ihr' – SchülerInnenvorstellungen zur Geschichte der Umwelt. In: H. Düselder and A. Schmitt, eds, *Umweltgeschichte: Forschung und Vermittlung in Universität, Museum und Schule*, Cologne: Böhlau, pp. 191–206.

Wider, M. (2018). *'Man muss es gesehen haben, um es zu verstehen' – Zur Wirkung von historischen Orten auf Schülerinnen und Schüler*, Hamburg: Dr. Kovač.

Winiwarter, V. and Knoll, M. (2007). *Umweltgeschichte. Eine Einführung*, Cologne: Böhlau.

Ludography

Limes Mittelfranken Mobil (2019). edufilm und medien GmbH. [Android].

England Originals (n.d.). Hex Digital Ltd. [Android].

Modelling and Simulation to Teach (Classical) Archaeology: Integrating New Media into the Curriculum

Erika Holter and Sebastian Schwesinger

Humboldt-Universität zu Berlin

Abstract

Digital modelling and simulation are increasingly becoming integral tools for historical research, making them relevant elements of any archaeological curriculum. In this chapter, we explore how creating reconstructions with these tools can be incorporated into programmes of study: modelling aids in critical analysis of source material, while simulations enable the critical integration of pragmatic, sensory aspects into interpretations. The use of each promotes specific forms of critical thinking that empower students to engage in historical interpretation and begin to ask their own questions.

Keywords

Modelling, Simulation, Digital Learning, Reconstruction, Virtual Environments

How to cite this book chapter:
Holter, E. and Schwesinger, S. 2020. Modelling and Simulation to Teach (Classical) Archaeology: Integrating New Media into the Curriculum. In: Hageneuer, S. (ed.) *Communicating the Past in the Digital Age: Proceedings of the International Conference on Digital Methods in Teaching and Learning in Archaeology (12–13 October 2018)*. Pp. 167–177. London: Ubiquity Press. DOI: https://doi.org/10.5334/ bch.m. License: CC-BY 4.0

Introduction

With digital tools such as 3D modelling or virtual simulation becoming increasingly accessible to makers and users alike, more and more non-specialists are taking advantage of them. These new formats present the field of archaeology with fresh opportunities to communicate the past and engage students. Not only can they serve to pique interest in archaeological topics; not only do they provide a different medium with which to impart the subject matter; digital modelling and simulation can themselves be incredibly productive research tools, which gives them an enormous potential in terms of training students for research.[1] At its foundation, research involves the use of critical thinking skills, which are becoming a core component of the teaching of archaeology – and the humanities in general – in universities today.[2] In addition to concentrating on mastering a set subject matter, the archaeological curriculum today aims to teach students how to learn, understand and analyse content independently. In this chapter, we would like to address how digital tools in the classroom – specifically the use of digital modelling and simulations to create reconstructions – can foster students' critical thinking skills that can be applied to their own studies, to research and beyond. This chapter deals specifically with the use of digital reconstructions in modelling and simulation as a teaching tool; using the results in order to mediate and communicate archaeological research for a broader public is dealt with elsewhere in this volume.[3]

Modelling: critical thinking in practice

When it comes to the fragmentary remains of ancient life, the process of reconstructing a whole out of the disparate pieces is itself a method with which students and researchers can begin to think critically about how to analyse the sources that are available to archaeologists. Creating a reconstruction model is therefore not focused on a (realistic) final product but rather on the process of weighing and interpreting the sources at hand. As Joshua Epstein (2008)

---

[1] On the use of digital models and simulations for research, see for example Favro (2012); Bartz, Holter and Muth (2016); Holter, Schäfer and Schwesinger (2020).

[2] On the importance of critical thinking in the archaeological curriculum (and humanities in general), see for example Lipe (2000: 19); Hamilakis (2001: 9); OKell, Ljubojevic and MacMahon (2010: 152–155).

[3] For example Quick or Hageneuer in this volume. Archaeological excavations also employ image-based digital 3D models in the field in order to aid in documentation (see for example Dell'Unto 2014). While this use of digital modelling requires greater scrutiny in a classroom setting to prepare students to understand its benefits and limitations, it is, however, not the focus in this chapter.

succinctly explained in his landmark article 'Why model?', the main goal for modelling is not, as commonly (mis)understood, prediction.[4] He determined 16 alternative reasons for modelling, and it is worth reprinting his list here in full because it makes clear how useful it can be for training archaeologists (or, in general, those studying objects and sites that can be modelled and simulated, such as art historians etc.):

1. explain (very distinct from predict);
2. guide data collection;
3. illuminate core dynamics;
4. suggest dynamical analogies;
5. discover new questions;
6. promote a scientific habit of mind;
7. bound (bracket) outcomes to plausible ranges;
8. illuminate core uncertainties;
9. offer crisis options in near-real time;
10. demonstrate trade-offs/suggest efficiencies;
11. challenge the robustness of prevailing theory through perturbations;
12. expose prevailing wisdom as incompatible with available data;
13. train practitioners;
14. discipline the policy dialogue;
15. educate the general public;
16. reveal the apparently simple (complex) to be complex (simple) (Epstein 2008: 1.9).

The task of creating a model provides the students with a structure to begin 'guiding data collection' (2), on which basis they can explain the site and their reconstruction of it (1). Continued work on the reconstruction in turn 'illuminate[s] core uncertainties' (8) within previously 'bracket[ed] ... plausible ranges' (7), leading to the students' questioning of prevailing theories (11) by 'exposing prevailing wisdom as incompatible with available data' (12).[5]

In order to illustrate how the process of modelling – specifically, the process of creating a digital reconstruction – can itself be a productive teaching tool, we would like to give a brief example of what this can look like in a classroom setting. These observations are based on seminars on digital reconstruction offered at the Winckelmann-Institut für Klassische Archäologie at Humboldt-Universität zu Berlin: one focused on the Forum in Rome and would go on to

---

[4] E. Holter would like to thank X. Rubio-Campillo for leading her to this article.

[5] An early example for the use of digital models (and CAD specifically) as teaching tools (in this case, in the field of art history) is Günther (2001), who mainly extols their benefits in training students to recognise and analyse elements of architecture. Further experiences with including the creation of digital models in archaeological or historical teaching have not to our knowledge been published.

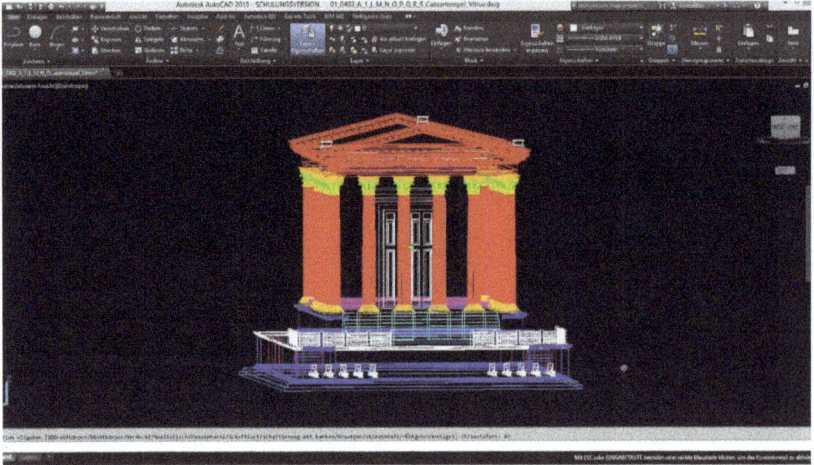

Figure 1: Screenshot of a reconstruction of the Temple of Caesar from AutoCAD. © E. Holter/S. Muth/A. Müller.

become the founding model of the *digitales forum romanum* project; the other built on the experience of the first and offered a course modelling the Athenian Agora.[6] The first step was to teach the students how to use the software with which the reconstructions were to be created: in our example, in cooperation with an architect, we used the architectural modelling software AutoCAD (Figure 1).[7] The students worked in teams, each team receiving a set of buildings that it was required to reconstruct in all of their building phases. For this, a documentation worksheet was developed with the class in order to structure the different evidence (archaeological, literary, comparative) on which the reconstruction was based as well as to explain each step.[8]

In addition to practical experience with gathering relevant material, the documentation of the sources – which is the first step of digital modelling – led to a clearer understanding of what information is available for a reconstruction –

---

[6] This is based on the experience of E. Holter, who can describe the two courses from two different perspectives: in the first, she participated as a student under S. Muth; in the second she was a teacher. She is grateful to the architect A. Müller for his patience and help in teaching the students of both classes. For more on the *digitales forum romanum* project, headed by S. Muth, see the project website www.digitales-forum-romanum.de and Bartz, Holter and Muth (2016).

[7] AutoCAD offers a free education licence for use in universities but it has a steep learning curve, which posed a significant barrier for some of the students in both classes. Other modelling software is possibly more suited to work with students.

[8] The documentation for the class that would lead to the *digitales forum romanum* project was later moved to an online wiki to make collaboration easier: https://wikis.hu-berlin.de/digiforo/Hauptseite. Several examples can be viewed there.

and how conjectural different elements of the reconstructions would be. The questions that arose, often without clear answers in the academic literature, were the launch pad from which the students could begin to learn to form their own individual judgements based on the available evidence, training them in historical interpretation. In the class, students were specifically encouraged to reconstruct alternatives within the plausible ranges determined by the sources in order to underline this: the validity of the alternatives was then assessed as part of the learning process in discussion with the lecturer and the class. Understanding the nature of the sources on which reconstructions (and interpretations in general) are based also led to an increased awareness of other historical and social factors and assumptions that go into each, reinforcing critical thinking skills.

Creating digital architectural models, especially with students, therefore makes gaps in archaeological knowledge visible; the gaps themselves represent free spaces open to interpretations, in which new questions are made possible. Accordingly, modelling allows the students to become active participants in the process of knowledge acquisition, not only their own but for the discipline as a whole.[9] Each free space represents a possible avenue of research that it is worthwhile to pursue. The creation of digital models can be integrated into departmental research projects for similar reasons, and serves as a means with which students can be directly included in the research process.[10] Students of archaeology have to deal with a wide variety of disparate evidence, and it is the goal of teaching archaeology to give them the appropriate skills to weigh the evidence in terms of specific research questions, a skill with applications beyond the study of archaeology. Digital modelling in the classroom is one method by which these skills can be put into practice.[11]

---

[9] Active learning specifically in the context of the archaeology classroom is dealt with in Burke and Smith (2007) (a survey of the ideas behind active learning is given in their introduction, followed by a series of examples).

[10] In addition to possible preparation for an academic career, see Ishiyama (2002) for the learning benefits to undergraduates who participate in faculty research. A prime example for this is the *digitales forum romanum* project (see above).

[11] The use of digital models created by others in the classroom is a question that needs to be dealt with in more detail elsewhere: reconstructions created by others are often especially difficult to analyse, as very few provide an extensive documentation detailing their research and design decisions. In addition, there is as of yet no widely accepted method for visualising uncertainties in digital models (Schäfer 2018). Integrating digital models into game engines could be a next step, as different models of the same building or space can be integrated into a single scene, thereby providing comparable alternatives and making the reconstruction itself dynamic. This underlines its uncertain elements and is a first step towards communicating the uncertainties to outside users, allowing digital reconstructions that have already been created to continue to be of use in communicating the past (on this, see Holter, Schäfer & Schwesinger 2020).

Simulation: engaging with the technology

The creation of various architectural models, while a research tool in its own right, leads to further uses with which to expand research questions, most notably through their integration into digital simulations. By creating the digital models themselves, students learned to critically analyse their sources – and any resulting reconstructions. In this section, we would like to turn to a further digital tool: digital simulations. Using simulations, we can expand what questions students can ask of the archaeological material: specifically, simulations enable the integration of sensory perception into historical interpretation.[12]

In a graduate course in which students developed and pursued their own research projects on ancient material public culture, we focused their attention on the Agora and the Pnyx in classical Athens.[13] Digital architectural models of these spaces were provided, and the students were instructed to reconstruct historical scenarios in these ancient spaces using a game engine (in this case, Unity 3D).[14] In addition to the ability to move freely through the reconstruction (from a first-person POV if desired), the use of a game engine allowed for the further embellishment of the virtual environment with textures, plants, people and equipment. In contrast to the rather sanitised aesthetic of architectural software, the game engine aesthetics enables a more 'realistic' look and feel. This impression is reinforced when using a head-mounted display for a VR set-up.

Especially the Pnyx as the location of the public assembly during the heyday of classical democracy proved to be a useful case study, and this scenario was reconstructed in the game engine (Figure 2). The Pnyx was renovated several times during this period, and, for the second building phase, there is no certain evidence for the location of the speaker's platform. Knowing its exact location is highly relevant, as it would have had an influence on the visual and acoustic communication between the speaker and the audience, a primary purpose of

---

[12] Sensory studies in classical antiquity, itself a relatively new field, is subject to similar considerations as those we raised here regarding digital modelling. As E. Betts (2017: 195) puts it, 'Interpretation (itself a "creative nonfiction") begins during archaeological fieldwork, and partial evidence in any area of classical studies makes the search for Truth redundant. Instead, sensory studies enable us to extract new meaning from our evidence as we strive for better understandings of human individuals and societies.'

[13] S. Schwesinger led this seminar in the Cultural History Department at Humboldt-Universität zu Berlin. He would like to thank the digital humanities scholar U. Schäfer for her inexhaustible patience while teaching rookies the principles and workings of a game engine.

[14] On the possibilities of game engines for historical research, see Holter, Schäfer and Schwesinger (2020). On the intellectual history and epistemic potential of scenarios, see Wolfsteiner (2018).

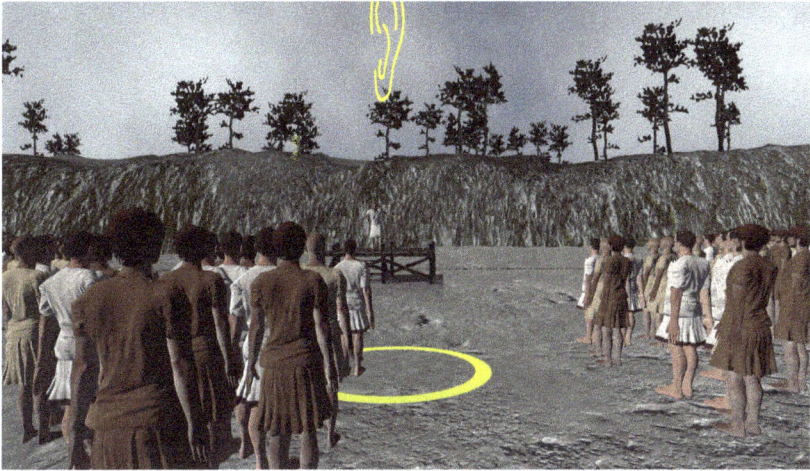

Figure 2: Screenshot from public assembly scenario on the Pnyx in Unity3D. © D. Mariaschk/U.U. Schäfer.

the assembly in this space. Consequently, we integrated an acoustic simulation of a speech signal for three different proposed locations of the speaker's platforms into the virtual environment in order to make the differences between these not only visible but also audible.[15] In this way, digital simulation tools provide a chance for comparing different architectural reconstructions by placing them in an environment that can be experienced with different senses (seeing, hearing), thereby expanding the scope of possible interpretation. Multisensory experience is thus used as a kind of spatio-functional performance test: if spaces like the Pnyx were built to serve the function of political communication, then moments where they failed to serve their purpose – for example, where the speaker could be only poorly heard by the audience – might have triggered architectural or procedural changes. When, with the help of simulations, the reconstructions of ancient spaces stop being simply static architectural structures, students can start to examine the dynamic and sensory space the buildings were a part of. This opens up functional or pragmatic interpretations

---

[15] In the research project Analog Storage Media – Auralization of Archaeological Spaces we developed this idea further into an interface within which it is possible to switch between the three different locations without exiting the play mode of the game engine. With this customizable interface, a user can toggle between variations not only for architectural but also for other uncertainties that concern, for example, the behaviour of the crowd or of the speaker, or the lighting due to the time of the day (Holter, Schäfer & Schwesinger 2020). For the application of acoustic simulations to archaeological research, see Holter, Muth and Schwesinger (2018) as well as Kassung and Muth (2019).

as opposed to symbolic or ideological ones.[16] In this sense, virtual environments become a tool by which static reconstructions are made dynamic in order to include pragmatic considerations. Therefore, we can widen the scope of students to interpret the spatial implications of different reconstruction proposals, i.e. how well each of them performs its assumed function.

The role that digital models can and should play in research is, however, a matter of ongoing debate, and it is important to prepare students for this discussion as well. Considerations on the scientific applicability and research value of digital tools concentrate on a critical understanding of them as an epistemic medium, i.e. how the things and techniques we use to gain, store, express and convey knowledge inscribe themselves into that knowledge.[17] This involves examining the means and formats of gathering and representing archaeological knowledge historically and contemporarily: one way to investigate the impact that digital modelling and simulation have on the way archaeologists work and think is to compare them to 2D line drawings and plaster models and consider how these might have done so as well. This perspective should help students to probe the limitations of simulations: what is their intended use? What aesthetics should they serve? Virtual environments, for example, often make use of a specific video game aesthetics that strives for a realistic impression in order to immerse users in a virtual world. But a virtual, computer game reality is not comparable to a historically perceived reality. While game engines today can accurately simulate the effects of many laws of physics (gravitation and optics are two examples that come to mind) – and future technology might come even closer to making virtual and physical reality indistinguishable – scholars and students will never be able to become a Greek or a Roman. Although the ancient spaces reconstructed should be interpreted within their cultural context, a critical position should always take the fact that we are evaluating it from a contemporary standpoint into consideration.

Coming back to the example of the Pnyx, the task for the listening student or scholar cannot be to use the audio-visual simulations in order to empathise with a Greek avatar but to determine and understand the important elements

---

[16] A good example of this is given by S. Muth (2014: 304–310; see also Kassung & Muth 2019: 199–201) for the Forum in Rome: Caesar moved the location of the speaker's platform from its traditional, republican location. Instead of considering this architectural transformation solely in symbolic, ideological terms (Caesar is showing his disrespect for republican tradition), a pragmatic, functional view considers whether or not this renovation improved the conditions for the political communication that was the primary purpose of the speaker's platform. For university teaching, H. Günther already predicted that the advantage of self-created digital models and environments would lie in illuminating functional contexts (2001: 121).

[17] For a media-critical perspective on cultural heritage, see Kassung and Schwesinger (2018).

of the historical scenario of the public assembly: how important was it to understand an orator word for word? How informed were participants of the public assembly about the content of the proposals? How interactive was the relationship between the speaker and the audience? What behaviour from the crowd was regarded as appropriate? Questions like these direct attention away from the simple textual content of the speeches that have survived to this day, instead focusing on the structural basis or situational components of the scene. In order to understand the function of architectural spaces students need to acknowledge the cultural foundations of the situation, which will come to their attention precisely through their experience of these historical spaces in digital simulations.

We believe that, in this way, virtual environments might serve as classroom tools for a sensory-based epistemology of archaeological reconstructions. Instead of trying to evaluate which simulated event and result is more 'true' than the other, students should be guided to experimentally investigate the conditions under which, for example in the case of political communication in classical Athens, such an auditory situation might have made sense to the people involved by bringing all possible resources together to study the structures, relations and sensory conditions that seem to have been important for political communication to function. This includes the (knowledge about the) role of architecture to acoustically support an orator as much as the different reception attitudes that may have guided a listener's understanding. Such findings can be used for listening trainings with students, helping them to reflect on their contemporary and mediated listening habits.[18] This might also support a more extensive approach to virtual sensory spaces and counterbalance careless claims of 'realism'.

Conclusion

How can and should digital modelling and simulation be integrated into teaching? Most important is training the users of these digital tools in how to critically understand them. This includes learning to recognise the sources of the reconstructions and applying the sources themselves to the creation of digital models. Here, uncertainties in the reconstructions should be understood not as dead ends but as the starting point for new research questions. The experience in simulations can be used to consider the material and cultural conditions of sensory perception, so that users (in this case, students) can better understand the historical specificity of the experience and what questions we need to ask of the evidence in order to better analyse sensory conditions in antiquity. As we hope to have shown, digital reconstruction and simulation tools are not so

---

[18] See Hamilakis (2001: 9–10), who also argues for more reflexivity in the classroom.

much for answering questions as they are for asking them. This is exactly the skill that we should want students of humanities to learn most of all, making the proper integration of digital tools into teaching a highly effective method.

Acknowledgements

The authors would like to thank the Image Knowledge Gestaltung Cluster of Excellence for their financial support, and all the colleagues in the Analog Storage Media – Auralization of Archaeological Spaces project for the rewarding collaboration that lies at the foundation of the views expressed here. E. Holter would also like to thank the Caroline von Humboldt Grant Program for a generous completion grant, which made further work on this chapter possible. She owes a debt to her teacher S. Muth, who provided to her as a student many of the opportunities discussed here.

References

Bartz, J., Holter, E. and Muth, S. (2016). Digitales Forum Romanum: Chancen und Grenzen virtueller Rekonstruktion und Simulation. In: K.B. Zimmer, ed., *Von der Reproduktion zur Rekonstruktion – Umgang mit Antike(n) II*, Rahden: Marie Leidorf, pp. 193–208.

Betts, E. (2017). Afterword: Towards a methodology for Roman sensory studies. In: E. Betts, ed., *Senses of Empire: Multisensory Approaches to Roman Culture*, London: Routledge, pp. 193–199.

Burke, H. and Smith, C. (2007). *Archaeology to Delight and Instruct: Active Learning in the University Classroom*, Walnut Creek, CA: Left Coast Press.

Dell'Unto, N. (2014). 3D models and archaeological investigation. In: I. Huvila, ed., *Perspectives to Archaeological Information in the Digital Society*, Uppsala: Institutionen för ABM, pp. 51–77.

Epstein, J.M. (2008). Why model? *Journal of Artificial Societies and Social Simulation*, [online] JASSS. Available at: http://jasss.soc.surrey.ac.uk/11/4/12.html [Accessed 6 November 2018].

Favro, D. (2012). Se non è vero, è ben trovato (If not true, it is well conceived): Digital immersive reconstructions of historical environments. *Journal of the Society of Architectural Historians*, 71: 273–277.

Günther, H. (2001). Kritische Computer-Visualisierung in der kunsthistorischen Lehre. In: M. Frings, ed., *Der Modelle Tugend: CAD und die neuen Räume der Kunstgeschichte*, Weimar: VDG, pp. 111–122.

Hamilakis, Y. (2001). Interrogating archaeological pedagogies. In: P. Rainbird and Y. Hamilakis, eds, *Interrogating Pedagogies: Archaeology in higher education*, Oxford: Archaeopress, pp. 5–12.

Holter, E., Muth, S. and Schwesinger, S. (2018). Sounding out public space in late republican Rome. In: S. Butler and S. Nooter, eds, *Sound and the Ancient Senses*, Abingdon: Routledge, pp. 44–60.

Holter, E., Schäfer U.U. and Schwesinger, S. (2020). Simulating the ancient world: Pitfalls and opportunities of using game engines for archaeological and historical research. In: C. Rollinger, ed., *Classical Antiquity in Video Games: Playing with the Ancient World*, London: Bloomsbury, pp. 217–231.

Ishiyama, J. (2002). Does early participation in undergraduate research benefit social science and humanities students? *College Student Journal*, 36: 380–386.

Kassung, C. and Schwesinger, S. (2018). Saxa Loquuntur. The function of (multi-) media for antique architecture. In: D. Singh, J. Sieck, H.N.-N. Muyingi, H. Winschiers-Theophilus, A. Peters and S. Nggada, eds, *Digitisation of Culture: Namibian and International Perspectives*, Singapore: Springer, pp. 171–185.

Kassung, C. and Muth, S. (2019). Plausibilisieren. (Re-)Konstruktion als Experiment. Sehen und Hören in antiker Architektur. In: S. Marguin, H. Rabe, W. Schäffner and F. Schmidgall, eds, *Experimentieren. Einblicke in Praktiken und Versuchsaufbauten zwischen Wissenschaft und Gestaltung*, Bielefeld: transcript, pp. 189–204.

Lipe, W.D. (2000). Archaeological education and renewing American archaeology. In: S.J. Bender and G.S. Smith, eds, *Teaching Archaeology in the Twenty-First Century*, Washington, DC: Society for American Archaeology, pp. 17–20.

Muth, S. (2014). Historische Dimensionen des gebauten Raumes: Das Forum Romanum als Fallbeispiel. In: O. Dally, T. Hölscher, S. Muth and R. Schneider, eds, *Medien der Geschichte: Antikes Griechenland und Rom*, Berlin: de Gruyter, pp. 285–329.

OKell, E., Ljubojevic, D. and MacMahon, C. (2010). Creating a generative learning object (GLO): Working in an 'ill-structured' environment and getting students to think. In: G. Bodard and S. Mahony, eds, *Digital Research in the Study of Classical Antiquity*. Farnham: Ashgate, pp. 151–170.

Schäfer, U.U. (2018). Uncertainty visualization and digital 3D modeling in archaeology: A brief introduction. *Digital Art History*, 3: 87–106.

Wolfsteiner, A. (2018). *Sichtbarkeitsmaschinen: Zum Umgang mit Szenarien*, Berlin: Kadmos.

Developing Digital Archaeology for Young People: A Model for Fostering Empathy and Dialogue in Formal and Informal Learning Environments

Sierra McKinney*, Sara Perry*, Akrivi Katifori[†] and Vassilis Kourtis[†]

*University of York
[†]Athena Research & Innovation Center, Greece

Abstract

While preconceptions of archaeology and cultural heritage are generally formed at a young age through exposure to mass media and teachings in formal and informal settings, the quality of these exposures is extremely variable and often fails to engage young people in meaningful ways. Although digital technologies may appear as tempting means to intervene in this meaning-making process, their application to archaeological pedagogy at the primary and secondary school

How to cite this book chapter:
McKinney, S., Perry, S., Katifori, A. and Kourtis, V. 2020. Developing Digital Archaeology for Young People: A Model for Fostering Empathy and Dialogue in Formal and Informal Learning Environments. In: Hageneuer, S. (ed.) *Communicating the Past in the Digital Age: Proceedings of the International Conference on Digital Methods in Teaching and Learning in Archaeology (12–13 October 2018)*. Pp. 179–195. London: Ubiquity Press. DOI: https://doi.org/10.5334/bch.n. License: CC-BY 4.0

level can be superficial or result in the replication of existing problematic peda-gogical approaches. However, while the challenges of weaving archaeological knowledge into primary and secondary education are considerable, the digital archaeology schoolroom is an untapped resource with potential for engendering individual learning, constructive group dialogue, good citizenship and larger social conscience.

After reflecting on common weaknesses with extant pedagogical methods, including the prevalence of digital tools that require solitary and passive use, we present an alternative approach to the archaeological education resource: a multi-component digital kit for use in formal and informal learning environments. Created as part of the EU-funded EMOTIVE Project, this kit's components (including 3D printed objects, a virtual museum, and chatbot, which are usable independently but ideally deployed in tandem over a period of days or weeks) seek to nurture perspective-taking skills, close looking and listening skills, critical dialogue, and self-reflection to foster empathy among young people.

Keywords

Archaeology in Schools, Digital Media, Young People, Historical Empathy, Facilitated Dialogue

Introduction

As a discipline and field of practice, archaeology offers a powerful tool for education. The inherent ability of archaeology to evoke wonder, enchantment and powerful personal connections results in a pedagogy that can simultane-ously engage, challenge and inform. While the potential for digitally mediated archaeological education is immense, recent research into the implementation of educational programmes has frequently privileged the post-secondary envi-ronment and, where primary and secondary studies have been attended to, the published literature primarily focuses back on the technological development of tools such as virtual reality and 3D modelling, rather than on their efficacy as teaching aids, suggesting gaps in understanding around current practice.

With the adoption of archaeology into formal curriculums for primary stu-dents in countries including Canada, England and Australia (Alberta Educa-tion 2007; Australian Curriculum 2015; British Columbia 2018; Department of Education 2013), and the continued presence of archaeology in informal learning environments such as clubs and museums, archaeological education for children and young people is an important area of development with the potential to engender individual learning, constructive group dialogue, good citizenship and larger social conscience. Furthermore, the growth of digital technologies has enabled archaeology to be taught to younger audiences using increasingly varied methods including virtual (VR) and augmented reality (AR), digital games, 3D modelling and printing, and virtual museums. However, these approaches can often replicate problematic elements of their analogue counterparts in that they provide solitary experiences, one-directional provision of information, and passive engagement. In such cases, the human elements of archaeology, and the associated benefits of an affective experience, can be lost. Instead, we argue for a model of archaeological education for children and young people that embraces the emotive elements of archaeology through the development of pre/historical empathy and the use of facilitated dialogue.

The following chapter grows out of the three-year European Commission-funded EMOTIVE Project (EMOTIVE n.d.a; Katifori et al. 2019), an interdisciplinary research programme uniting eight institutional partners through work at cultural heritage sites across Europe, including two UNESCO-listed World Heritage Sites and various popular local attractions serving tens to hundreds of thousands of visitors per year. EMOTIVE is premised upon a growing body of scholarship that demonstrates the direct relationship between visitors' emotional experiences (e.g. feelings of wonder, provocation, and resonance generated through their engagement with these sites) and their heightened understanding of, attachment to and care for the sites and their exhibits in the short and longer term (see Perry 2019; Perry et al. 2017). In other words, the evidence suggests that it is through personal, emotional connections that humans are most likely to be primed to acquire knowledge about, protect and promote the archaeological record. EMOTIVE, then, aims to research, design, develop and evaluate methods and digital technologies that support cultural sites and interested communities (interpreted broadly to include museums, schools, heritage and archaeological destinations, spiritual and religious settings, galleries and other local and tourist destinations, community centres, citizen/interest groups, and more) in creating such emotional connections with heritage.

Our concern is that typical pedagogical approaches to heritage tend not only to devalue, ignore or misunderstand the importance of emotion but also neglect or misapply the capacities of digital media, therein undermining the learning outcomes and broader transformative social prospects of the subject matter. We outline here a conceptual model that aims to respond to this predicament, using dialogue fostered through children's social engagements with digital technologies to cultivate historical empathy. Below, we contextualise our work in relation to extant digital heritage initiatives for young people before going on to define historical empathy and facilitated dialogue, drawing particular inspiration from Endacott and Brooks (2013), Bormann and Campt (in Smithsonian n.d.) and the US National Park Service (2019b), and extending their approaches to address the more distant past via a focus on pre/historical empathy. We offer a summary of the application of our conceptual model in informal educational environments in the UK (tested with eight- to 15year-olds), noting that detailed analysis of our evaluations is available in McKinney (2018) and McKinney et al. (forthcoming). We then conclude with brief reflections on some of the key challenges confronting such work (and echoed by other researchers), which suggest the importance of informal learning environments for pursuing emotively engaging heritage outcomes.

Overview of existing digital heritage for young people

Preconceptions of archaeology and cultural heritage are formed from childhood, typically in relation to exposure to the media, formal classroom lessons and informal educational experiences. The quality of these exposures is extremely variable in their ability to be relevant and impactful for young people. In attempting to connect with children, many museums, schools and cultural institutions have turned to digital media – and digitally hosted resources that are available for printing – seemingly under the assumption that such resources will afford more resonance for students, not to mention convenience for teachers. Yet, the availability and quality of digital tools for children's archaeological education vary considerably, tending to privilege extremes – e.g. highly technical and expensive tools or simple pdfs; melodramatic narratives or a series of didactic facts.

Seeking to contextualise our work in relation to comparable pedagogical efforts, we conducted a cursory review of online educational resources, evaluating them against Beetham and Sharpe's (2007) expansion of Laurillards's (2002) typology of digital resources for learning. This typology outlines five basic forms of resource: narrative, productive, interactive, adaptive and communicative. Narrative resources ask users to engage with a representation (such as text, images or videos), which may be assimilative, in the sense that the user passively consumes them, or productive, wherein the user partakes in their creation. Productive resources consist of tasks that ask the user to manipulate or provide data, but, by our reckoning, this form of resource is very uncommon within the existing corpus of archaeological digital educational tools. Interactive resources return information on the basis of user input, such as quizzes or search engines. Within the existing corpus, interactive resources appear frequently, often as part of virtual museums or in the form of searchable artefacts or museum databases. Adaptive resources require continuous input from the user, such as virtual worlds or games, and, owing to the nature of this type of resource, they are becoming increasingly common with the rise of archaeogaming and VR/AR technology. Finally, communicative resources include tasks that emphasise interaction between individuals and groups, such as social media or messaging. As it relates to digital archaeological educational tools, digital communicative resources tend to occur in the form of public outreach on social media by archaeological sites or museums. However, the extent to which these offerings provide the opportunity to engage in bilateral communication can vary, resulting in resources that may be communicative or alternatively may be narrative in nature, depending on the level of engagement from the owner (e.g. the museum) of the social media site. An alternative and smaller subsection of communicative archaeological digital tools are chatbots, which offer an opportunity to engage in discussion with a virtual interface or robot even if their current implementations leave a lot to be desired (see Tzouganatou 2018).

Our review indicates that digitally hosted analogue materials are the most prevalent learning materials available for those seeking to teach about archaeology to young people. This category, which falls under the digital resource typology's assimilative narrative type, includes worksheets, lesson plans and other assets that are created with the explicit intention that they be printed prior to use. While these materials may be useful and engaging, their adoption of the affordances provided by digital technologies is minimal. As such, they often utilise formats traditionally found in the classroom, with a heavy emphasis on reading, identifying and reiterating facts, and solitary, passive use. Yet, the benefit of these digitally hosted analogue materials is their ease of use: they require few to no advanced or costly resources and can be employed by large groups of children simultaneously. Furthermore, they can be retrieved from many locations, including museum websites, archaeological professional societies and government-sponsored sites (Archaeology Scotland n.d.; National Park Service 2019a; Society for American Archaeology n.d.; University of Leicester n.d.), making them accessible to a seemingly wide audience. An excellent example of this type of tool is the Star Carr resource created by Henson (Star Carr Archaeology Project n.d.), which utilises storytelling and interactive activities to emphasise the human nature of prehistoric peoples.

An alternative approach can be found in the use of virtual museums and exhibits for pedagogical purposes. Virtual museums have the ability to embrace the affordances of the internet, including 3D walkthroughs, 3D artefact reconstructions, hyperlinks, videos, mini games and virtual digs (Friends of Bonnechere Parks 2006; Leicester City Council 2019; SFU Museum of Archaeology and Ethnography 2009). As such, depending on their application of these affordances, virtual museums can be adaptive or interactive, and even have the potential to be communicative. However, an iconic example, the Virtual Museum of Canada (VMC n.d.), reveals the often-disappointing implementation of these resources, wherein many fall into the assimilative narrative type. The majority appear to mimic a textbook rather than the halls of a museum, as they consist of a series of text-heavy pages with a small scattering of images, and their primary technological innovation consists of the inclusion of video. Indeed, many simply replicate existing analogue materials in html code. While this limited technical complexity of the VMC is likely due to lack of resources, the end result remains an uninspiring and, at times, onerous tool to use (but cf. the VMC's unique Journey into Time Immemorial (SFU 2008)). At the opposite extreme, large institutions, such as the Louvre and Vatican (Louvre

Museum n.d.; Mvsei Vaticani n.d.), have digital museums that consist solely of virtual walkthroughs, which allow the user to digitally 'see' the museum but provide no information, interpretation or ability to focus on a specific work of art or artefact.

Furthermore, adaptive resources, such as VR, AR, serious games and 3D models and prints, are increasingly being deployed for teaching and learning, sometimes via web-based repositories and sometimes through offline services and bespoke projects. Indeed, existing research on digital tools for primary education has arguably favoured these technologies. However, the research typically explores them as isolated elements and focuses on the function of technology itself rather than its efficacy as a means of educating. Additionally, many of these approaches require expensive technology, access to research prototypes and/or a degree of digital expertise, which limits accessibility for users. Important recent exceptions include Di Giuseppantonio Di Franco et al.'s (2019) combination of the affordances of 3D models with an historical inquiry-based learning methodology, which has demonstrated positive results in encouraging complex and critical forms of historical understanding among Tunisian primary and secondary students.

Even if easily accessible, the nature of the technology itself may manifest in problematical forms of engagement that limit pedagogical potential. For instance, VR is almost exclusively experienced by its users in an isolated, solitary fashion, and it frequently consists of passive engagement with the virtual environment. An exception to this predicament is Google Expeditions (Google 2019), which allows a teacher to 'guide' a class of students through a virtual environment augmented with information and text. However, even in this instance, in which the children are simultaneously participating in the same tour, each student remains isolated within their own headset. This is mitigated to a certain extent with the application of AR, as users can more easily share in the experience. However, AR presents its own challenges, as it is frequently designed to be used in a site-specific location, potentially limiting its accessibility.

Perhaps the most dynamic of the above-listed digital resources for children's education are archaeological games. As adaptive tools, with the potential to also become communicative, archaeological games have the ability to enable user agency and multiplayer social interaction in an immersive experience. Recent examples of this type of educational resource include Hiriart's (2019) sophisticated archaeogame prototypes that explore the lives of Anglo-Saxon families. Hiriart's work not only establishes the potential for games (played in formal educational settings) to foster higher-order thinking, challenge preconceptions and counter naïve conceptualisations of the past but also furnishes a wider theoretical model and design guidelines for others to create effective gaming-based 'personal encounters' that are meaningfully integrated with extant formal learning resources.

The argument for *pre/historical* empathy

In contrast to the passive, didactic and solitary pedagogical techniques that are the basis of many of the resources discussed above, we suggest that a human-focused practice, such as archaeology, requires a human-focused pedagogy. The concept of historical empathy offers a meaningful intellectual grounding upon which to build such a pedagogy, and it has obvious parallels with both the inquiry-based approach of Di Giuseppantonio Di Franco et al. (2019) and the historical thinking approach of Hiriart (2019). Collectively, these models seek to nurture richer personal engagements with heritage through methods that oblige students to see – or, indeed, embody – difference and to take the lead in navigating their own learning. Importantly, these methods also demand a degree of faith from educators, trusting in students to steer the process and negotiate complicated topics among themselves. The advantage of historical empathy, as we see it, is its measurable, tripartite nature (which also maps neatly onto the facilitated dialogue model that we outline below) and its future action orientation (forcing children's attention onto next steps and subsequent acts on the world).

Specifically, historical empathy is the 'process of students' cognitive and affective engagement with historical figures to better understand and contextualize their lived experiences, decisions, or actions' (Endacott & Brooks 2013: 41). First introduced by archaeologist R.G. Collingwood in England (Collingwood 1939), the concept was subsequently developed internationally, with key research undertaken in Canada, the United States and Denmark, in addition to the UK. Studies have demonstrated that the application of historical empathy results in increased interest in the taught content (Endacott 2010; Kohlmeier 2006); an improved ability to retain content knowledge (Brooks 2011; Endacott & Brooks 2013; Kohlmeier 2006) and to understand complex ideas (Endacott 2010; Foster 1999); and the development of the ability to establish connections and relationships between the past and the present (Brooks 2011).

The most recent model of historical empathy, created by Endacott and Brooks (2013), consists of a framework with three 'interrelated and interdependent endeavors' (p. 43): historical contextualisation, perspective taking and affective connection. This model was recently applied in a heritage context by Savenije and de Bruijn (2017) and has been more widely employed within the field of history education (de Leur, Van Boxtel & Wilschut 2017; Efstathiou, Kyza & Georgiou 2018; Ellenwood 2017).

The first of the three components, historical contextualisation, aims to provide students with critical information about significant historical events, figures and practices, in order to assist students in understanding cultural norms and perspectives informing the views of historic peoples. The second element, perspective taking, challenges students to view the past from alternative perspectives, considering their own personal experiences and beliefs in relation to

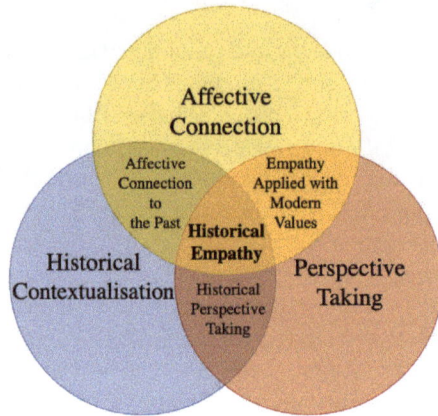

Figure 1: Diagram of historical empathy and its components (adapted from Endacott & Brooks 2013: 44).

those of others, in order to better understand how a historical individual may have viewed their circumstances. The third component, affective connection, prompts students to recognise the human nature of past peoples, as individuals with their own emotions and complexities. In viewing the past through the lens of complex people, students are prompted to connect these experiences to their own lives and, in doing so, consider their actions in the future. It is in this final element that a key aspect of historical empathy is introduced: care. The ultimate aim of historical empathy is to develop a sense of care: a care to learn about the past, a care that events happened, a care for other people (past and present) and, lastly, a sense of care to apply the lessons learned from the past into the present (Barton & Levstik 2004).

However, the historical empathy model has been applied almost exclusively in relation to the historical period (drawing upon historic sources, especially the written word), leaving out the vast majority of the human past and its empathetic potentials. The lack of engagement with this model in archaeology is perhaps unsurprising given the fragmentary material evidence available to connect people in the present with people from the distant past. Yet, other – more intangible – mechanisms to forge such connections are widely available and are virtually unexplored within the discipline. Here we are referring to dialogue, and specifically the Arc of Dialogue – a model for facilitating dialogue developed by Tammy Bormann and David Campt (International Coalition of Sites of Conscience n.d.). Dialogue encourages individuals to share their unique views and experiences with the 'express goal of personal and collective learning' (Smithsonian n.d.: 4). As facilitated dialogue challenges participants to share personal experiences and beliefs, listen and examine factual

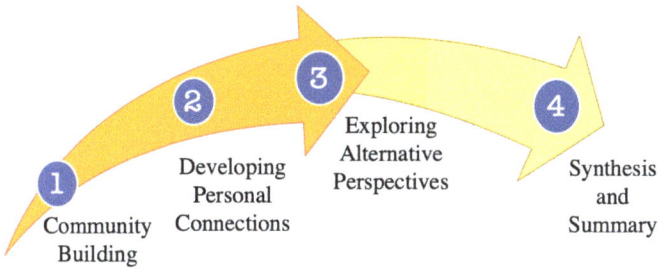

Figure 2: Arc of Dialogue (adapted from National Park Service 2019b: 11).

information presented to them, and consider the perspectives of others, it is a natural complement to historical empathy, and one means by which deep time and more distant human pasts may be explored. Furthermore, dialogic methods, including group discussion and debate, have been successfully used when teaching historic empathy in classroom environments (Endacott & Pelekanos 2015; Jensen 2008; Kohlmeier 2006).

The Arc of Dialogue consists of four phases: community building, sharing personal experiences, further exploration of alternative perspectives, and summary and synthesis (National Parks Service 2019b: 11; Smithsonian National Museum of the American Indian n.d.: 4–5; Smithsonian n.d.: 6–10). The first phase introduces participants to the topic and one another, with the intention of developing an environment that invites and encourages participation. The second phase asks participants to share their personal connections with the topic, fostering a sense of care and affective connection. This is followed by the third phase, in which participants are challenged to listen to alternative views. They are encouraged to ask questions, reflect on the topic more broadly, and view things from the perspectives of others. Finally, the fourth phase summarises the discussion and prompts the participants to reflect on the discussion, their own beliefs and what they have learned.

Pre/historic empathy through dialogue: EMOTIVE's digital education kit

We have tested the efficacy of a dialogue-based pre/historic empathy model via the development of a digital education kit for the UNESCO World Heritage Site of Çatalhöyük in Turkey (whose components are extensible to other sites, contexts and audiences).[1] The Exploration of Egalitarianism Digital Education

---

[1] While we discuss here our specific adaptation of the pre/historic empathy model for Çatalhöyük, we are separately developing each of the model's three components

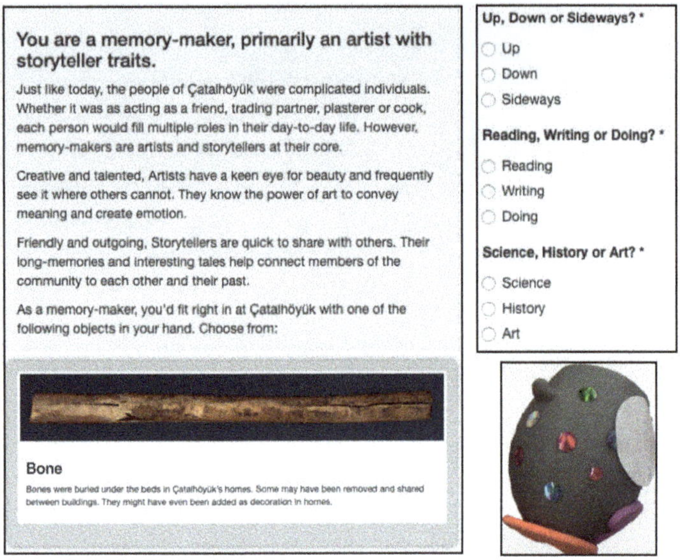

Figure 3: Elements of the Personality Quiz.

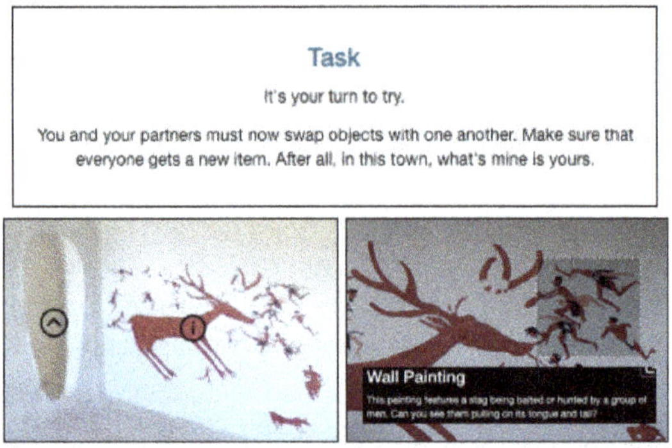

Figure 4: Example task and screenshots of the Egalitarian Trading Experience.

as generic tools that other sites, teachers and interested organisations and individuals can use to tailor the Kit to their needs and learning objectives. These tools
include: (1) the Personality Quiz (a profiling quiz used to connect users to a specific
role and related objects), created with EMOTIVE's Profiling Quiz Editor; (2) the
3D-moulded prints (replica artefacts that can be crafted quickly (in minutes) by
the site or a user with plaster of Paris or modelling clay), created with EMOTIVE's
Meta Moulds; (3) the Web Experiencing Tool (a web-based virtual representation of
a site, visualised through interactive 360-degree photos), created with EMOTIVE's
Floorplan Editor; (4) the Narralive Mobile App (an interactive digital storytelling

Kit (hereafter referred to as the Kit) consists of three phases: the Welcome to Çatalhöyük Personality Quiz, an Egalitarian Trading Experience, and a Discussion with Bo the ChatBot (Figure 3). Each stage broadly correlates to one of the entwined components of historical empathy and a phase of the Arc of Dialogue (Figure 2). At the time of writing, the Kit is accessible for public use through the University of York Archaeology Department's Educational Resources webpage and on EMOTIVE's website (EMOTIVE n.d.b; University of York n.d.).

In the first stage, the Personality Quiz, participants answer a series of questions about themselves in order to reveal their own complex Neolithic personality and three potential 3D printed objects (Figure 3). These personalities have the dual purpose of matching a participant with an object and developing an affective connection by establishing a link from the object to their own personality. This introduces the users to the topic, as established in the first phase of the Arc of Dialogue.

Following on, participants tour a series of virtual houses (360-degree digital photographs of physical replicas of Çatalhöyük's Neolithic period buildings) in groups of two or three (Figure 4). The houses are visualised on computers through an interactive web-based app (using the Floor Plan Editor, a tool in development by members of the EMOTIVE team) wherein panoramic 360-degree photos are enhanced with points of interest that offer a closer view of specific features as well as more information. The virtual walkthroughs are led by a mobile-based narrative (created via a digital storytelling authoring tool, also in development; Figure 5), which guides participants through an embodied experience of egalitarianism, in which they are asked to exchange and leave behind objects via collective decision-making. Through this embodied experience, participants are able to recognise and develop connections to their own lives, as outlined in the second phase of the Arc. During this component of the experience, the participants are provided with additional factual information to assist with historical contextualisation.

Finally, larger groups of five to eight users then come together to engage in a facilitated dialogue session with a chatbot (whose rules-based format is being elaborated by the EMOTIVE team for generic application; Figure 5). The chatbot replicates the Arc of Dialogue, resulting in a 'nesting doll effect' (Figure 6). As the chatbot guides the users through the dialogue, they are challenged to engage in perspective taking and synthesise what they learned throughout the entirety of the experience. In doing so, the chatbot fulfils the third and fourth phases of the Arc of Dialogue.

Thus, using the established pedagogies of historical empathy and the Arc of Dialogue as our guide, we have developed a resource that simultaneously applies

---

app for mobile devices), developed with the Narralive Storyboard Editor; and (5) the EMOTIVE Bot (a rules-based chatbot), built using the third-party SnatchBot (2019) software and grounded in EMOTIVE's Bot of Conviction model (Roussou et al. 2019).

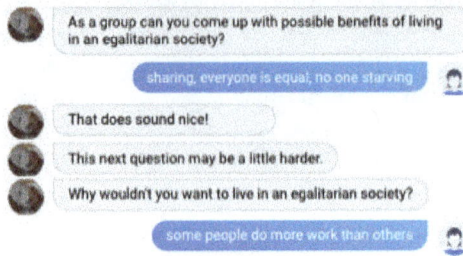

Figure 5: Screenshot of a conversation with Bo the Chatbot.

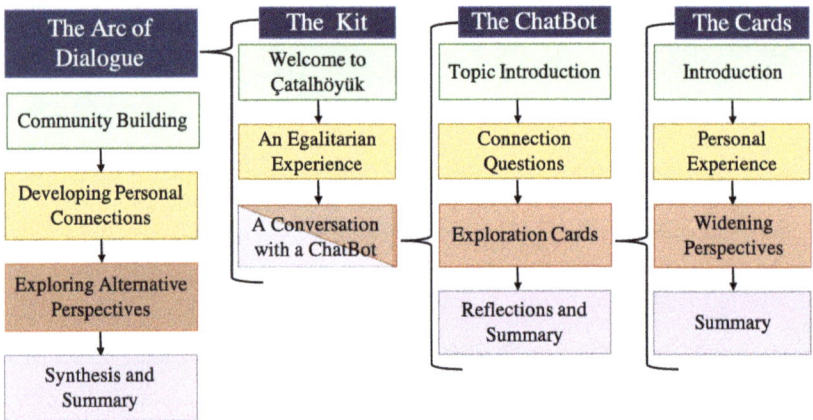

Figure 6: Schematic of the Digital Education Kit mapped onto the Arc of Dialogue. 'The Cards' refer to a specific component of the chatbot experience, whose specifics are outlined in McKinney (2018).

multiple digital technologies, including 3D prints, a chatbot, webpages and virtual walkthroughs, to create a digital resource for archaeology that emphasises collective, embodied and affective learning. In doing so, we aim to avoid replicating the problematic pedagogical strategies discussed at the beginning of this chapter. Indeed, we seek to bridge the extremes, creating an approach that develops resources that are both communicative and adaptive through the application of an affectively engaging and dialogic framework. Under this framework the technical educational tools are applied in a manner that is social, immersive, informative and encourages active bilateral engagement while all remaining accessible through a single webpage (McKinney 2019). Although it is complex in its various parts, we have simultaneously developed generic tools (see description in note 1), including a how-to guide for the creation of dialogic chatbots, to enable others to experiment in other contexts – playing with their content, adjusting how, in which order and when (if at all) they are deployed, and otherwise remixing them, knowing that individually and collectively they function to enhance emotive outcomes among users.

Our tests of the pre/historical empathy model suggest that it is best applied in informal educational environments, owing to the challenges of integrating any new resource into the formal learning setting (also see comparable discussions in Di Giuseppantonio Di Franco et al. (2019) and Hiriart (2019)). While this point requires further exploration (see McKinney et al., forthcoming), the informal application of this approach is arguably its strength, as young people are empowered to survey ideas that might otherwise sit awkwardly within their formal schooling, and that might more fluidly fold into their home lives, where empathetic (or non-empathetic) relations are so strongly created and reinforced.

However, in presenting our model, we do not wish to dictate a strict framework that must be followed. Rather we hope here to have provided a small degree of inspiration for future possibilities for digital archaeological educational resources: accessible tools that foster a sense of personal connection or care, empathy, dialogue, and enchantment.

Acknowledgements

This work is part of the EMOTIVE Project, which has received funding from the European Union's Horizon 2020 research and innovation programme under grant agreement No. 727188. The authors would like to thank Angeliki Tzouganatou and Sophia Mirashrafi for significant intellectual contributions that laid the foundations for our work, as well as the larger the EMOTIVE team. We also wish to thank the young people and leaders of the Young Archaeologists' Clubs who participated in our formative studies.

References

Alberta Education (2007). *Social Studies Kindergarten to Grade 12*, [pdf] Available at: https://education.alberta.ca/media/3273004/social-studies-k-6-pos. pdf [Accessed 1 April 2019].

Archaeology Scotland (n.d.). *Heritage Resources Portal*. [online] Archaeology Scotland. Available at: https://archaeologyscotland.org.uk/learn-resources [Accessed 20 March 2019].

Australian Curriculum (2015). *History: Sequence of Content 7-10 Strand: Knowledge and Understanding*. [pdf] Available at: http://docs.acara.edu.au/resources/History_7-10_-_Sequence_of_content.pdf [Accessed 1 April 2019].

Barton, K.C. and Levstik, L.S. (2004). *Teaching History for the Common Good*, London: Routledge.

Beetham, H. and Sharpe, R. (2007). *Rethinking Pedagogy for a Digital Age*, Abingdon: Routledge.

British Columbia (2018). *BC's New Curriculum Social Studies 3.* [online] Government British Columbia. Available at: https://curriculum.gov.bc.ca/curriculum/social-studies/3 [Accessed 1 April 2019].

Brooks, S. (2011). Historical empathy as perspective recognition and care in one secondary social studies classroom. *Theory & Research in Social Education*, 39(2): 166–202.

Collingwood, R.G. (1939). *An Autobiography*, London: Oxford University Press.

de Leur, T., Van Boxtel C. and Wilschut, A. (2017). 'I saw angry people and broken statues': Historical empathy in secondary history education. *British Journal of Educational Studies*, 65(3): 331–352.

Department of Education (2013). *National Curriculum in England: History Programmes of Study.* [online] Government UK. Available at: https://www.gov.uk/government/publications/national-curriculum-in-england-history-programmes-of-study/national-curriculum-in-england-history-programmes-of-study#key-stage-3 [Accessed 1 April 2019].

Di Giuseppantonio Di Franco, P., Winterbottom, M., Galeazzi, F. and Gogan, M. (2019). Ksar Said: Building Tunisian young people's critical engagement with their heritage. *Sustainability*, 11(5): 1373, DOI: https://doi.org/10.3390/su11051373.

Efstathiou, I., Kyza, E.A. and Georgiou, Y. (2018). An inquiry-based augmented reality mobile learning approach to fostering primary school students' historical reasoning in non-formal settings, *Interactive Learning Environments*, 26(1): 22–41.

Ellenwood, T.D. (2017). Historical empathy: Judging the people of the past in a secondary social studies classroom. *Learning to Teach*, 6(1). [online] University of Toledo. Available at: https://www.utdl.edu/ojs/index.php/learningtoteach/article/view/233/115 [Accessed 29 April 2019].

EMOTIVE (n.d.a). *Emotive.* [online] Emotive Project. Available at: https://emotiveproject.eu [Accessed 18 February 2019].

EMOTIVE (n.d.b). *Exploration of Egalitarianism: A Digital Education Kit.* [online] Emotive Project. Available at: http://athena.emotiveproject.eu/schoolkit [Accessed 22 August 2019].

Endacott, J.L. (2010). Reconsidering affective engagement in historical empathy. *Theory & Research in Social Education*, 38(1): 6–47.

Endacott, J.L. and Brooks, S. (2013). An updated theoretical and practical model for promoting historical empathy. *Social Studies Research and Practice*, 8(1): 41–58.

Endacott, J.L. and Pelekanos, C. (2015). Slaves, women, and war! Engaging middle school students in historical empathy for enduring understanding. *The Social Studies*, 106(1): 1–7.

Foster, S. (1999). Using historical empathy to excite students about the study of history: Can you empathize with Neville Chamberlain? *The Social Studies*, 90(1): 18–24.

Friends of Bonnechere Parks (2006). *How to Dig*. [online] Virtual Museums. Available at: http://www.virtualmuseum.ca/sgc-cms/expositions-exhibitions/esprits-spirits/English/Dig/digdown.html [Accessed 23 March 2019].

Google (2019). *What Is Expeditions*. [online] Google. Available at: https://support.google.com/edu/expeditions/answer/6335093?hl=en [Accessed 15 March 2019].

Hiriart, J. (2019). *Gaming the Past: Designing and Using Digital Games as Historical Learning Contexts*. PhD. University of Salford, UK.

International Coalition of Sites of Conscience (n.d.). *Facilitated Dialogue*. [pdf] Sites of Conscience. Available at: https://www.sitesofconscience.org/wp-content/uploads/2019/01/Dialogue-Overview.pdf [Accessed 30 April 2019].

Jensen, J. (2008). Developing historical empathy through debate: An action research study. *Social Studies Research and Practice*, 3(1): 55–66.

Katifori, A., Roussou, M., Perry, S., Drettakis, G., Vizcay, S. and Philip, J. (2019). The EMOTIVE Project – emotive virtual cultural experiences through personalized storytelling. In: *CIRA@EuroMed 2018*, Dublin: IEEE, pp. 11–20, [pdf] Available at: http://ceur-ws.org/Vol-2235/paper2.pdf [Accessed 29 April 2019].

Kohlmeier, J. (2006). 'Couldn't she just leave?': The relationship between consistently using class discussions and the development of historical empathy in a 9th grade world history course. *Theory & Research in Social Education*, 34(1): 34–57, DOI: https://doi.org/10.1080/00933104.2006.10473297.

Laurillard, D. (2002). *Rethinking University Teaching: A Conversational Framework for the Effective Use of Learning Technologies*, London: Routledge/Falmer.

Leicester City Council (2019). *The Jewry Wall*. [online] Government Leicester. Available at: http://jewrywallstory.leicester.gov.uk [Accessed 21 March 2019].

Louvre Museum (n.d.) *Experience Louvre*. [online] YouVisit. Available at: https://www.youvisit.com/tour/louvremuseum [Accessed 20 March 2019].

McKinney, S. (2018). *Generating Pre-Historical Empathy: An Examination of a Digital Classroom Kit*. MSc. University of York, UK.

McKinney, S. (2019). *Exploration of Egalitarianism Digital Education Kit*. [online] GitHub. Available at: slmck.github.io [Accessed 20 March 2019].

McKinney, S., Perry, S., Katifori, A., Kourtis, V. and Lougiakis, C. (forthcoming). Generating Pre-Historic Empathy in Classrooms. *Journal of Community Archaeology and Heritage*.

Mvsei Vaticani (n.d.). *Raphael's Room*. [online] Vatican Museum. Available at: http://www.museivaticani.va/content/museivaticani/en/collezioni/musei/stanze-di-raffaello/tour-virtuale.html [Accessed 20 March 2019].

National Park Service (2019a). *Teacher Resources*. [online] National Park Service. Available at: https://www.nps.gov/archeology/Public/teach. htm#plans [Accessed 20 March 2019].

National Park Service (2019b). *Forging Connections through Audience Centered Experiences Workbook*. [online] Google Drive. Available at: https://drive. google.com/file/d/1vvAsiyORvBI1kDOU6SXVk76DWmHfR6lV/view [Accessed 8 April 2019].

Perry, S. (2019). The Enchantment of the Archaeological Record. *European Journal of Archaeology*, 22(3): 354–371.

Perry, S.E., Roussou, M., Economou, M., Young, H. and Pujol-Tost, L. (2017). Moving beyond the virtual museum: Engaging visitors emotionally. In: *23rd International Conference on Virtual Systems & Multimedia (VSMM)*, Dublin: IEEE, pp. 1–8.

Roussou, M., Perry, S., Katifori, A., Vassos, S., Tzouganatou, A. and McKinney, S. (2019). Transformation through provocation? Designing a 'bot of conviction' to challenge conceptions and evoke critical reflection. In: *Proceedings of the 2019 CHI Conference on Human Factors in Computing Systems*. ACM Digital Library, 627.

Savenije, G.M. and de Bruijn, P. (2017). Historical empathy in a museum: uniting contextualisation and emotional engagement. *International Journal of Heritage Studies*, 23(9): 832–845, DOI: https://doi.org/10.1080/ 13527258.2017.1339108.

SFU Museum of Archaeology and Ethnography (2008). *A Journey into Time Immemorial*. [online] Simon Fraser University. Available at: http://www.sfu. museum/time. [Accessed 10 April 2019].

Smithsonian (n.d.). *Beyond Bollywood: Indian Americans Shape the Nation*. [pdf] Sites Archives. Available at: http://sitesarchives.si.edu/exhibi-tions/exhibits/beyondbollywood/BeyondBollywoodDialogueToolkit.pdf [Accessed 16 April 2019].

Smithsonian National Museum of the American Indian (n.d.). *Americans: A Dialogue Toolkit for Educators*. [pdf] Available at: http://nmai.si.edu/sites/1/ files/pdf/education/NMAI-Americans-dialogue-toolkit.pdf [Accessed 16 April 2019].

SnatchBot (2019). *SnatchBot*. [online]. Available at: https://snatchbot.me [Accessed 19 April 2019].

Society for American Archaeology (n.d.). *K-12 Activities & Resources*. [online] Society for American Archaeology. Available at: https://www.saa.org/edu-cation-outreach/teaching-archaeology/k-12-activities-resources [Accessed 20 March 2019].

Star Carr Archaeology Project (n.d.) *Schools*. [online] Starr Carr Project. Avail-able at: http://www.starcarr.com/schools.html [Accessed 15 March 2019].

Tzouganatou, A. (2018). Can heritage bots thrive? Toward future engagement in cultural heritage. *Advances in Archaeological Practice*, 6(4): 377–383.

University of Leicester (n.d.). *Teaching Resources.* [online] University of Leicester. Available at: https://le.ac.uk/archaeology/outreach/for-teachers/teaching-resources [Accessed 20 March 2019].

University of York (n.d.) *Educational Resources for Schools.* [online] University of York. Available at: https://www.york.ac.uk/archaeology/schools [Accessed 16 August 2019].

Virtual Museum of Canada (n.d.). *Virtual Exhibitions.* [online] Virtual Museum of Canada. Available at: http://www.virtualmuseum.ca/virtual-exhibits/type/virtual-exhibits [Accessed 20 March 2019].

Index

www.ingramcontent.com/pod-product-compliance
Lightning Source LLC
Chambersburg PA
CBHW040829300326
41914CB00059B/1292